THEATER
IN THE
AMERICAS

A Series from
Southern
Illinois
University
Press
ROBERT A.
SCHANKE
Series Editor

American Political Plays after 9/11

AMERICAN POLITICAL PLAYS AFTER 9/11

Edited by Allan Havis

Southern Illinois University Press / Carbondale and Edwardsville

The Guys, copyright © 2001 by Anne Nelson. *At the Vanishing Point*, copyright
© 2002 by Naomi Iizuka. *The Venus de Milo Is Armed*, copyright © 2003 by Kia
Corthron. *Back of the Throat*, copyright © 2006 by Yussef El Guindi (all rights
reserved). *Three Nights in Prague*, copyright © 2004 by Allan Havis. *Question 27,
Question 28*, copyright © 2004 by Chay Yew, East West Players version.

13 12 11 10   4 3 2 1

Library of Congress Cataloging-in-Publication Data
American political plays after 9/11 / edited by Allan Havis.
      p. cm. — (Theater in the Americas)
Includes bibliographical references.
ISBN-13: 978-0-8093-2954-0 (pbk. : alk. paper)
ISBN-10: 0-8093-2954-9 (pbk. : alk. paper)
ISBN-13: 978-0-8093-8555-3 (ebook)
ISBN-10: 0-8093-8555-4 (ebook)
1. Political plays, American. 2. American drama—21st century. I. Havis, Allan.
PS627.P65A437 2010
812′.54080358—dc22   2009035629

To a special mentor
  DEREK WALCOTT
And in memory of
  HAROLD PINTER AND JOE CHAIKIN

CONTENTS

ACKNOWLEDGMENTS

I thank many individuals for helping bring this anthology to publication. Karl Kageff, editor-in-chief for Southern Illinois University Press, was more than hospitable when the project came to his attention. Extremely supportive, wise, and insightful was Kristine Priddy, the book's acquisition editor, at Southern Illinois University Press, who gave tremendous time, energy, and astute guidance to every step toward publication. Further, I thank Robert Schanke (Theater in the Americas series editor), who presented many constructive ideas along the way and enriched the direction of the essay that frames the book. I acknowledge my friend and theater colleague Provost Steven Adler of Warren College, University of California, San Diego, for his kind role in this anthology's publication. Heartfelt gratitude and admiration go to Julie Morris, executive key staff at Thurgood Marshall College Provost Office, for giving excellent, sustained professionalism in the formatting of the book, in communicating with the many playwrights, in her amazing editing artistry, and with her beatific patience. To my wife, Julia, and my family, I must give tribute to their daily encouragement, love, and good humor. Finally, I thank the generous contributing playwrights, allowing such a volume of work to come into existence.

given without obtaining, in advance, the written permission of Dramatists Play Service Inc., and paying the requisite fee; inquiries concerning all other rights should be addressed to Morgan Jenness, Abrams Artists Agency, 275 Seventh Avenue, 26th floor, New York, NY 10001. Regarding *Three Nights in Prague*, contact author's agent, Susan Schulman, A Literary Agency, 454 West 44th Street, New York NY 10036 (212-713-1633).

American Political Plays after 9/11

INTRODUCTION

Obvious to our society is the sharp turning point America has experienced, not by entering the year 2000 but by enduring the event and the aftermath of September 11, 2001. The great trauma to our nation has touched every aspect of American life, from commercial air travel to basic safety in our neighborhood schools and shopping centers. Clearly, the public trust had been undermined by lax security and by the unaffordable luxury of our complacency in a mercurial global situation. Although the Cold War has subsided with the dramatic reunification of Germany in 1989 and the transformation of Communist Russia in the 1990s, stateless enemies of the United States have created a new polarity that effectively supplants the long-standing superpower rivalry. From a national perspective, America's criminal-justice system has been severely tested and compromised by our detention camp for suspected terrorists in Guantanamo Bay, our civil rights and privacy have been challenged by the USA Patriot Act enacted October 26, 2001, and our image in the world has been altered perhaps irrevocably by our invasion of Iraq and our soldiers' misconduct with Abu Ghraib prisoners.

Stating this as a prelude to this anthology's introduction, the inspiration to form an artful kaleidoscope of revelatory dramatic texts was first and foremost a way of approximating the American zeitgeist as this millennium decade unfolded in cascading waves of shock, pain, and reawakening. Looking at our national character and our social challenges vis-à-vis new plays often yields pungent truths about a shifting culture, and yet the treasured record of political literature for our theatrical heritage has elements of abundance and occasional deficiencies reflecting American denial. Further, the examination of playwriting trends is a worthwhile effort in the nation's self-analysis. There is concrete correlation among community activism, aesthetic sensibilities, and the pulse of the national theater scene as early as the 1920s, as the suffragette movement, Prohibition laws, and socialist energies brought plays to the public eye: Elmer Rice's *Adding Machine* (1923), Eugene O'Neill's *Hairy Ape* (1922), and Sophie Treadwell's *Machinal* (1928).

Beginning with the Federal Theatre and the Group Theatre in the 1930s, political performance in the United States had taken root for at least one generation, and the reflection today holds a degree of veracity all the way back to the once-banned, 1937 leftist labor musical *The Cradle Will Rock* (by Marc Blitzstein and direction by Orson Welles). Harold Clurman, the renowned founder of the depression-era Group Theatre and respected theater critic, once declared that all outstanding plays are political, be they the family plays of Eugene O'Neill (*Desire under the Elms*, 1924), Tennessee Williams (*Glass Menagerie*, 1947), and Arthur Miller (*All My Sons*, 1947) or the more demonstrative political works from German dramatist Bertolt Brecht (*Mother Courage and Her Children*, 1939) and American John Howard Lawson (*Processional*, 1925). Is it the audience's obligation to provide the larger social context when nothing within the narrative is politically overt? Clurman's statement begs the question of themes both explicit and implicit. Certainly, his Group Theatre made every attempt to foster social and ideological change. But if the play's intention is quietly implicit of political content, does the writer's message have the commensurate power and provocation of more brash drama? Was there a considerable risk personally or economically in staging the play? Should an autobiographical playwright ask nakedly, "Is my life someone's propaganda?"

It's axiomatic to say that political theater has often played, at best, a secondary role in American stage life. Still, the value of political theater is indisputable to our cultural dialogue, our notion of freedom, and our artistic collective identity. Seventy years after Blitzstein's legendary production, it is eye-opening to consider Connecticut's Wilton High School and the controversy engendered by the principal's cancellation of the student-composed play *Voices in Conflict* for being too inflammatory and partisan about the Iraq War. The text was inspired in part by the emotional letter from a 2005 Wilton High graduate killed in the war. Bonnie Dickinson, who has taught theater at Wilton for thirteen years, explained to the *New York Times*, "If I had just done *Grease*, this would not be happening."[1] Some First Amendment attorneys have defended the principal, saying that he had latitude to intervene because of public disruption and controlling "educational merit" during the school day. This was not the only censorship issue at the high school; the student newspaper ran into trouble for criticizing the school administration, and the Gay-Straight Alliance had to take down posters hung in the school stairwells. In response to this action, the Public Theatre and the Vineyard Theatre in New York City invited the high school students to present the play at their prestigious theaters in June 2007.

The Wilton case was not the only publicized example of accusations involving theatrical censorship of political works in recent years. Off Broadway's New York Theatre Workshop encountered a storm of protest by cancelling Alan Rickman's production of *My Name Is Rachel Corrie* originally scheduled for March 2006, after a notable London premiere in 2005. Using diary entries, *My Name Is Rachel Corrie* documents the life and death of activist American Rachel Corrie protesting Israeli actions against Palestinians. Complicating the matter was not the literary material per se but the various groups and media interpreting the play's propaganda value in light of the current crisis in Israel. Furthermore, New York City has the largest concentration of American Jews who figure prominently in the cultural life of the city. When the play went on to a New York opening at another venue, many key critics were unconvinced of the play's aesthetic voltage, objectivity, and theatrical necessity.[2] Certainly, the greater drama occurred outside the play rather than within the play.

What became apparent to the world after September 11, 2001, was the paradoxical reality of United States' vulnerability and majesty—which is to say that our country as the one remaining superpower was overripe as a target for terrorism and unwilling to give full attention to the warnings of terrorism. After the trauma of the four jet hijackings, we were rendered a helpless and wounded giant in pursuit of an invisible nemesis. Prior to the direct threat from Islamic radicals, federal authorities were widely focused on the grass-roots militia and separatists movements that, in part, spurred badly handled stand-offs at Waco, Texas, and Ruby Ridge, Idaho. Regrettably, the demonic shadow of terrorism could be delineated from afar and within our own backyard. The April 19, 1995, bombing of the Alfred P. Murrah Federal Building in Oklahoma City, Oklahoma, the first attack on the World Trade Center on February 26, 1993, and the anthrax scare just months after September 11 had cautioned the nation about stateside catastrophe; still, the magnitude of the Al Qaeda airline scheme had surpassed the imagination of our best defenses. Beyond the realm of homeland security, a cry from the heart was heard from our cultural elite, with many pundits calling for the "end of irony" in our literary life. Included in this circle were Graydon Carter, *Vanity Fair* editor, and Roger Rosenblatt of *Time* magazine. Had irony died as a result of September 11, or was societal cynicism just knocked down senseless?

Notable faux-news shows such as Jon Stewart's *Daily Show* and Stephen Colbert's *Colbert Report* on basic cable Comedy Central provided redoubtable witty relief despite the temporary weight of cultural probity. Comic Dave Chappelle flourished for a short period on the same cable channel, proving that our nation had little patience for church mourning. Around the same time, former sports newscaster Keith Olbermann would reinvent himself on MSNBC as the quintessential sarcastic counterpunch to Fox cable's self-righteous Bill O'Reilly. Olbermann's protégée Rachel Maddow (in her spinoff MSNBC show) elected to apply a sweeter posture of intellectual irony and moral indignation to complement his *Countdown with Keith Olbermann*.

Six days after September 11, comedian Bill Maher on his ABC TV show *Politically Incorrect* generated a firestorm of controversy by parrying in so many words that the Al Qaeda plane hijackers were not cowardly (he admitted they may have been stupid), but *we were cowards* for lobbing cruise missiles two thousand miles away. Maher's remarks triggered his show's cancellation instantaneously and launched a sensational media debate on free speech, patriotism, and a new variation of McCarthyism.

Coming to Maher's defense was *New York Times* Sunday columnist Frank Rich. The argument by a *Times* writer for "unpunished" free speech in our media was not surprising. Rich's career metamorphosis into politics was significant, since he initially found fame as the *Times*'s first-string, acerbic theater critic throughout the 1980s. One of Rich's running themes in the last few years is the unsavory cross-pollination between American entertainment and the transparent market strategies of political camps and their campaigns. The George W. Bush administration's theater of war in Iraq and the president's exploitation of the September 11 tragedy, according to Rich, have gone on for years despite numerous statements from Bush's own party about the folly of this endeavor.[3]

The matter of entertainment colliding with news-headline dignity has all the algebraic features of an inappropriate cocktail joke. Jay Leno, Dave Letterman, and the rest of the late-night television comics fell into a 9/11 moratorium for many days. Yet, to many political and cultural analysts, theaters reacted dully, cautiously, and slowly to the seismic action of the newly emerging threats from foreign terrorists and from our government's responses to these threats. With hundreds of professional regional theaters scattered around the continent, few institutions commissioned or presented shows to acknowledge recent events. Hollywood's response was equally measured with a few films such as Spike Lee's *25th Hour* (2002), Oliver Stone's *World Trade Center* (2006), and Paul Greengrass's *United 93* (2006). Of course, other powerful issues were also impacting this period of history. Our nation's confidence had been punctured in 2000 after a phenomenal burst in the Internet economic bubble, anticipation of the tsunami from Massachusetts (granting legal gay marriage in 2004), shock in 2005 from a hurricane called Katrina, and unnerving in 2001 by Enron's colossal corporate fraud that became a modest prelude to the nine-hundred-billion-dollar Wall Street bailout in 2008, along with comparable bailouts for the banking industry and two major car companies in 2009. The end of the Bush years signaled to many leading economists a Herbert Hoover depression of untold proportion. Moreover, older controversies such as abortion and affirmative action were back in the news along with futuristic concerns regarding stem-cell research and cloning. Quite telling of our society's race and sexual relations was CBS management firing radio personality Don Imus, on April 12, 2007, for loutish remarks directed toward the champion female Rutgers University basketball team. The corporate decision was slow in coming, despite the public uproar about "nappy-headed hos," and the daily media circus enacted perfect unscripted political theater. In addition, star political figures such as then-senator Barack Obama were saying that they would *never again* appear on Imus's show, *Imus in the Morning,* as if Imus had never misspoke before.[4] Finally, Vice President Dick Cheney's unmarried, lesbian daughter, Mary, gave birth to a boy in 2007. American conservatism and every organization that touted family values braced for anything worse. Dramatic irony was resuscitated and looking rather good again—but would our theater pick up the cue now?

Perhaps it was inevitable that the British had to come to the rescue. One of the most discussed and celebrated overt plays about September 11 and our nation's military misadventure in Iraq was from a British playwright, David Hare. Hare's *Stuff Happens* (the bald title comes from U.S. Defense Secretary Donald Rumsfeld's response to the unchecked looting of Iraqi museums) triumphed in London before moving to nonprofit theaters in Los Angeles (2005) and New York (2006). The biting, satirical play premiered in London to sensational houses and a long sell-out run. The playwright explained in an interview, "I describe it as a play about how a supposedly stupid man, George W. Bush, gets everything he wants—and a supposedly clever man, Tony Blair, ends up with nothing he wants."[5]

Hare's caustic script (more proof that irony's alive and well) was not the sole political production that commanded attention outside the scope of the national theater community. Just months after the September 11 attack, Tony Kushner's prescient *Homebody/Kabul*—his first significant work after his Pulitzer-winning *Angels in America*—was produced by New York Theatre Workshop. In Kushner's play, the profound corruption and hardship in contemporary Afghanistan are witnessed in an extended, brilliant monologue by a middle-aged British woman as if attempting to reconcile the various historical accounts, guidebooks, and her own fragile common sense. Certainly, the Taliban was in the international news before the Al-Qaeda affair on our jets; in March 2001, the Taliban ordered the demolition of two massive Buddhist sacred statues (circa 507 and 554 A.D.) in Bamiyan, Afghanistan, and in 1996 the Taliban invited Osama bin Laden to leave the Sudan. Al Qaeda found a perfect, new alliance inside Afghanistan. Kushner's ambitious drama intensified the warped Western lens of scrutiny on a major hot spot halfway around the world. Islamic fundamentalism, as an underestimated theatrical character on the global stage, was ready to make an unmistakably striking presence. Toward the end of the decade, other leading American playwrights weighed in on the imploding militaristic terrain rocking our nation. In 2007, Craig Lucas's *Prayer for My Enemy* highlights with sentience the damage stateside facing an American soldier from Iraq. A year later, Michael Weller's morbidly funny *Beast* imagined disfigured U.S. war dead returning home for an encounter with the Supreme Commander in Crawford, Texas. That same year, Steven Dietz's *Last of the Boys* reflected on the undying Vietnam War syndrome forty years later.

Other lesser-known and minor theater offerings arose on the heels of September 11. Irish singer/song writer Larry Kirwan's *Heart Has a Mind of Its Own* places emphasis on Lieutenant Brian Murphy of New York's Police Department, who perished in the line of duty that fateful day. Elena K. Holy, artistic director of a tiny New York group (the Present Company), commissioned several writers to cover the event known as 9/11—the end result was *Response: Stories about What Happened* (works by Julia Lee Barclay, C. Rusch, and Leslie Bramm). From New York's Stuyvesant High School, a respectable work was assembled by testimony from student peers and faculty and edited by their high school teacher Annie Thoms. Stuyvesant's *With Their Eyes* had productions outside of New York in Kansas City, Missouri, and in Los Angeles. Robert Maese's *Fallen 9/11* is a supernatural story about an attorney trapped inside an elevator shaft and saved by firefighters and Saint Barbara. Seen on the west coast and developed at the Sundance Theatre Lab, actress/playwright Adiana Sevan dramatized in *Taking Flight* her own experiences of assisting a dear friend who nearly died on September 11.

Wall Street Journal drama critic Terry Teachout wrote a scolding treatise in 2005, *When Drama Becomes Propaganda—Why Is So Much Political Art So Awful?* in which he lost all patience for politically relevant theater.[6] Analyzing Sam Shepard's Bush-baiting *The God of Hell* (2004), Teachout declared the satire from one of the best contemporary American playwrights half-baked and wholly unfunny. The critic classified the burden on the political dramatist to be both a good artist and a competent journalist. Moreover, Teachout faulted gifted authors such as Kushner for unabashed self-righteousness and Shepard for club-thumbed sententiousness. He slammed actor/writer Tim Robbins for his antiwar play *Embedded* (2003) and marked down Jules Feiffer's McCarthy-era story *A Bad Friend* (2003) for idealizing the "progressives" of Feiffer's Brooklyn youth. Teachout's key criticism in the piece was to blame the artists not for their leftist identity but for coasting on their leftism and their respective self-satisfaction. He did have words of praise for Doug Wright's 2004 Pulitzer Prize–winning play, *I Am My Own Wife*, about a German transvestite who survived the Nazis and the Communist regime in East Berlin and for Heather Raffo's one-woman show titled *Nine Parts of Desire* (2004) covering a range of Iraqi women's lives impacted by Saddam Hussein.

On the other hand, in 2003 *New York Times* theater reviewer Bruce Weber wrote a well-regarded, Friday-edition *Critic's Notebook* piece with respect to the explosion of political plays hitting the American scene.[7] He quoted Alexis de Tocqueville on the visitor's point of view on our nation as a way to weigh British playwright David Edgar's two-play-cycle *Continental Divide* upon its recent U.S. premiere. Although Weber praised the erudite work (ostensibly a statehouse election drama set in California) and Edgar's venues at prestigious Oregon Shakespeare Festival and La Jolla Playhouse, the relevance of Edgar's saucy political commentary and plotting felt eclipsed, if not by the unexpected gubernatorial victory of film star and bodybuilder Arnold Schwarzenegger, then by the four missile jets in September. Weber cited a positive direction for American dramatists (sensibility left of center) in response to the rise of George W. Bush, September 11 infamy, the undefined war in Iraq, the shifting composition of the Supreme Court, and the discernible realignment of the political forces from *blue* to *red* states. In addition, he identified the historical liberal proclivities of the professional-theater community. The article highlighted Richard Greenberg's *Take Me Out* (2002)—a Broadway play with sustained frontal nudity and winner of a Tony Award about a gay ballplayer—and seven other mostly New York–based shows with distinctive political overtones. John Patrick Shanley's *Dirty Story* and A. R. Gurney's *O Jerusalem* were two 2003 tales centered on America and the Middle East conflict. Gurney also updated his older play *The Fourth Wall* from 1992, which pokes harsh fun at George H. W. Bush's presidency and the hideous callousness of the GOP toward those Americans struggling to make ends meet. Presented around the nation with many Hollywood stars enacting the script, *The Exonerated* (2002) by Erik Jensen and Jessica Blank depicted an unflinching indictment of the death penalty in their "docu-drama." At the Guthrie Theatre in Minneapolis, Arthur Miller's *Resurrection Blues* (2002) satirizes the notion of a second coming inside a third-world, Latin American police state and attracting a callow American camera crew. In its 2002 New York premiere, *Book of Days*, Lanford Wilson's reinvention of Wilder's classic *Our Town* links the web of corruption from corporate America to church, home, and the Republican Party. British playwright Caryl Churchill's *Far Away* (2000)—a cautionary fable about an unnamed authoritarian regime—was showcased at New York Theatre Workshop. Of course, Kushner's *Homebody/Kabul* appeared in the pedigree roundup.

With enthusiasm, Weber's *New York Times* article asserted that this new wave of political theater in the United States had not been rivaled since the Vietnam War/Watergate era. Weber selected an apt quotation from playwright Greenberg:

> You do see American theatre that by default, by what it accepts, promotes conservative thinking. But activist to the right? Theatre doesn't seem to be the medium for that. Maybe it's not the right place for demagoguery. Nobody ever wrote *Waiting for Righty*, did they?

The seventy-year jump from Clifford Odets's 1935 classic "call to action" play, *Waiting for Lefty*, is instructive about what remains timeless in our society and what strains of change we must confront. Union membership battles and unfair labor laws of the 1930s are a far cry from what conditions face the American wage earner today. American theaters continue to support soft-edge, social narrative over heated, political, accusatory tracts. Even Shanley's 2005 Pulitzer Prize–winning script *Doubt*, which bears down on the Catholic Church's sex scandals, is constructed in a restrained and quiet temper. The recent spate of successful agit-prop (agitation-propaganda) documentary films by Michael Moore (*Sicko*), Morgan Spurlock (*Super Size Me*), and Al Gore and David Guggenheim (*An Inconvenient Truth*) suggest what might appear as a more attractive and influential medium for politicized entertainment.

What was curiously missing in Weber's essay in linking the present artistic activity with theater life during the Vietnam/Watergate period: the plethora of influential, ideological theater groups that helped define that epoch and the splendid unfolding known as "off-off Broadway" that includes Julian Beck's Living Theatre, Joe Chaikin's Open Theatre, the San Francisco Mime Troupe, Richard Schechner's Performance Garage, Peter Schuman's Bread and Puppet Theater, Squat Theatre, Luis Valdez's Teatro Campesino, Charles Ludlam's Theatre of the Ridiculous, Lee Breuer's Mabou Mines, Andre Gregory's Manhattan Project, Richard Foreman's Ontological/Hysterical Theatre, the Talking Band, and the Wooster Group. Some of these theater groups have endured with sheer tenacity and sweat equity. The health of these groups is not unrelated to the continuum of political plays by political playwrights. The scrappy, site-specific, political group from the 1980s and 1990s—New York's En Garde Arts—folded when funds dried up and its artistic director Anne Hamburger nabbed a royal salaried position with Disneyland.

The economics of survival for experimental/political theater groups is rudely Darwinian. New York real-estate escalations have made low-budget, loft theater virtually unthinkable. The same can be said of most major theater cities such as Los Angeles, San Francisco, Chicago, Boston, and Seattle. While the dollar continues to shrink in value, funding organizations and state agencies prioritize grants to the larger artistic enterprises over the "bottom fish." Typically, the larger theaters play it safer than the small ones. In addition, the attraction of premium television cable productions and the rise of independent films have drawn a good deal of theater talent away from live performance. For most stage actors and artists, there are no health insurance and no 401(k) retirement annuities. Toward a poor man's theater was a more acceptable idea during the hippie revolution. Nonprofit theater and corporate business have merged after a courtship in the 1980s. The results are convoluted, but clearly the bean-counting CPAs are running much of the show. Hence, regional theaters have been careful about selecting political work first seen in New York since the days of Wallace Shawn's controversial *Aunt Dan and Lemon* (its closing monologue argues sardonically for genocide) and again a dozen years later with Paula Vogel's 1998 Pulitzer Prize–winning play on incest, *How I Learned to Drive*. Steering the life and the artistic decisions of regional theaters is the preservation of the subscriber base; loading up the season with "lush upholstery drama" and avoiding confrontational art make wise sense to the board members of any large cultural palace with an operational budget of five million dollars and upward. To quote a famous campaign line from the 1992 Bill Clinton arsenal, "It's the economy, stupid!"

Another observation that may be very insightful: commercially successful playwrights such as David Mamet and Paddy Chayefsky made their most blatant political and wisely satirical statements in film scripts such as *Wag the Dog* (1997) and *Network* (1976) respectively, reaching an audience in the millions. When British playwright Harold Pinter received the Nobel Prize in 2005, his acceptance speech was a long diatribe aimed squarely at George Bush's foreign policy and questionable American values. Likewise, activist American dramatists such as Eve Ensler, Naomi Wallace, and Larry Kramer have no qualms mixing their daily politics with their body of works.

Despite the harsh realities facing American political drama today, this volume of literate plays calls attention to something exceptional and conscientious on the theatrical landscape. This collection forms a fascinating meditation on our mortality, our geography, our hidden mood, and our destiny. The plays do not lay blame at any one doorstep, but something unsettling resonates in their inclusive company. The six scripts chosen all do not focus on the tragedy of September 11, but they reverberate in the wake of our nation's ordeal and our economic uncertainty. Half of the plays resound with themes of social injustice masked by false alarms on national security, border hysteria, and the tyranny of our cultural biases. With poetic clarity, authority, and distinction, this constellation of work heralds American perseverance, defiance, and anxiety. We see America's silhouette from foreign eyes and from native eyes. Perhaps to a majority of onlookers the silhouette is mainly a Rorschach test in projection. Some of the dramatic texts redirect the political problems in unexpected directions in the examination of war, intolerance, identity, sexuality, our faith in God, and our national well-being. Our country's unwieldy militarism continues to beat hard as a determinant along with America's troubled history regarding race and class relations, universal health care, global ecology, and xenophobia. The volume begins with the conundrum facing our cities' working-class heroes in the fire department, our underclass Kentucky citizens in Butchertown, and an African American family with injurious ties to the first Gulf War. The second half of this book proceeds to jump a metaphoric fence by giving difficult points of view of an Arab American at risk in a large American city, an Egyptian named Mohamed Atta visiting Prague, and a Japanese American community during World War II. The common thread throughout these six plays is a profound delineation on human strife and aspiration in a failing world. It makes sense then to begin the anthology with a drama on unsung heroism seen among our cities' firefighters.

The Guys

On a chance encounter between Anne Nelson, a journalist, and stage director Jim Simpson at a Human Rights gala in New York's Chelsea Piers, a play's genesis took hold. Simpson heard from Nelson about her time spent with a New York fire-department captain who requested help composing eulogies for his eight men after September 11. Simpson encouraged her to imagine a play with that theme in mind. Defying the logic of time, Nelson finished a draft in nine days, and the script went into rehearsals with film stars Sigourney Weaver and Bill Murray for production at a tiny, downtown-Manhattan space blocks away from ground zero. All of the above is rather remarkable. Nelson's sustained career as a journalist and Columbia University professor clearly assisted her honest interpretation and interaction with the real-life analogue to The Guys. Her elegant drama concentrates its energies on Nick, a damaged captain, who relies reluctantly on Nelson's fictional surrogate, Joan, with the task of building fitting tributes for the officer's fallen colleagues. In her role as compassionate listener, Joan evokes from Nick the towering portraits of courage and individual vitality unique to each friend and member of the firehouse station. The odd pairing of Nick and Joan lends an element of poignancy and humanity outside the devastation that destroyed the World Trade Center.

The compact play is rendered in the most careful light, neither sentimental nor calculated. The conflict within the event is not a power struggle between two souls but the necessity to merge with a total stranger. Nelson's language respects the vernacular and mines the depth of simple expressions artfully. *The Guys* captures an elusive essence about heroism and survival that mitigates the catastrophic loss for so many American working-class families.

At the Vanishing Point

Inspired in part by the life and the startling work of photographer Ralph Eugene Meatyard from Lexington, Kentucky, and using historic Butchertown, a very rough section of nearby Louisville, Naomi Iizuka's *At the Vanishing Point* presents a tapestry of raw, unpunctuated, singular voices. This site-specific play was commissioned by Actors Theatre of Louisville. Make no mistakes about it; Butchertown is a contemporary hog-killing neighborhood that maintains little vanity or pretension. Brecht had captured much of the bloody atmosphere of the urban slaughterhouse in his Chicago fantasy *Saint Joan of the Stockyards* (1931); Iizuka maintains an equal texture of grittiness and uncouth behavior without passing judgment on her characters. Iizuka's ability to build brilliant enigmatic theatrical events has added immensely to her renown. Her play's haunting structure is something of a choral tone poem based on real lives, sparing a plot engine or any chronological necessity to stay linear. Iizuka starts with The Photographer, who in turn announces the other figures and establishes the curious facets of the narrative. Meatyard's imagery (he died in 1972) was acclaimed for the ingenious use of rejected dolls and doll parts, broken mirrors, all forms of masks and papier-mâché busts, dead fowl, and many other props. In the same spirit, Iizuka has assembled an aesthetic collage of human debris and detritus, systemic of America's underclass and compassionate as the works of Studs Terkel. Specific to the philosophic journey of *At the Vanishing Point* are the interplay of memory and vision, conversation and photographic expression, teleology and the banishment of death. The play quietly taps into the myth of Orpheus and also relies respectfully on the voices of The Photographer's three children. The eclectic pastiche of music comes from Louis Armstrong, Sun Ra, Tara Jane O'Neil, and Mozart's German lieder. The subtle political essay in the play reveals itself in Maudie Totten's concluding monologue:

> when we got married, roy was working the cut floor, pulling loins. that's a bracket one job. good money hard work. you gotta be quick and strong. the speed of the rail is 300 hog an hour. you got 25 men workin the rail, that's five hogs per minute, 12 second per hog. and you gotta do it right the first time, cause I'll tell you, you don't get a second chance. Roy had

a friend name frank henzel. he worked the kill floor splitting hogs. they used chainsaws, and they didn't have the automatic brakes back then, and the saw, it got away from him, and it's on a pulley right, on a chain, and it flew up and coasted see, turned all around, turned back on him and tore him up, it tore him to pieces.

The Venus de Milo Is Armed

Playwright Kia Corthron has earned an esteemed reputation here and in England as a decisive and prolific political dramatist. She brings to life vivacious characters. Her wide range of social issues is not hidden; she is happy to expose the full force of her conscience. *The Venus de Milo Is Armed*, which premiered in Montgomery, Alabama, at the Alabama Shakespeare Festival, is a distinct southern story that entails, at first glance, the coming together of an African American family riddled by secrets. Rin, her protagonist, is a young woman obsessed with land mines and missing body parts. She keeps land mines, and she knows too well about her brother's disquieting business. Taking a clue from the playwright's title, readers may still be surprised to see the incongruity of the filial reunion set against the universal horror of land mines. Collateral damage, like friendly fire, has become a hideous euphemism in postmodern military parlance; the moral complications to modern warfare transcend the combatant armies. The delayed destruction and indifference to the victim set this passive weapon into a league of its own. Corthron's canvas pulls disparate elements together, defeating our expectations in gradations. Family lies can unify or demolish society at random, which makes this a tragic story. Her script was commissioned by Southern Writers' Project based at the Shakespeare Festival, and it is interesting to note that the theater signed the contract on September 10, 2001. Admirers of Corthron commend her for her civic passion, lyric realism, and exceptional rhythmic dialogue that delineate her characters but rarely revert to the author. At times, Corthron risks sounding polemical, but her unflinching poetic expressiveness, adroitness, and fidelity to human relationships deflect the problem handily.

Back of the Throat

In *Back of the Throat*, two government agents wreak havoc on the life of obliging Khaled, seemingly a luckless Arab American. The importance of the play is aided and abetted by the Federal Patriot Act; our government can be the agency for terrorism and not its sorry victim. Other political plays from overseas have applied some wry variation of intrusion by two government officials (Nikolai Gogol's *Inspector General*, 1836, and Václav Havel's *Largo Desolato*, 1985), but specific to Yussef El Guindi's drama is the comic paranoia of ethnicity post 9/11. The odd title to this script reflects an absurd moment where Khaled instructs the agents in how to pronounce his name. Khaled demands to know who submitted his name to them. Was it a friend or a neighbor? An innocent past encounter by Khaled with a known terrorist fuels the inquiry. Essentially an interrogation drama, the agents, Bartlett and Carl, begin politely, persistent in bagging their quarry by insinuation and distortion. Their routine is classic good cop, bad cop. Carl finds a music box that plays "Oklahoma," and Khaled responds, "I've never been able to identify the tune." Adding to his pain, Khaled experiences animus in an alternate reality provided by flashbacks. These hallucinatory scenes remove us from the claustrophobia of his apartment, but there is no respite from the atmosphere of persecution. The story ends with ambiguity; Khaled might be more culpable than not, meriting the law's tag "a person of interest." El Guindi belongs to a circle of new Arab American writers (Nathalie Handal, Jamil Khoury, Heather Raffo, and Betty Shamieh) who have emerged on the national stage. To mention Franz Kafka hovering above El Guindi's sky would be a truism, as it would be remiss to forget Harold Pinter's *Birthday Party* (1958). Pinter's Stanley is not that different from Khaled, unless one cites racial profiling. El Guindi's production note tells the actors to avoid broadness and menace until the text firmly arrives at that station.

Three Nights in Prague

With *Three Nights in Prague*, the elliptical mindset of Al Qaeda's Mohamed Atta al Sayed became the play's initial rationale. After the first reports alerted the world about the nineteen airborne terrorists, it was the unforgettable searing photograph of Atta—cold hostile eyes, tight serious mouth, and arrogant brow—that most captured my attention. His absolutism could not be any more intense. Atta, college-educated engineer and the sole Egyptian, stood apart from the other hijackers—most of the men were from Saudi Arabia. Months after the American tragedy, intelligence reports from the Czech Republic underscored the fact that Atta was seen in Prague in dialogue with a high-level Iraqi consulate member five months before 9/11. Dick Cheney seized on this esoteric news item to make the strategic connection between Osama Bin Laden and Saddam Hussein. In May 2002, *New York Times* columnist William Safire devoted an op/ed piece on Atta's time in Prague.[8] Safire identified Iraq's chief espionage agent in the Iraqi embassy—Ahmed al-Ani—as the operative who might have had extensive consultations with Atta. In addition, Safire discussed the reasons why the CIA and media outlets such as *Newsweek* and the *Washington Post* sought to discredit the accounts. Assuming said intelligence on Atta was true, according to Safire, the report would establish a casus belli, justifying the war on Iraq. The play I wrote probes that fantasia from sundry angles and applies an overlay of speculation on Atta's published will and the rumors of his closeted homosexuality.[9] Although there is an absence of an American character, the dramatic events adumbrate our nation's image as though looking at a mysterious photographic negative inside a darkroom. Complicating the proposition of the play's viability in America's professional theaters is the declared concern from many artistic directors and literary managers that a provocative Mohamed Atta narrative on stage is simply an invitation for trouble from a myriad of groups and individuals. The discreet worry expressed was not unlike that of bookstores unwilling to stock Salman Rushdie's novel *The Satanic Verses* in 1989. The *fatwa* commanding Moslems worldwide to kill Rushdie issued by Iran's principal leader, the Ayatollah Ruhollah Khomeini, had a powerful impact on the book-buying public and the international media. Rushdie had to spend nearly a decade in hiding, and he employed every measure of personal safety imaginable. Hitoshi Igarashi, the Japanese-language translator of *The Satanic Verses*, was killed in 1991; Ettore Capriolo, the Italian-language translator, was stabbed the same month as Igarashi, and William Nygaard, the publisher in Norway, survived an attempted murder in 1993. Fifteen years later, Sherry Jones's novel *The Jewel of Medina*, showcasing the life of Islamic prophet Muhammad's prepubescent wife, was quickly pulled by Random House in August 2008 (fearing another *Satanic Verses* reception). With that said, what assurances can you give a professional theater company that no disruption and no harm will come to this public institution if you portray an Islamic zealot in harsh light?

Question 27, Question 28

Perhaps most removed from the literal time frame and cultural landscape within this anthology, *Question 27, Question 28* is rich in allegorical power and moral paradox. One of the play's strategies is to test the notion of tolerance and trust by a historical conduit. Certainly, it was a gambit that worked quite well when Arthur Miller wrote *The Crucible* (1953). San Francisco's Asian American Theatre Company commissioned Chay Yew, noted writer and director, to revisit the disconcerting World War II internment camps that held Japanese Americans living on the West Coast. Reports identified over 110,000 civilians who were removed from their homes as early as 1942. Sadly, President Franklin D. Roosevelt authorized this action through an executive order. *Question 27, Question 28* navigates the full controversial chapter of behavior stateside, beginning well before the attack on Pearl Harbor December 7, 1941, and broad stepping to President Ronald Reagan's signing the 1988 bill that provided financial restitution to each remaining Japanese American who had lost his/

her rights. The play's title is a direct reminder of the two numbered questions about "United States loyalty" put to the encamped individuals. Yew's artistic and political instinct brought about a testimonial drama referencing archival matter and, in the main, the recollections of women. His theatrical result was a "recital" text for three Asian actresses and one Caucasian actress, not wholly unlike Brecht's "learning plays," or "*Lehrstücke*," from the late 1920s and early 1930s. Yew's production notes specify a staged reading atmosphere with scripts and music stands rather than fully designed enacted drama. The script's directorial approach clearly is understated and intellectual. Several Caucasian women are in the repertory of *Question 27, Question 28*, and their proclamations and asides run the gamut from sensitivity to intolerance toward Asians. Yew also highlights generational differences among Asian women, and the shading of attitudes provides a complex illustration of American life for minorities. The parallels to the experiences of Islamic and Arabic communities after September 11 may not be as egregious and reprehensible, but it would be hard to not examine the periodic cycle of governmental abuses toward whole communities in a land as diverse as ours. Finally, Yew's international reputation as an energetic, socially agitated dramatic writer is enhanced by telescoping back into history in order to reinterpret pressing contentions today that will not fade away.

Political theater in America has a great obligation in helping our society understand what is truly at stake in democracy, security, and the ethical economy for the next generation. We expect too much from glitzy media journalists, bloodless Internet discourse, and traditional Sunday newspaper pundits, all the while giving little attention and far less faith to passionate actors on the cusp of a continental proscenium. This volume of idiosyncratic, uniquely signature plays provides ample evidence about the inequities and contradictions within our culture and the valuable mission to stay focused on a national dialogue free from talk-radio platitudes and the bromides of politicians. When the 2008 Republican candidate's campaign for the presidency referred to the nonessential celebrities such as Paris Hilton and "Joe the Plumber" while framing an argument against the Democratic opponent, one must have a degree of despair about democracy in America and the terrible blurring between vapid entertainment and imposing societal decisions. Likewise, the exquisite media confusion between comedian Tina Fey's send-up of Governor Sarah Palin and Sarah Palin (in the real) provided a Pirandellian vortex on the nature of political identity.

In future years, the American stage, as is its wont, will revive favorite plays and musicals from our time and the major plays of Shakespeare. The collective intentions of our regional theaters and the commercial theater on and off Broadway will determine what relevance remains of live performance. The final wave of our digital age may reduce the spirit of live drama and social editorial beyond the pale. The trenchant politics of our new age may become passé and irrelevant, along with the vain fashions of our time. That wish to some sounds exceedingly refreshing and perhaps long overdue. Indeed, the recent nostalgia for Clifford Odets's *Awake and Sing* (1935) at Lincoln Center and the retro-musicals of *Hairspray, Cry-Baby, Jersey Boys*, and *A Catered Affair* on our Great White Way may have little to do with anything politically angry today. But in the precise mirror of our cultural face, we must account and accept our blemished, political features. Theater is our life. An unexamined life is not worth living. Our archival memory resides inside this mirror and, in some profound capacity, so does our unmistakable destiny.

Notes

1. Alison Leigh Cowan, "Play about Iraq War Divides a Connecticut School," *New York Times*, March 24, 2007.

2. Ben Brantley, "Notes from a Young Idealist in a World Gone Awry," review of *My Name Is Rachel Corrie*, Alan Rickman, director, New York Theatre Workshop, *New York Times*, October 16, 2006; Jeremy McCarter, "Stand and Don't Deliver," review of *My Name Is Rachel Corrie*, Alan Rickman, director, New York Theatre Workshop, *New York Magazine*, October 30, 2006.

3. Frank Rich, *Someone Tell the President the War Is Over*, New York Times Op/Ed, August 14, 2005.

4. Jake Tapper, "Obama: Fire Imus," *ABC News: Politics*, April 11, 2007, http://www.abcnews.go.com/Politics/story?id=3031317&page=1. The article discusses Senator Barack Obama's calling for the firing of Don Imus.

5. Ina Jaffe, *"Stuff Happens": The Iraq War as History Play*, NPR, August 26, 2005.

6. Terry Teachout, *When Drama Becomes Propaganda—Why Is So Much Political Art So Awful? Wall Street Journal*, June 6, 2005.

7. Bruce Weber, "Critic's Notebook: Political Plays, Alive and Fiery," *New York Times*, March 14, 2003.

8. William Safire, *Mr. Atta Goes to Prague, New York Times* Op/Ed, May 9, 2002.

9. Michelangelo Signorile, "The Mohamed Atta Files: The Hijacking Ringleader Was Gay (BARF!)," *MSNBC/Newsweek Web Exclusive*, http://www.freerepublic.com/focus/f-news/562450/posts, October 31, 2001.

THE GUYS

Anne Nelson

Production Notes

THE GUYS, Nelson's first play, is based on a true experience. It opened at The Flea Theater, only a few blocks from Ground Zero, on December 4, 2001, twelve weeks after the September 11th attacks. It played to thirteen months of sold-out houses, featuring a rotating cast that included Sigourney Weaver, Bill Murray, Susan Sarandon, Tim Robbins, Bill Irwin, Amy Irving, and Anthony LaPaglia, among others. The play drew more than twelve thousand people to the seventy-four-seat theater and has subsequently been produced in forty-eight states and at least twelve foreign countries. The 2002 recorded version, featuring Irwin and Swoosie Kurtz, won the Best Audio Drama award from the Audio Publishers Association. The 2003 feature-film version premiered at Lincoln Center's New Directors series and received Special Recognition for Excellence in Filmmaking from the National Board of Review. Scores of theatrical productions of *The Guys* have been presented as benefits for local firefighters.

> *Landscape plotted and pieced—fold, fallow, and plough;*
>
> *And all trades, their gear and tackle and trim.*
>
> *All things counter, original, spare, strange;*
>
> *Whatever is fickle, freckled (who knows how?)*
>
> *With swift, slow; sweet, sour; adazzle, dim;*
>
> *He fathers-forth whose beauty is past change:*
>
> *Praise him.*
>
> —*Gerard Manley Hopkins,*
> *"Pied Beauty," 5–10*

Part 1: Are You OK?
Opening Monologue

(A tall woman, simply dressed in pants. She stands, spotlit at center stage, and addresses the audience directly.)

JOAN: New York. My beautiful, gleaming, wounded city.

When I was a little girl in Oklahoma, I'd wait every week for *Newsweek* and *Life* magazine to plop into the mailbox. What were they doing this week in New York City? Going to plays written by Eur-o-pee-ans. Listening to jazz and string quartets. All those things you weren't supposed to do in Oklahoma. I thought you probably needed a passport to get into New York. I had this picture in my mind of people lined up at the bridge, paying a fee for admission.

I was right.

I hit New York when I was seventeen. I never really went back.

Stone by stone, I built my life. A prewar apartment on the Upper West Side.

(Conspiratorially.)

Rent stabilized.

Filled with music and books. A husband who liked opera more than football. Two charming children in a good private school. An interesting job.

Oh yes, my career. I started out, as a young woman, traveling to Latin America and writing about the dirty wars. I was a brave, foolish twenty-five-year-old girl—yes, girl, though I would have fought that word at the time. I saw bodies, talked to refugees, dodged bombs. The only time I was really afraid was on nights before I got on the plane to go back down. I'd cut my deal with God. If I got killed this time, someone would have to feed my cat.

That was before I had human dependents.

After a few years, I burned out. I settled down. I made my mother happy. And when I got my normal life, my apartment, my family, it was like a gift. Every time I took a hot shower I was grateful. Gradually, I stopped reporting. I found work as an editor. I became—theoretical.

(Beat.)

"Where were you September 11th?" Question of the year. I was at home, getting ready to go vote for Mark Green.

18

How many times did I vote for Mark Green? It was like Catholics and the weekly obligation.

The phone rings and it's my father in Oklahoma, "Is your TV on?"

"No," I want to say. "Only people in Oklahoma have their TVs on at nine o'clock in the morning."

(Changes demeanor to talking-to-father mode.)

"No," I say. "Why?"

"A plane crashed into the World Trade Center. Musta been one of those little planes, pilot had a heart attack."

"Dad," I said. "Maybe it's terrorism."

He thought about it. "Why would someone do that?"

(Long beat.)

So I turned on the television and joined the witnesses of the world. I called my husband, who works on Thirty-first Street. So he could tell his office mates and they could all go watch it out the window.

Note this—my Dad calls from Oklahoma so I can call my husband so he can watch it out the window.

That moment marked the end of the Postmodern Era.

So we all, in our assigned places, watch the second plane hit. We watch the towers go down.

And then, because I don't know what else to do, I go to the corner polling place and vote for Mark Green. . . .

The week after the attack, I visit my sister in Park Slope. She lives in Park Slope because she's ten years younger than me. Over the ten years between us, the Upper West Side got priced out of the market.

I like Park Slope. It's more like my neighborhood used to be.

They just had another kid, three months old, and I needed to hold that baby. It was primal. That week you could have scored big in the rent-a-baby trade.

The phone rang, my sister answered. It was her friend the masseuse. Park Slope—you have friends who are masseuses. You meet them at the bookstore coffee shop during poetry readings.

This friend was giving emergency massages to rescue workers. "Look," she said. "I've been working on this guy. Bad shape. He's a fire captain, and he just lost most of his men. He's got to give the eulogies. The first one is on Thursday. He—can't write them. He needs a writer."

"Well," I said. When was the last time I heard someone say they *needed* a writer. In fact, that was just when we were all discovering our "crisis of marginality."

Everyone wanted to help. But we couldn't. They didn't want amateurs wandering around the site. They didn't want our blood. Even surgeons felt useless. A friend of mine went to volunteer. Plumbers and carpenters first, they said. Intellectuals to the back of the line.

The firefighter needs a writer.

I called him. He lived down the block. "Come now," I said. "I have a few hours." My sister took the baby out for the day.

I knew exactly what to expect. Fire captain. Big guy. Works out.

(A knock. Lights come up to reveal a modest living room. There are two chairs with side tables that hold a coffee pot, half full, and two cups. It is early afternoon. Over the course of the play, the lights gradually dim towards evening.)

(JOAN walks stage right to meet NICK. He is in his late forties, no taller than JOAN. He is dressed in blue jeans and tennis shoes. He holds a folder of files in his hand. He looks around him uncertainly, with an apologetic, disoriented expression, then offers his hand. They shake.)

NICK: Joan?

JOAN: Hi.

NICK: Hi.

JOAN: I . . . I'm really sorry about . . . what happened.

NICK: *(Unfocused gaze.)* Oh. Yeah.

(Comes back into focus and looks at her anxiously.)

Look, I feel really bad about this. It's a beautiful afternoon. It's the weekend. You should be with your kids. You don't need to be doing this.

JOAN: My kids have playdates. I'm useless. It's fine. Hey, do you want some coffee?

NICK: Yeah, sure, if you've got some going.

JOAN: *(She gets up.)* Milk? Sugar?

NICK: Just black.

(She goes to the kitchen and brings back two mugs. They sit down at the table. He puts the files down on the table. They both place their hands on the cups and look down at them in silence.)

See, I just don't know what to do. These guys . . . the call came, and they went off, and . . . they haven't found them yet but . . . some of the

families, they want to have the service now so they can try to move on.
. . . I got to get up and talk in church. . . . I been sitting down in front of
a piece of paper all day, and I haven't been able to write one sentence.
Not a thing—I keep going into a clutch.

(He looks at her helplessly.)

    I mean, I'm no writer under normal circumstances. But now. . . .
What can I tell the families? What am I going to say?

JOAN: Hey, it's OK. Maybe I can help. I . . . I've never written a eulogy before,
but I've written some speeches. It's OK. Now, how many did you say
there were?

NICK: *(He sighs.)* Eight.

JOAN: Eight.

NICK: Eight men. I lost eight men.

JOAN: So . . . eight eulogies.

(She stares at the paper in front of her.)

    Well, we'll just take it a step at a time, do what we can. You say that
one of the services is this week?

NICK: Yeah, Thursday.

JOAN: So we'll do that one first.

NICK: You see, the department has 350 men unaccounted for. It's been ten days,
but they haven't found any bodies. Some of the families, they're still
waiting, they say they're going to find them alive in some air pocket or
something. But the other families, they say no, they're gone. They want
to go ahead and have the service. But they don't have bodies.

JOAN: *(Slowly, taking it in.)* Right.

NICK: Some of the families are putting a picture up where the coffin is supposed to go. And we'll just do the eulogies up there with the photograph.

JOAN: Uh huh.

NICK: . . . but the thing is, we're talking about 350 men—you got to understand,
over a bad year we might lose maybe, six. This was in one day. One hour.

(Pause.)

    So. That means 350 services. But if they keep digging and find some
bodies, the families might want funerals to bury them, and if every guy had
a service *and* a funeral, that would be 700. . . . We'll be doin' this for a year.

(Thinks for a moment.)

    I hope they don't all want funerals, too.

JOAN: *(She shakes her head absorbing the thought. They sit silently.)* So which services are scheduled so far?

NICK: *(Pause while he tries to think.)* I've got the list here.

(He opens the file and looks through several papers.)

Bill Dougherty, he's first. That's Thursday. Then Jimmy Hughes. He's next week. After that there's Patrick O'Neill. That's a real hard one. My best friend. What a fine man. His wife wants to do his on his birthday. And the next day is Barney Keppel. Barney. Everybody loved Barney. The guys are going to take that one hard.

JOAN: *(She writes the names down on a list and looks at it.)* So that makes four we need to do today. Well, we'll just try it a step at a time. Thursday?

NICK: Thursday. Yeah. Bill Dougherty.

JOAN: *(She sits with pen poised over notepad.)* Catholic service?

(NICK nods mutely.)

Did you talk to the priest? Do you know how long the eulogy's supposed to be?

NICK: Oh, not too long. Four minutes, five max. No, not even that long. There'll be other people talking, too. But the families want me to say something. I'm the captain. What can I say to them? How can I explain it?

JOAN: Hey, it's OK.

(Softly.)

I mean . . .

(She reaches a hand toward his shoulder but awkwardly withdraws it; he doesn't see. She fetches a box of paper tissues and puts them unobtrusively on the table and sits down. He takes one and grips it tightly in his hand.)

Human beings have been giving eulogies for thousands of years. You're doing this for the families. You'll comfort them. It's for them. It won't be about what happened that day. We'll talk about who they were, make it about them. That's what you can give the families.

NICK: I keep hearing all these speeches from the politicians on TV. The pictures in the papers. Hero this, hero that. I don't even recognize them.

JOAN: So that's why it's good *you're* doing this. You can give their families and friends something they can recognize. You can do that. So, hey, tell me about Bill.

NICK: *(He takes a deep breath.)* Bill. Yeah, Bill. Well, see, that's the problem. There's just not much to say. This hero stuff, like they were some guys in a movie. But Bill—he wasn't like that. He was just an ordinary guy. A *schmo*. If Bill walked into a room, nobody would even notice.

(Looks up to her helplessly.)
You can't say that in a eulogy.

JOAN: Hey, it's OK. Don't worry. We'll do this. I mean, people who are ordinary . . . in a . . . an extraordinary situation—that's what this is about. Now back up a little bit. Tell me about him. What did he look like? When you think of him, what comes to your mind?

NICK: Look like? He looked like—a plumber. Not a big guy. Reddish hair. Mid-forties. But he was the senior man. All the junior men relied on him. They had their eyes on him to know what to do. "My men," he called them.

JOAN: When you close your eyes, where do you see him? What's he doing?

NICK: *(Thinks.)* In the kitchen.

JOAN: The kitchen?

NICK: The guys spend a lot of time in the kitchen between runs. There's a lot of downtime. Bill's there saying, "I'm looking out for my men. . . . My men need this. . . ." Yeah, Bill spent a lot of time talking in the kitchen. He was real good with the younger guys, he was always taking them and pointing things out to them.

JOAN: *(Writing it down, encouragingly.)* Uh huh . . . yeah?

NICK: See, someone like Bill—he's real senior, he's been there sixteen years. There's always new guys comin' through, and sometimes they can be a pain in the ass for the older guys. They're a little nervous, and they don't know where things are. A guy like Bill could have blown them off, but he was always lookin' out for them. Here's the gear, here's the tools, here's how you handle it, no, not like that, like this . . .

JOAN: *(Writing.)* Was he a family man? Religious?

NICK: Oh, Bill was quiet. Never talked about himself. Half the company didn't even know he was married. I know he went to Mass, but he never made a show of it. But he was proud of being Irish. You know, I think that's why he was a fireman—it's thick in the Irish blood. *(Pauses.)* He loved New York, all its nooks and crannies. You know, these guys see the city from the outside and the inside, underground and in all the hidden places. Bill wanted to know the history of everything. I remember him telling me, "Nick, just got this great book—*A Walking Tour of Flatbush Avenue*."

JOAN: Flatbush Avenue!

NICK: You want to have a guy like that around, especially downtown, with all these crazy streets. Nowadays you get a computerized map when you get a call. But somebody can still call in and give you bad directions, or a building name with no address, or no entrance on that side of the street . . .

JOAN: I never thought of that.

NICK: On that day . . . I still don't know what happened. I can't find anyone who saw the company. They got off the apparatus, and the officer told the driver, "We're going to Tower 1." They're running down West Street in full gear about the time the second plane hit. And maybe they peeled off and went to Tower 2. But we don't know where to look for them.

(Stops, choked.)

JOAN: *(After a moment.)* What else did Bill love? Any sports? Music? You said he hung out in the kitchen—did he like to cook?

NICK: Oh, Bill wasn't exactly a cook. The guys take turns making meals for everybody. Sometimes it's OK, but it can get pretty bad. I call their cooking "valiant attempts, and dismal failures."

JOAN: *(She smiles.)* Yeah?

NICK: Every guy has his specialty, and they usually cook it every time it's their turn. We're talking undercooked chicken and *nasty* Rice-a-Roni. Bill would sit there and try it and come up with some real zingers.

JOAN: So he was more of a critic.

NICK: Yeah, yeah!—he was the firehouse food critic. And he could zap 'em but good. But not mean. He was never mean.

JOAN: OK, OK. . . . Yeah, this is good. This works. 'Cause you know, Nick, you want to give people someone they recognize. Not just a plaster saint. This is good. Wait a minute.

(She writes, crosses out, draws some arrows on the page.)

NICK: *(Watching her.)* I'm really sorry. I'm not giving you anything to work with here. I shouldn't be doing this to you.

JOAN: *(Still focused on paper, shaking her head.)* No, no, just wait.

(She tears off a sheet, copies from one sheet to another, then quickly numbers paragraphs.)

Here.

(She hands two pages to NICK.)

Try this. Start here, and it jumps to there. And . . . if you could read it out loud so I can hear it?

NICK: *(Reads slowly.)* "I'm Nick Flanagan, captain of Ladder Company 60.

24

I've worked with Bill Dougherty for a long time. I want to give my condolences to all of Bill's family here with us today."

(Nods.)
    OK.

(He resumes reading.)
    "We've been hearing a lot about heroes, and Bill was one of them. He gave his life for others, and that is a noble thing. But Bill was a quiet hero. Never one to show off, never blustered. He was a firefighter for sixteen years, and he was a good one. He had the most important quality for a firefighter. He was absolutely dependable."

(He looks up and smiles at her.)
    Yeah. That's right. Dependable.
    "Over time, we realized how important he was for the newer guys at the firehouse. Sometimes it can be hard for the experienced men to show the young ones the drills year after year. But Bill was always looking out for the new guys, showing them the ropes. And he did it in that quiet way of his, never made them feel small. 'My men,' he called them. 'My men.'"

(Looks at her.)
    Yeah. You got it. You got it. That's him.
JOAN: They're your words. I just put them in order.
NICK: No. You got the craft. You know how to put it.

(He reads on.)
    "He was like an older brother to them, looking out for them. They appreciated it, and I appreciated it. You got to have guys like Bill to build a strong team. They may not say much, but they hold things together.
    "If Bill hadn't been a fireman, he could have been a food critic. Bill used to spend a lot of time in the kitchen, talking to the guys and evaluating the cuisine. When Bill tried out a questionable dish, he could come up with some real zingers. The restaurants of New York are lucky he went into another line of work."
    Yeah. The guys'll like that.

(Nods. Looks from one page to the next, finds his place.)
    "What did Bill love? He loved his family, and he loved this city. On September 11, he was the senior man. The younger men could look to

someone who was steady and professional, to show the way. We know that Bill and the other firefighters of New York saved hundreds—maybe thousands—of lives that day. That means that there are thousands of people and their family members who are able to go on because of them. We can only thank them and ask for God's kindest blessing on those they have left behind."

(He absorbs it.)

JOAN: *(Pause. She looks at him anxiously.)* So it works?

NICK: You got it. I can do this. I'll have this in front of me when I get up there, something to give them.

*(*JOAN *takes a breath, closes her eyes, and slumps back into her chair.)*

NICK: You OK?

*(*JOAN *stands up and breaks the fourth wall.)*

Monologue 2

JOAN: "Are you OK?" That was what we all kept asking each other, the rest of September. What was the answer? The pebble's dropped in the water. The point of entry is you, yourself. Were you present at ground zero and wounded, suffocated, or covered in white ash? No? I guess you're OK. The first ring around the pebble: "Is your family OK?" Did you lose someone in the towers or on the planes?

The next ripple—friends. "Are your people OK?"

Next ripple: If someone died in the Tower that you had dinner with once and thought was a really nice person, are you OK?

Next: If you look at a flyer of a missing person in the subway and you start to lose it, are you OK?

(Pause.)

If all the flyers are gone one day. They're—gone. Are you OK?

Is anyone OK?

That first week I bought a coffee at Starbucks on the way to work, and the guy at the counter handed me my cup and said,

"Here's your change. God bless America."

And I took a breath, and said, "Are your people OK?" And he said, "Only two missing."

Only two.

And I said, . . .

(In strained voice.)

"I hope you can find comfort."

Only people in Oklahoma talk to servers in coffee shops. But at least there you can say, "God bless." Here you don't know if they have a God, or if you have a God—or if anyone *has* a God, it's the same God. That wants the same things. . . .

We all travel in our track. Neighborhood, job, friends. Parents of your children's friends. No matter how big a city gets, the only way to live in it is to live in your village. You get to a certain age, the next person you meet has a logical connection to the ones that came before. Friend of a friend.

Nick and I weren't supposed to meet. You couldn't create another sequence for his life that leads to me. Or for my life that leads to him. After September 11th, all over the city, people were jumping tracks. (NICK *and* JOAN *are back at the table.)*

Part 2: Pain Has Its Price

NICK: Jimmy. What can I say about Jimmy? He was the new guy. Still on probation. I hardly knew the guy. I never even got to meet his family. His girlfriend came down to the firehouse last week, nice girl. Said he was a bicycle racer. The bike club out in Flushing had a memorial for him, put flowers on the handlebars and everything.

(He stops short.)

But that's all I know about him.

JOAN: How long was he there?

NICK: Oh, he was only with the ladder company for a couple of weeks. He had been with the engine company for seven weeks before that. That's what they do with the probies—seven weeks engine, seven weeks ladder. But when they flip 'em to ladder, they come into my office the first day, we shake hands, and then we might not see each other that much for a while.

JOAN: Ladder?

NICK: The ladder company. See, there are two companies side by side. The mission of the engine is to put water on the fire. They got the hoses, they work like a team to get it where it has to go. Ladder—we do ventilation, entry, and search.

JOAN: *(Feeling a little slow.)* So your engine has the ladder thing.

NICK: No, no. You call the engine an engine and the ladder a truck. Oh yeah, the big ladder, sure. But a lot of other things, too. All kinds of ladders.

Suitcase ladder—beautiful, folds up so you can carry it like a suitcase. Axes. Electronic sensors. We got the forcible-entry team that breaks down the doors so the guys with the hoses can get in. Engine and truck, we work out of the same firehouse, and sometimes we hang out together, but we don't know all each other's guys the same way.

JOAN: I see. So Jimmy just got there. What was it like for him?

NICK: *(Struggling.)* He had to learn fast. He was willing to learn—it was always "Show me more, show me more." I think he had a lotta friends that were firemen.

JOAN: How old was he?

NICK: I got it here.

(He opens the file in front of him for the first time and leafs through a couple of pages, squinting.)

I think . . . let's see. . . . Yeah, he was . . . uh, twenty-six.

JOAN: Oh.

(She writes slowly.)

What kind of things did he like? What did he look like?

NICK: *(He turns the pages in the file slowly, in consternation.)* I don't know, I just don't know. He wasn't there that long. And with everything that's happened . . .

(He looks at her desperately.)

This is terrible. This is a terrible thing. But I have to tell you, right now, I can't even remember his face.

(He is anguished and ashamed.)

JOAN: Hey. Hey. We'll do this. We'll figure it out.

(She studies her notes.)

Now you say they come into your office on the first day.

NICK: Yeah, they all do. They come in, and I shake their hand, and I say, "Welcome to the company. This is the best job in the world."

(He stops.)

Two weeks before this happened, I shook his hand. But I didn't tell him he'd be dead.

JOAN: *(Gently.)* You didn't know.

(He's still silent.)
> So how was he doing at the job?

NICK: I'm not real sure. He was still learning.

JOAN: I mean, if he was screwing up, you would have heard about it, right?

NICK: Oh yeah. I always hear about it if they screw up. *(Pause while he thinks.)* I didn't hear anything like that.

JOAN: *(Writing.)* So he wasn't screwing up. So he was doing fine. And he went through probation, and every guy goes through probation, so we can put that in, too, right?

NICK: *(Tentatively.)* Yeah . . .

JOAN: So how does it work?

NICK: Well, first they got to take the test. And then there's this brutalizing physical. And paperwork, lots of paperwork. Piles of paperwork. And then they go home and wait. Long, long wait. They think it'll never end. Most of the guys get rejected. But if you're lucky, you get the call. "This is fireman so-and-so. Come on down. You're in."

JOAN: *(Writing and smiling.)* Yeah. And then what?

NICK: And then you start. And you sit down, keep your eyes open, and shut up.

JOAN: Right. What are the senior guys like with the new ones?

NICK: Well, you know. They show 'em around. Some are more patient than others. They give 'em a little bit of a hard time. Not exactly hazing—it all goes with the territory. Jimmy was doing fine. He was a regular guy, low-key. Well-liked. He came in same time with another probie. Hipólito Díaz. I love that name. You gotta love that name. Where do they get these names. Sounds like a ballpark.

(He assumes a sports-announcer voice.)
> "Now batting for Jorge Posada, Hipólito Díaz."

(Pause.)
> Hippo's missing, too. He's missing with the guys from the engine.

JOAN: So they started in the summer, right? Was it a long, hot summer? What was it like in the firehouse in the weeks leading up to it?

NICK: Oh, nothing special. Some little stuff. False alarms, wastebasket fires. The guys were a little restless. This was the day. They were chomping at the bit. This was the day they were waiting for.

JOAN: So Jimmy hadn't really been in many fires before.

NICK: No, no, this was it. September 11th.

(He shakes his head slightly in wonder. He is shocked at the realization.)
This was his first real fire.

(JOAN breaks the fourth wall. She stands up and addresses the audience—angry, sarcastic.)
JOAN: Of course, everyone has their own description. Myself, I favor the idea
that it's like a massive boot, stomping right here.

(She thumps her outstretched hands across her chest and diaphragm. Struggles to take a deep breath.)
Knocks the wind out. "Heartbreak" sounds too pretty, too fragile
for this sensation. It's a body blow. And then you just can't breathe, not
really. Not for a long time.

(She assumes a pedagogical voice.)
Brain Chemistry for Dummies. Lesson 1. The science of pain.

(She's in a pseudo-medical authoritative demeanor. She goes to the shelf and picks up a book, opens it, and reads from it.)
"Cortisol is released in response to stress. Cortisol is sometimes
called a 'stress hormone.' A variety of psychological stressors can cause
cell death in the nerves affected by the cortisol system . . ."

(She shakes her head.)
Cell death. Don't like *that*.
"Trauma is translated into anatomical changes in the brain. . . . Stress
can cause changes in the neural architecture—the hard wiring—of the
brain. . . . Diminished blood flow to the brain causes comparable brain-
cell death. And so does normal aging."

(She looks at the audience. Bitter.)
That explains a lot.
Put simply. We've got a nerve fibers running through our brains
like lines strung across telephone poles. Our brain sends out chemical
messages that leap from pole to pole. And when we experience devastation—trauma—toxins spill out and . . .
God, can you imagine what it looks like in there?

(She stops short. Then she resumes reading.)
When monkeys are subjected to severe forms of stress, they show

signs like passivity, cries of distress, and self-directed behaviors like huddling and rocking . . .

(She absorbs it.)
. . . The animal model seems to say that pain has its price. The victim carries his scars."

(She closes the book. The lights come up on the stage, and she takes her place in the chair at the table, where NICK *is still sitting. She reenters the scene.)*
JOAN: Here. Try this.

(She hands NICK *her notebook.)*
NICK: *(He traces the sentences with his finger, reading through the boilerplate passage sotto voce.)* "I'm Nick Flanagan of Ladder Company 60 . . . " Yeah. "Honor the memory . . . condolences . . . " OK, here.

(More formally.)
"Jimmy's job was to learn as much as possible, as fast as possible. We could tell he was going to be good. He was quiet, helpful, and hardworking. The guys liked him, and they're good judges of character."
Yeah, this is working.
"On that morning in September, Jimmy was going out on his first big fire. He was serving with the cream of the crop, and he was holding his own. They were ready for this day. It was the work they had chosen, work that was about risking everything—risking your life—in order to save others. In our grief, let us remember that."

(He nods to himself.)
"When Jimmy first came to the firehouse, he came into my office, and I shook his hand, telling him what I tell all the new men. 'This is the best job in the world.' Now I would say, 'This is the most important job in the world.'"

(He's shaken by this, and she's distressed. They sit quietly and motionlessly.)
JOAN: I . . . I'm sorry. Maybe that last part's not right.
NICK: *(Staring into the middle distance.)* "The best job in the world." Can I say that in front of his folks?

(He looks at her.)
But it's true! I've been doing it for more than twenty years. I can't imagine doing anything else.

JOAN: I believe you.

NICK: These guys, you just wouldn't believe these guys.

JOAN: *(A long beat.)* More coffee?

NICK: Why not.

JOAN: *(She takes his cup and refills it.)* Here you go. It's a little cold.

NICK: You should try the coffee at the firehouse. It's really bad.

JOAN: Oh, I drink a lot of bad coffee.

NICK: No, I mean really bad.

(He grins.)

      Disgusting.

JOAN: *(Smiling.)* I usually don't drink it this late in the day anyway.

NICK: *(He's suddenly anxious, looking around.)* It is getting late. Hey, I should be getting outta here. It's your weekend. You got plenty of other things you need to do.

JOAN: Nick, when we were talking on the phone, I thought about what I was going to do this afternoon. Nothing more important than this. But next week, once I'm in the office, with the kids and everything—then it might be hard to get back. Let's see what we can do today.

NICK: Patrick. We got to do Patrick. The thing is, I think I'm—what do they call it—denial, in denial, about Patrick. I swear, I'm sitting in the office and the door opens, and I think he's gonna walk in.

JOAN: *(She looks down at her notes.)* Patrick O'Neill.

NICK: Oh, Patrick. This man had a full, full life. This man always had something going on. His work, his family, his church. I say to him one time, what are you doin' this weekend? And he says, going to the church picnic. I didn't know they still had church picnics!

JOAN: Kids?

NICK: Four. Christie, she just got married. I think she's twenty-five. The twins, they're fourteen. And Theresa's ten. Wife Mary Rose. He's got a birthday coming up, he's gonna be forty-seven next month.

JOAN: How long was he with the company?

NICK: Patrick came into the company as a brand-new lieutenant four years ago. I got to see this man grow. When you're new, you're shaky about everything, but over time I saw him grow. He had conviction, that was the thing about Patrick. He knew this was the job for him. He was sure he could do it. That's what makes a leader. The troops eat it up.

JOAN: So the men looked up to him.

NICK: Oh, yeah. So they wanted to follow. That's the difference between being a boss and a leader. Patrick was two weeks away from taking his captain's test. No doubt about it, he had it.

JOAN: Are the men ever—afraid?

NICK: Afraid. People are afraid, but they never admit it.

JOAN: You can't admit it. Everything would fall apart. You can't afford that.

NICK: They need someone to follow. Good decisions. Calm under fire. I don't like the cowboy hotshot type, never did. Pat wasn't like that. When I think of him, I think of when I was in the army infantry, they had this motto, "Follow me." That's what he was like. Confident. "Follow me." And they did.

(He pauses briefly.)

    That morning, too.

JOAN: What picture do you have of him? When you think about him, what do you see him doing?

NICK: Oh, I see him walking. With these giant strides—you're not gonna stop *this* train. He could cover a room in two steps. Yeah, I see him leading five guys up to a building, sizing it up—first thing he does when he gets to a fire, walk around, size it up. And these five guys behind him, running to keep up. And all the time, they're listening to him, thinking what does he want, how do we do this job right.

JOAN: How does he motivate them? Criticism or praise?

NICK: Oh, there's lots of praise, back in the kitchen. But he kept an eye on them, too, especially the new guys, the probies. "This one's good," he'd say if he liked him. But don't try to pull anything over on him. If you got a square rooter, Pat picked up on that right away. He knew.

JOAN: A square rooter?

NICK: That's what we call them, a guy that's just out for himself. You know, an operator. Me times me.

JOAN: So Patrick was a real straight arrow.

NICK: Oh yeah. "Work, church and home." That was the motto. He was a real role model for the men. Last year, when Barney Keppel had his little brush with the law, Patrick helped him out. Barney goes to him and says, "OK, Lieutenant, from now on, I'm a new man. Work, church, and home. Just like you."

JOAN: He must have liked that.

NICK: Oh yeah. He didn't believe it—not for a minute. Barney was, "Work, church, and home—at least until Friday." But that was OK. Barney didn't mean any harm, he just got into scrapes. Him and Dave. Barney and Dave.

JOAN: So Patrick talked a lot about his kids?

NICK: Oh yeah. It was always, "I got Frankie's soccer practice this weekend, gonna meet Christie's in-laws on Sunday, tonight we're going to Theresa's recital." This man had a full life. One day he says, "I made Waldorf salad for the church picnic. You gotta try it sometime." He goes to the church picnic. I tell you, I didn't know they still *had* church picnics.

(He shakes his head in wonder.)

JOAN: Well, I can't say that I've been to any lately.

NICK: *(Mournfully.)* Nobody's having any fun anymore.

JOAN: We're all walking under this cloud.

(There's a silence. Then she brightens.)

But there was something last night. A tango wedding party. No, really, I went to a tango wedding party. Only in New York. He's Japanese, she's a blonde from California, and they met at their tango club in Central Park.

The party was in this restaurant down on Thirty-eighth Street. The whole place was done up all white and silver, with candlelight. They had a little tango trio—real Argentines. And they played, and after the dinner people danced—ten couples, the bride and groom. They were really good!

NICK: Tango. That's a difficult dance.

JOAN: And the women were all dressed up, with their hair up, wearing little high-heeled shoes with pointy toes. You don't see that any more. When they got going on the dance floor, their feet just flashed. It was so beautiful. It was like a dream intermission in the middle of—all this.

And there was drama, too. On the 11th the groom was flying in from the West Coast, and the bride was working downtown. And there were hours and hours when each one thought the other one was dead. But they weren't. So they had this incredible evening. It was beautiful. They were beautiful. They made us all beautiful. For a few hours.

NICK: I dance, you know. That's my big thing.

JOAN: You dance? Really?

NICK: Yeah. I've been taking lessons for years. I don't do the competitions. I just like learning new stuff and perfecting my steps. And the people. The people are great.

JOAN: What kind of dancing?

NICK: Lots of kinds. Swing, ballroom. Tango is the top dance, that's really at the top. Very difficult dance. You can study tango for a long time. You like to dance?

JOAN: Oh, I like to. But my husband doesn't, so I don't get the chance. But watching them made me want to. Their teachers were there—I never saw dancing like that before.

NICK: Usually you don't get to dance with your teacher socially. But once we were at this party and my teacher said, "Yeah, c'mon, let's do it." What an experience. You looked at her, and it was all there—the frame. She was perfect—you can't make a mistake when you're dancing with perfection.

JOAN: The frame?

NICK: The frame. It's the invisible box you're standing in, and how you hold yourself inside it.

JOAN: *(Uncomprehendingly.)* Oh.

NICK: Like if you push your partner's hand—here, give me your hand—

(She is still seated. He takes her right hand with his left, in ballroom posture.)
If you push your partner's hand . . .

(He pushes her hand, palm to palm, and it gives way easily.)
. . . and it's like cooked spaghetti, that's no good. Here, put up your hand again.

(She does, and he takes it. This time it's firm but pliant.)
You gotta have some resistance, you got to feel the whole body move in the same direction. Cha, like this.

(Now when he pushes, her torso turns a bit to the side.)
Otherwise it's no good.

(They drop hands, smiling self-consciously.)

JOAN: Yeah, I see.

NICK: And if you're lucky, it all comes together. When people move in synch. Sometimes it's real hard for these modern women, you know. They're professionals, they're educated, they're used to be in charge. But when you're dancing, you got to be able to follow. You've got to be able to feel the lead.

JOAN: You've got to let go.

NICK: Yeah. It's not so hard. You just follow. Here, like this.

(He gently takes her hand. The lights slowly dim, except for a spot on them. Soft music rises—a few strings playing "Hiro's Tango.")

You know, there are only eight steps to the basic tango. Just lean into me, feel where I'm going. Yeah, step step cross step, step step step foot up. There you go, you're getting it.

(They go through the steps several times. They do not hold each other close. Their posture is slightly formal but friendly. At first he is encouraging, and she is tentative and awkward in the steps.)

Don't look down.

(After a few tries, the dance becomes gets smoother, more fluid—but never melodramatic. The dance becomes more confident. Their movements synchronize. Then the music fades. NICK *retreats into the darkness to his chair.* JOAN *turns to the audience, still in the light.)*

Monologue 3

JOAN: *(Addressing the audience quietly.)* Of course, that never happened.

We didn't dance. He just gave my hand that little push, like a demonstration of a cantilever. It was all—proper. I never even got up from my chair.

But after that touch, whenever I watched him, I noticed how light he was on his feet. I could imagine him moving quickly and usefully across a landscape of flame and broken glass. I could see him at a dance class, swinging his partner, smiling as their feet snapped, synchronized, into place.

I could see Jimmy Hughes, cresting a hill on his bike. And Patrick O'Neill with his kids and his salad at the picnic. It made me wonder what I used to see every time I walked past a firehouse. I never thought about a kitchen back there.

I knew then that every time I saw a person on the street, I saw only his public shadow. The rest, the important part, lives in layer after layer beyond our view.

We have no idea what wonders lie hidden in the people around us.

*(*JOAN *sits down in the dark, and the stage lights come up on the two of them.)*

JOAN: Nick, where were you that morning?

NICK: At home. In Brooklyn. When it happened, I went outside to the street. I could see the towers on fire.

JOAN: You were off-duty?

NICK: I wasn't due in until 6 P.M. that night. We work tours. Patrick was on that morning.

JOAN: *(She's not writing. She's looking at him intently.)* You went to the fire-house?

NICK: *(Shaking his head slightly.)* I made an entry in the log at 10:15. I got there twenty minutes after the second tower went down . . .

(Long pause.)

The engine and truck left at 8:52. We've got a video camera at the door with a time clock. You see them go out. We lost fourteen—eight from 60 Truck, six from the engine. Two survived. Both drivers. One driving the engine, one driving the truck. The last thing Pat said was, "We're going into Tower 1."

You see, there was a really stupid thing. You know those big orange plastic cones they use for traffic? Well, the ladder truck ran into one on the way, and it got wedged under the fender. You can't go anywhere 'til you get the cone out. Steve, the driver, he's out there wrestling and cursing that cone, and it just wouldn't come out. So Pat says, "Come on, guys, we'll go on, it's just a couple of blocks, and Steve can meet us down there. We're going to Tower 1."

Steve finally gets the cone out and heads down. He makes it to the lobby of Tower 1, and he's trying to find out where the company is. And then he's blown out the lobby of Tower 1 by the collapse of Tower 2. He's blown clear out of that lobby. Hitting that stupid cone saved his life.

(They sit silently.)

JOAN: An orange plastic traffic cone.

NICK: They still haven't found the guys. I don't know where they are. Maybe after the second plane hit Tower 2, they went there. I just have no idea. I keep trying to figure it out.

JOAN: We can't figure any of this out. It's too big for us. People used to have religion. Something terrible would happen, and they'd say, "Oh, it was God's will." But we don't . . . buy that now. God's will? This wasn't God's will. There's no reason. No explanation.

NICK: Yeah. No reason. I say to Pat the night before, you want to work first tour or second tour. We do this all the time, trade off. And always before he has a reason. "I'll take today, you take tomorrow." "I'll take tomorrow, you take today." He'd say, "I got my daughter's soccer practice, I got this I got that," there was always a reason. But that day, he just said, "Oh, I'll take Tuesday morning." This time he didn't give a reason. There's no reason. I'm alive and he's dead and I don't even know why. I lie awake nights thinking, "What was the reason?"

JOAN: No reason.

(She takes a drink of cold, bitter coffee, makes a face. Then she looks at her notes.)
     Nick, this guy sounds too perfect. I mean, he must have had some flaw. C'mon.

NICK: Flaw. *(He thinks hard.)* Well, I guess he was a perfectionist.

JOAN: OK.

NICK: *(He smiles.)* It used to drive him nuts if something wasn't working right, if something was messy. If he saw the probies loafing around the firehouse. "Do something useful. Sweep or something!" Or if they were sitting in the kitchen. He'd say, "Don't just sit there. Read something!" That was Patrick.

JOAN: *(She smiles as she writes.)* Yeah, OK. Is that a flaw. . . . But at least it's human. We got to make him human.

NICK: *(Wistful.)* I tell you, every day at the firehouse, I still think he's going to walk in that door.

JOAN: *(She reviews the page.)* Tell me what you think of this.

(She stands up and holds the page before her, pacing a few short steps as she reads aloud.)
     "I want to offer my condolences to his family, who are here with us today. It is impossible to think of Patrick without thinking of you. Even when he was working all out, Patrick always had his family in mind."

(To NICK.)
     That's the sense I have of him.

NICK: *(He nods with an expression of satisfaction.)* Yeah, that's good.

JOAN: "Patrick was a fine father. It was a quality he brought to the firehouse. He had that calm presence you look for in a leader. "Follow me," he'd say, and they would. The men looked up to him—for the way he did his job but also for the way he lived his life. 'Work, church, and home' was his motto."

NICK: *(He corrects her.)* Well, that's what Barney always *said* was Patrick's motto. I don't know if that's what *Patrick* said was his motto.
     But no, no, leave it in, it sounds good.

JOAN: "Patrick O'Neill was a big man. He covered the ground in long, sure strides. When he went out to a fire, he led the way. The other guys had to walk double-time just to keep up."

NICK: That's right. I was one of them.

JOAN: *(She looks at him inquiringly.)* We could put that in.

(Pause. She gets no response. She goes on.)

"He took special pride in the new guys, the probies. He expected the same sense of purpose in them that he had himself. If one of them was taking it easy around the firehouse and Patrick walked in, he'd need to find an emergency broom."

NICK: That's good. "An emergency broom."

JOAN: *(She starts to read more haltingly, to have trouble.)* "On September 11th Patrick was two weeks away from taking his captain's test, and there's no doubt about it. He would have aced it. When I think of Patrick, I think of the infantry motto, 'Follow me.' I'm sure that's what Patrick said that morning when he got the alarm. 'Follow me'—with his long stride that gave so much confidence and purpose to his men that day.

"And I don't care whether Patrick ever took that captain's test. In my book he earned it. And captain's the least of it. Patrick O'Neill was many things to many people. Leader, friend, brother . . . husband, father . . . And none of us here will ever forget him."

(As she finishes, her voice starts to quaver. But her face is distorted. Perhaps she is in tears. NICK is still listening, looking into an abstract distance. He turns to look at her after she finishes.)

NICK: That's . . . hey, what's . . . ?

(He stands up and makes a motion to comfort her but is uncertain what he should do. He regards her, awkward and distressed.)

Aw, look what I've done. I've dragged you into this. I shouldn't 'a' done that. I come along and unload all this stuff on you, and now you're wrecked, too. I had no right to do that.

JOAN: No, you don't understand.

NICK: You're hurting. This hurts you.

JOAN: This is nothing, less than nothing, compared to what's happened to you.

NICK: That doesn't mean you should suffer.

JOAN: Can you use this?

(She holds up the paper.)

NICK: Yes. Yes! Now I'll have something to say when I get up there. And the words. They're the right words. But that doesn't mean I should drag you into this. You were outside of it, and I dragged you in.

JOAN: If you can use it, that's all I ask. Was I outside of it? I don't want to be—not so far.

This is my city, too. I can't just watch it on TV. I want to do something. But this is all I know how to do. Words. I can't think of anything else.

NICK: *(Wonderingly.)* That's OK. They're your tools.

Monologue 4

(The lights dim to a spotlight, and JOAN *addresses the audience.)*

People need to tell their stories.

I know you absorb some toxins listening to the pain. It's like the print of a hand in raw clay. Even the people who tell the stories know this.

In Chile, some people who were tortured couldn't tell their families what happened. It caused the listeners too much pain. The people didn't want to hurt anyone with their stories—but they needed to tell them. So some shrinks gave them tape recorders and had them tell their stories to the machine. It helped.

You know, when it first happened, I'd wake up every day cleansed—of the memory. There would be these fresh moments after sleep. Then I'd remember. And another thought would resist. No. That's absurd. But the first thought would win. Yes, it happened, and now I have to go through another day living that reality.

I thought, "It would be good to get away."

So when they asked me to come to Argentina, I said yes. I was meeting with some Argentine writers. They told me what it all meant.

"The United States is living under total military censorship," they said.

What?

"The military won't let the newspapers publish pictures of the bodies."

"Wait, wait," I said. "The newspapers—they're still trying to figure out what happened. What happens next."

Pictures of the bodies? There aren't any bodies. Do you want pictures of pieces of bodies? Censorship—that's when information is blocked. They're not blocking that information. We know they're dead. People don't need pictures. People don't *need* pictures.

There was one woman in Argentina—her son was one of the disappeared. She told the newspapers there that when the planes hit the towers she felt . . . glad. We all know who was in those towers, she said. American imperialists . . . had it coming.

(She shakes her head despairingly.)
    I wanted to tell her.

(Beat.)
    They were civilians. They were massacred. And if there's one thing we've salvaged from the bloody twentieth century, it's the idea of human rights. For everyone. Even Americans.

(Bitterly resolute.)
    Now, it may sound strange to say Americans were victims of a human-rights abuse. But. Strange. Things. Happen.
    I couldn't wait to get back to New York. Where everyone understood.
    But I kept thinking about it. I realized that everything the Argentines were saying was about their own war twenty years ago. They thought it was about them.
    Everybody, all over the world, was talking about it. Writing about it. And they all—they all—thought it was about them! But it's not. It's about us!
    Isn't it?

Part 3: The Deal

(The light comes up on NICK *at the table.* JOAN *returns to her seat. The light in the room is dimmer.)*
NICK: *(He glances to the window.)* It's getting dark.
JOAN: Yeah.

(She gets up and turns on a lamp.)
    We're rounding the bend.
NICK: You're tired. You're fried. I can tell by looking at you. Let's stop.
JOAN: *(Wearily.)* One more. Didn't you say there's one more service scheduled?
NICK: Barney. Barney and Dave, my two wild men. But they haven't scheduled Dave.
JOAN: OK, Barney. Tell me about Barney.
NICK: Oh, Barney. Everybody loves Barney. He and Dave were always getting into trouble.
JOAN: *(She writes. She's worn down.)* Yeah?
NICK: See, these two guys had—*es*-ca-pades. Always together.
    You know, Barney wasn't even supposed to work that morning—he just came down to the firehouse to meet Dave.

41

(He grows expansive.)

Dave. You wouldn't want to live next door to Dave, oh no. He had this house on Long Island, yard full of old cars, he loved to mess around with wrecks. More wrecked, the better.

So one day Dave hears about a '69 Thunderbird convertible in Wyoming. "I'm gonna go buy it," he tells us, and off he goes with Barney. These guys go driving their beat-up old T-bird cross-country. They're supposed to be back at work, and we keep getting these calls—from South Dakota. Places like that. "Don' worry, Cap, we're coming, we're almost there." And afterwards they tell us the story. One of those firehouse tales in the kitchen, gets riper every time you hear it.

JOAN: So they fixed it up?

NICK: Oh yeah. Barney was a metal worker. He could do anything with metal. And a big sense of humor. He had this banter that kept you rolling. His jokes were pretty bad. And he would tell the same tired old one-liner over and over again. But somehow he always had everyone in stitches. Maybe it was the way he laughed at them himself.

(Shakes his head.)

This was a guy that you loved.

JOAN: Popular.

NICK: Well—yes and no. You gotta understand, this was a guy in his mid-thirties. He still lived at home with his parents. An older couple. German. They never called him Barney. "Bernhardt," it was.

(He tries for a German accent.)

His mom always said, "Bernhardt." Very orderly, very precise. Barney was like that. He had his own private workshop at the firehouse, did all the firehouse welding. He had all these tools. He collected old tools, machines from the twenties and thirties. He'd bring them in, nobody knows from where, nobody knew what they were for. Big things—drill presses, all kind of blades and stuff on them. Barney would take that old machinery, take it apart, clean it, and make it like new.—And we still didn't know what it was for!

JOAN: My dad's like that.

NICK: Yeah? And you know, up above the bench, where he hung his wrenches. Every tool had a spot on the wall with a . . . a . . . silhouette of the tool. It's that German precision. How did he get along with *Dave*? Dave's yard was a mess. Dave moves in next door, the property value goes down. That's what we always used to say.

JOAN: What did Barney look like?

NICK: Oh, you know, tall guy. Light hair. Kinda beefy. Not exactly hand-some. He and Dave would go out drinking, try to meet some nice women, but Barney never had much luck. Barney would say, if he could only meet a woman welder. That was the girl of his dreams. Whenever Barney met a new woman, the guys would say, "Yeah, but Barney, can she weld?"

(A pause.)

Flashdance. That was his ideal woman.

JOAN: Was he a good fireman?

NICK: As a fireman? I thought he was real good. He was a man who worked with his hands, respected his tools. Asked questions. He knew what was going on . . . analytical. He was interested in everything, he took his talent and used it for the company.

JOAN: *(She writes with a little more energy.)* Can you give me an example?

NICK: Let me think. OK, we have this giant generator—power source. Took two guys to move it. Hurst Tool. You use it for traffic accidents.

JOAN: *(Taken aback.)* Hearse tool? For hearses?

NICK: Hurst. H-U-R-S-T. Sometimes they call it "Jaws of Life" but it's a Hurst Tool. It's got these big jaws for cutting through metal, but it needs a lot of power. Generator weighs a ton, really hard to move around. So Barney takes his tape measure, whips it around, and he builds a brand-new hand cart for it that fits right into the truck compartment. On wheels. One guy can handle it on his own. No sweat.

JOAN: Sounds ingenious.

NICK: We didn't even know we needed it. Nobody asked him to do anything. He just thought of it and did it.

JOAN: He could have been an inventor.

NICK: Oh, he woulda been a great inventor. Everything this man built was made out of metal, and it was made right. We'd send him to the hard-ware store to buy something, and he'd say, "Nah, it was too flimsy." And he'd make it himself.

And he made it to last. His bench—it's bolted to the floor. You can't move that thing. One guy transferred in to the company, he brought this rack—you rest barbells on it—and put it up in the workout room. All the guys used it. He gets transferred out, and he says, "I'm taking my equipment with me."

Barney looks at Dave and says, "Oh no he's not." So Barney goes and welds it all together. You can use it, but you can't take it apart and get

43

it out the door. That thing will be there forever. Nothin' that guy could do about it.

(He relishes it.)
   He was mad.

(He pauses.)
   Everybody else was on duty. But I wasn't sure about Barney. He wasn't on duty. But he never called in. The whole time I was getting all the other reports, part of me was thinking, "Where's Barney?"
JOAN: What happened?
NICK: *(He stands and looks into the distance.)* The time went by. And we remembered the videotape from the security camera in the firehouse. And we watch the tape. It's almost nine in the morning, and Barney pulls up in his van and gets out. Then he's there talking to Dave. And you see the street and the sidewalk . . . suddenly filling with papers . . .

(Slowly, watching it in his inner eye.)
   The companies go. Barney and Dave go. You see them both turn and walk away. Helmets . . . Equipment . . . They walk away . . .

(The lights dim, then come up as two spots. JOAN *faces the audience on stage left.* NICK, *in uniformed funeral attire, stands and faces the audience formally, with the written eulogy in front of him.)*
JOAN: When do we go back to normal? I asked someone that the other day. Will we go back to normal? He said, "Yes, we'll go back to normal. But normal will be different. This *is* the new normal."
   The city is different. We lost our—jazz. We're muted. We lost—a lot.
NICK: *(He begins the oratory, in a simple, unpretentious, dignified way. He reads well and confidently, with affection. He's in control.)* "I am Nick Flanagan of Ladder Company 60. I am here to honor the memory of our dear friend and brother Bernhardt Keppel. I want to offer my most sincere condolences to his parents, Mr. and Mrs. Keppel, with us here today.

(He nods to the side.)
   "I hope that these few words can give you some sense of how much we thought of Barney, and of the light he brought into our lives."
JOAN: Some days I can almost go without thinking about it. But to really pull that off, I'd have to avoid the newspaper, not watch TV news. Not do a lot of things. Not hear a siren, not smell smoke.

NICK: "What can I tell you about Barney? He lifted your heart. He had an unstoppable sense of humor. He was fun. He had a happy laugh. It rose out of him and took you along. For Barney, humor was as natural as breathing.

"But Barney also had an art, the metal-worker's art. He recuperated things. There was nothing he loved more than fatigued metal.

JOAN: I get angry. How do you cut deals with God. Under these conditions.

NICK: Barney was a genius with metal. He could weld it, bend it, bolt it, drill it—you name it. And then he brought in—creativity. He'd notice something around the firehouse that didn't work very well, something we just took for granted. And he'd think up a solution. Like the huge generator—the Hurst Tool—that's mounted on the rig for car accidents. One day Barney builds us a specially designed hand truck that fits right into the compartment. He's fixed something before we even defined the problem. That's the kind of guy he was.

JOAN: I know my terms. I realized it the other day getting on the subway.

(She changes to a defiant tone.)

I want them back. I want them back. All of them. That's all I'll settle for. I want them back, just the way they were. I want them all back, together again. That's final.

NICK: We depend on our tools. They're all important. When you go out on a call, sometimes you break through metal, sometimes wood. You need different tools. When you're answering an alarm, every tool counts.

JOAN: *(Desperate, methodical.)* I'll tell you how it can work. I read about it in a book. Let's just play the tape backwards. Start with the shot of the rubble. The dust and steel rise and untwist and form back up into the buildings. The flames are sucked back into Tower 2, then Tower 1. The planes fly backwards across the river, take a curve, and land backwards in Boston.

Everybody gets out of the plane and drives backwards home.

NICK: But it's also how you use your tools. Barney set up his own workshop at the firehouse, and it is a thing of beauty. A tool for everything, and every tool in its place. He built the workbench himself and bolted it to the floor. I can tell you, that workbench isn't going anywhere. If Barney built it, he built it well. Meticulous. Barney had a unique talent, he used it for the betterment of the company. Here was a man who worked magic with his hands, respected his tools, and respected his job. The department can't ask any more than that. Yet he brought so much more. He made us smile—and he still does, just thinking of him. He made us laugh. He made us feel good about who we were. About working with each other.

JOAN: The guys from the ladder truck run backwards. Barney's there. He's next to Dave. This time Jimmy's in front and Patrick's in back. They all get into the truck, back up. The orange traffic cone falls out on the street, and the truck backs into the firehouse. Barney gets into his van and backs off home.

That's it. That's the deal.

But. I just . . . I just have nothing to bring to the table.

(She wilts.)

NICK: But trust Barney to leave us something more earthly, too. His careful hands built things to last. The tools he built for us are still in the firehouse. They're with us. They're anchored. They're welded. They're bolted. They're grounding us. We use them every day. And every time we touch them, we are grateful we could share his light.

(They look at each other across the stage. He is consoling, she is distraught. The lights go out.)

AT THE VANISHING POINT

Naomi Iizuka

Production Notes

AT THE VANISHING POINT had its world premiere at the Twenty-eighth Annual Humana Festival of New Plays at the Actors Theatre of Louisville in 2004. It was directed by Les Waters. The play was commissioned by Actors Theatre of Louisville and was made possible by an NEA/TCG Artist in Residency grant.

The original typescript of the play contains several inconsistencies in capitalization, spelling, punctuation, and grammar. These have been retained in the script presented here.

Special thanks to Dan Basila, Holly Becker, Turney Berry, Laura Lee Brown, the Butchertown Neighborhood Association, Emilya Cachapero, Helen Carle, John Catron, Claire Cox, Finn Curtin, Frederic and Julie Davis, Michael Dixon, Susannah Engstrom, Caitlin Ferrara, the Filson Club, Mike Flynn, Kendra Foster, Peter and Sarah Fuller, Jen Grigg, Jon Jory, Gene Hewitt, Fran Kumin, Damon Kustes, Dan LeFranc, the Louisville Public Library, Trey Lyford, Frazier Marsh, Marc Masterson, Guy Mendes, Bruce McKenzie, Elizabeth Nolte, Carrie Nutt, Tara Jane O'Neil, Tom Owen, Tanya Palmer, Alexandra Peterson, Martha and Richard Rivers, Ted and Jackie Rosky, Jim Segrest, Edward P. Seigenfeld, Sharon Sparrow, Sandy Speers, Terry and Mandy Tyler, United Food and Commercial Workers Local 227, the University of Louisville Library, Nancy Vitale, Les Waters, Madeleine Waters, Chloe Webb, Amy Wegener, James Welch, Steve Wilson, all the people at ATL who helped and advised during this residency, and most of all, thank you to the residents of Butchertown past and present for telling me their stories.

At the still point of the turning world.

Neither flesh nor fleshless;

Neither from nor towards; at the still point, there the dance is.

—T. S. Eliot, "Burnt Norton," Four Quartets

CHARACTERS (IN SPEAKING ORDER)
the PHOTOGRAPHER

PETE HENZEL, a guide at the thomas edison house
also: MARTIN KINFLEIN, an accountant at oertels brewery

RONNIE MARSTON, a bacon packager at fischers
also: IDA MILLER, a retired schoolteacher

MAUDIE TOTTEN, the owner of a bar near the stockyards
PHOTOGRAPHER'S WIFE

NORA HOLTZ, a student at the school for the blind
also: TESSA RHEINGOLD, a painter at hadley pottery

MIKE TOTTEN, an employee at the impound lot and a painter
also: FRANK HENZEL, a loin puller at fischers

CHORUS OF CHILDREN (three children):
PHOTOGRAPHER'S OLDER SON
also: MARTIN KINFLEIN'S FATHER AS A YOUNG BOY
the YOUNG FRANK HENZEL

PHOTOGRAPHER'S YOUNGER SON
also: the YOUNG PETE HENZEL

PHOTOGRAPHER'S DAUGHTER
also: the YOUNG NORA HOLTZ
the YOUNG RONNIE MARSTON

PLACE: Butchertown.
TIME: Past and Present.
Inspired by the photographs of Ralph Eugene Meatyard, 1925–72

SONG LIST
"The Raven" by Edgar Allen Poe, instrumentals by Buddy Morrow and his
    Orchestra with vocals by the Skip Jacks
"When Angels Speak of Love" by Sun Ra
"River Song" by Tara Jane O'Neil

"If Chaos Were a Song" by Tara Jane O'Neil
"Flood Song" by Tara Jane O'Neil
"Your Long Journey" folk song by anonymous, sung by Tara Jane O'Neil
"O God Our Help in Ages Past"
"Stardust" sung by Louis Armstrong
Mozart
German Lieder

PROPS LIST
A record player circa 1972
A box of old LPs
A projection screen
A slide projector
A bottle of bourbon
A tumbler
A gym bag
An old shoe
An old shirt
An old comb
A six pack of beer
A stuffed hooded merganser
A mirror
A pack of cigarettes
A lighter
An ashtray
A painting of a hooded merganser
A neon beer sign

1. self portrait

(darkness. the PHOTOGRAPHER *turns on a slide projector. his features are part in light, part in shadow.)*
PHOTOGRAPHER: i want to show you something.

(the PHOTOGRAPHER *clicks the projector forward. a projected image, a pixilated blur of dark and light.)*
PHOTOGRAPHER: now i could ask you what you see, and you might say, well
        you might say i don't know what i'm looking at, i don't know what that
        is, what the hell is that. and i could press you on it, and you might think

it was some kind of a trick i was playing on you, if you were inclined to think that way, if you were a suspicious sort. but maybe if you kept looking at the thing, after a while, you might begin to see the shape of something, and maybe i tell you it's a person, and so you start looking at the image with that in mind, and you begin to discern the features of some famous figure, some illustrious soul like thomas edison, say. or maybe you see the face of an anonymous stranger, a stockyard worker or a soldier or a young girl in a school play. i think it's about a kind of focus. when you focus on something, what happens is your eye frames it in what is called the fovea which is a section of the retina made up of these cones that are connected to the brain's optical cortex and then your brain takes all your experience and knowledge of the world, and it forms a kind of context by which to process and make sense of that information. so that say you're standing in the middle of a field, and you hold up your hand in front of your eyes

(the PHOTOGRAPHER *lifts his hand.)*
PHOTOGRAPHER: and everything else, the field and beyond, it becomes a blur, and all you see are the particulars of your own hand, the lines embedded in your palm, the whorls and ridges of your fingertips, and that makes you think of the time you cut yourself with the coping saw or the way the inside of a baseball glove, the way it feels, or the feel of your wife's hair warm from the sun, all of these things, more, and so you understand what it is you're seeing because of all the associations and memories of a whole lifetime, everything that makes you who you are comes together in that instant. but then let's say, let's say you shift your gaze to what lies beyond your hand, and so the frame, it changes, and what was a blur is now clear and distinct. and what you see is a field, and in the distance,

(a glimpse of a human figure in the darkened place.)
PHOTOGRAPHER: a human figure slowly walking away from you, towards a point far in the distance, a point beyond the horizon line, beyond where you can see, and yet you try. i'm trying to sort this out right now, how the eye selects and organizes the immensity of the world i guess you could say, those parts that stay with you and those that fall away.

(the figure vanishes. the PHOTOGRAPHER *clicks forward on the projector. a point of light in a field of darkness. it becomes gradually brighter as he speaks.)*

PHOTOGRAPHER: i'm an optician by training, but i'm also, i'm a photographer. i'd say i'm fascinated by light, by the properties of light, by what the eye sees, and also what it misses, and i guess that's how i've gotten to where i am now. there was a young man came into my shop the other day. he was in the army, hundred and first airborne. grew up in louisville he told me. his mom and dad, his wife and kids, they all lived there still. now as it happens, i got family, some of my wife's family, they live in louisville. so we got to talking and we figured out he knew my sister-in-law. she owns a bar just east of downtown, down near where the stockyards are at, and he knew her. anyway this guy, he said he thought he might need glasses. turned out he had a severe astigmatism. how he lived that long seeing so poorly i cannot understand. you'd think someone woulda asked him what he saw when he was trying to read a blackboard or aim a gun. you'd think they would've, but i guess no one did. afterwards he said he never saw so clearly in his life. said he could see the leaves on the trees where before it had just been a wash of green. he could see people's faces really see them. he said it hurt to see everything so sharp and clear. to be that aware was almost too much, it was almost too much to bear. i tell you what, i'm going to pause here for just one second.

(the PHOTOGRAPHER *goes to another table upstage on which sits a phonograph circa late 1960s and a cardboard box of lps.)*

PHOTOGRAPHER: i have this hi fi right here and some music. sometimes, sometimes i like to listen to music when i'm looking at my photographs. my wife says the music, it's like the music opens up a valve in your brain so more ideas can flow in, and sensations, too, all different kinds of sensations, and i have to say i'm inclined to agree. i have about a thousand lps i've collected over the years, jazz mostly. duke ellington, louis armstrong, dizzy gillespie, max roach, ornette coleman, you name it. i have it all cross-indexed by title and musician and then by record label, and then i have it cross-referenced so i can see who played on what track, and that's great because that way i can know that fats navarro played on this particular charlie parker song and bud powell was on the piano and i can know that right away. i like knowing that. i like having that information readily accessible. it lets me, it lets me see a bigger picture of how all these different people how they all fit together and intersect in this larger pattern, hold on here. i wanna, i wanna play you something, something you probably never heard before, and may never hear again.

51

(the PHOTOGRAPHER *pulls a record out of the box, slips the record out of its sleeve, and puts it on the turntable with care.)*

PHOTOGRAPHER: edgar allen poe's "the raven." as interpreted by buddy morrow and his orchestra with vocal accompaniment by the skip jacks.

(the PHOTOGRAPHER *places the needle on the record. the song plays for a bit. he listens.)*

PHOTOGRAPHER: isn't that the craziest thing you've ever heard. listen to those harmonies.

(the PHOTOGRAPHER *listens for a moment longer. lifts the needle, returns the record to its sleeve, puts it back in the box.)*

PHOTOGRAPHER: o man i love that. the craziness. the sheer improbability. i could listen to that all day long. just makes me smile. i stumbled across it in a yard sale. i couldn't believe it. somebody was going to throw it away, consign it to oblivion.

(the PHOTOGRAPHER *slips another record out of its sleeve and puts it on the turntable. he places the needle on the record. the music begins a piece of jazz plays.)*

PHOTOGRAPHER: i guess i like things a little off the beaten path. i like strange names you can pick out of phone books. i keep a list in this little notebook i have.

(the PHOTOGRAPHER *retrieves a small notebook from his pocket.)*

PHOTOGRAPHER:
> lummy jean licklighter.
> t. bois dangling.
> margaret a. ditto ditto.
> pharaoh feedback.
> connie fongdong.
> everette derryberry,

alright that's enough of that. i could go on for hours i tell you. you think i'm kidding you ask my wife, i'm not.

(the PHOTOGRAPHER *returns to the slide projector. he switches off the light. he clicks forward the slide projector. a pixilated blur of dark and light takes shape. similar to the first image but also different.)*

PHOTOGRAPHER: this is a self-portrait right here. i took it not too long ago. some fifteen years ago i said i'm going to learn how to take a picture. i'm going to give myself as long as it takes, i'm going to apply myself, and so that's what i did. i use a rolleiflex these days, but my first camera, that was a bolsey 35 mm reflex. i bought it when my oldest son was born.

(a young boy, the PHOTOGRAPHER'S OLDER SON, *is gradually revealed in the space.)*
PHOTOGRAPHER: i wanted to have a memory of him growing up because, well because i loved him very much and i wanted, i wanted to understand what i was seeing when i looked at him. it goes so quickly it seems to me, and there's so much, there's so much to take in.

(a younger boy, the PHOTOGRAPHER'S YOUNGER SON, *is gradually revealed in the space.)*
PHOTOGRAPHER: i have all different kinds i do. i have, well i have a whole series i took of light on water. i have a series i did of twigs that are close ups of twigs. they don't much look like twigs. get that close to anything, and it doesn't look like what you think it does. my younger son calls them zen twigs and i think that's a pretty good name for them. i have photos of red river gorge i took for a friend, for a book he's writing. mainly, though, i take photos of my wife and kids.

(a young girl, the PHOTOGRAPHER'S DAUGHTER, *is gradually revealed in the space.)*
PHOTOGRAPHER: somebody asked me once why it was i took so many photos of my family, and i guess i'd have to say because they're right there. they're with me every single day of my life, and with my kids, well i'm their father and they kinda have to do what i tell them to—or at least that's the assumption i labor under. i got three of 'em. two boys and a girl.

(a flurry of movement. like birds shifting in the eaves. the three children vanish.)
PHOTOGRAPHER: i like to take photos of them in old, derelict buildings mostly, where you get nature kinda reclaimin the place, and there's vines and weeds pushin through the windows, and maybe some young, impertinent oak tree shootin up through the floorboards. i like the quality of light in those buildings, and also, of shadow.

(the PHOTOGRAPHER *clicks forward the projector. a square of darkness. a deep enveloping velvet darkness.)*
PHOTOGRAPHER: there was a time, i couldn't take a picture in the sunlight to save my soul. there were all these shadows you had to contend with, and i couldn't figure it out, and i was lost. then after a while, i got a little

older, i guess, and well, well it's not that hard to do anything anymore. you make your peace with whatever it is. you find your way.

(the sense of shadows in a ruined, cavernous space. the space grows darker as the PHOTOGRAPHER *speaks. the light on his face grows brighter.)*

PHOTOGRAPHER: i started using masks in my photographs not too long ago, the kind you get at the five and dime. i have this one photo i took of the kids in masks. we were out in a wooded area not too far from where we live, and my younger son had gotten into some poison ivy, and there were tears and fussing, as there often were in those days, and he didn't want to wear his mask, he just wouldn't do it to save his life, and i remember i was pretty mad at the time 'cause he wasn't doing what i had it in my mind he should be doing, and i had an idea in my head of how this picture was supposed to be, and it wasn't turning out that way at all, and the whole thing was getting on my last nerve, but finally i just took the photo and called it a day. and what struck me, what struck me when i finally got around to developing it—well, it turned out to be a pretty good picture. there's something about seeing a person put on one of those masks, and you can't really see their faces, and there's a kinda mystery and strangeness that comes out of that that i think, well i think is there all the time, it's just the mask, it lets you see it in a way that you couldn't otherwise.

(the jazz begins to fade away. underneath the jazz, the sound of the needle scraping against the void.)

PHOTOGRAPHER: all the everydayness, the realness of it is still there. the poison ivy and the tears and the ice cream afterwards, that's all still there. but it's as if inside of all of that, the masks, they let you see this other thing. for me, i guess, it's about how you see. it's about the act of seeing a thing, and how it connects to other things and is part of a whole. because on some level, how we form connections, how we see a thing and shape it in our minds, it's very personal, i think. it's about who you are and everything that makes you who you are, and how that comes together to form a certain way, a way of looking at the world.

(the PHOTOGRAPHER *clicks the projector forward. a square of light. as he speaks, the* PHOTOGRAPHER'S WIFE *becomes visible. she wears a mask. she wears a dress with sky-blue flowers.)*

PHOTOGRAPHER: this is a photograph of my wife maddie. madelyn. i call her maddie. we've been married twenty-five years. that's a quarter of a century. that's a pretty long time. she's very patient with me and i thank her for that, because sometimes, well sometimes i can be difficult. other people might not know this about me, but maddie does and she's kind enough not to remind me of it too often. we met at her sister's wedding in louisville. my wife has a twin sister lives in louisville. she got married over at st. joes, then they had the party afterwards down by the old water tower. that's where i met maddie. she was dancing with this guy she was going with at the time. i forget his name. he worked at fischers, i remember that. he had scars all along his hands, cuts and burns, the skin all white and smooth, translucent-like. he liked her, too. i could tell. i could tell by his eyes. how he looked at her, shy and hopeful. she was wearing a dress with blue flowers, sky blue, and the way it was cut, you could see her shoulders, the nape of her neck, a wisp of hair, a single strand. and all i wanted, all i wanted was to touch the back of her neck. like this. and i thought, i thought this girl, she's gotta be the most beautiful girl i will ever know in this life or the next, and she doesn't know me yet, but i'm seeing her now across a room of strangers,

(the PHOTOGRAPHER's WIFE *takes her mask off.)*
PHOTOGRAPHER: and i know, i know i'm going to marry her and we're gonna have children together and grow old together, and we're gonna, we're gonna have us a life, a whole entire life together.

(the PHOTOGRAPHER's WIFE *recedes from view.)*
PHOTOGRAPHER: this is a memory. a kind of photograph.

(somewhere in the darkness, a woman begins to sing a cappella a song of eastern mountains and northern seas. as she sings, the PHOTOGRAPHER *clicks the projector again and again. with each click, we see points of light in a field of darkness in different formations.)*
PHOTOGRAPHER: if i were to give you the facts of my life, i would tell you i was born in normal illinois in the first part of the twentieth century. i would tell you i was an optician and a photographer, and that i've lived in kentucky most all my adult life, and that it is the most beautiful place i know, and i am lucky to call it home. i would tell you i have friends who write poetry and paint, and drink and break bread together, and take long walks in the woods, and raise a little hell because sometimes you need to raise a little hell, you just need to, and that's alright, that's as it should be. i would tell you that i was a husband and a father and that's, that's maybe the most important thing. i would tell you that some-

times, sometimes i think i wasn't as conscious as i should've been. it's something i think about, whether i have taken sufficient care, whether i have done what i should've done. i would tell you that my kids are all grown up now, and that i look at them and i can't even believe it. what a remarkable thing to have your children become people you like and respect, people you would choose as friends. sometimes i wonder what they'll remember, the things they'll take with them. what stays. what falls away.

(the PHOTOGRAPHER *clicks the projector forward one last time. a pixilated blur of light and dark like the first image. the* PHOTOGRAPHER *is part in shadow, part in light. the woman's singing transforms into the song of the river. a wordless song that is the essence of the ohio river on a day in late spring, sunlight on water, the drone of bees, and the sound of unseen birds in the trees, hundreds of birds invisible in the leaves.)*

PHOTOGRAPHER: louisville kentucky. april 1972. down by the point. late afternoon. a field of trees, giant oaks and cotton wood, weeping willow and sycamore. sunlight through the leaves. the sound of birds high above, hundreds of starlings invisible, unseen. the sound of the creek flowing into the river, the sound of water rushing, sunlight shimmering on the water. the scent of livestock and dead leaves and earth, the scent of earth. in the distance, i see my wife. she's standing on the edge of the woods, and beyond the trees, sky as far as the eye can see. i go to her, across a field of tall grass, the sssssh of the grass, and the wind, the sound of the wind like voices from across the river, and when i get to her at last, i lean in close, i lean in close and whisper in her ear. this is what i say.

(the PHOTOGRAPHER *recedes from view. the song of the river ends.)*

2. snapshots from a family album

(projection: pete henzel, edison house. PETE HENZEL *enters the space. he's carrying a small gym bag. he begins disassembling the projection screen and putting away the slide projector.)*

PETE HENZEL: so what it is alright, what happened was, i was walking out on the point, and i saw this thing that i can't explain in a logical way, and it's been on my mind, and the more i think about it, the more i'm convinced, the more i know, i just know, i just know in the way you know when you really know a thing—well, ok, let me backtrack here for a second because i think in order for you to process what it is i have to say to you, it's important to say up front that i'm a very sensitive individual. i have been all my life. i've always been predisposed in some way or maybe more aware, i'm more aware of certain vibrations, i guess you would say, vibrational movements in the atmosphere. i'm talking about a kind of energy, a kind of manifestation of displaced energy and the harnessing of a kind of flow or wave of charged particles of human consciousness—are you following me here? cause you're lookin at me like you're not following me. let me put it another way: you know how like some folks, how they have perfect pitch? i had an uncle like that used to sing in the choir over at st. joes when he was a little boy, he could pick out an d sharp or a g flat or middle c, just hear it in his head and he'd come back and go:

(PETE HENZEL *vocalizes a note.*)
PETE HENZEL: or

(PETE HENZEL *vocalizes another note.*)
PETE HENZEL: or

(PETE HENZEL *vocalizes another note.*)
PETE HENZEL: and it never failed, he always got the note, he always got it, he got it perfect. my uncle he used to work over at the old hellmuellers bakery. it's closed down now, but it used to be, you could smell the bread a block away, and everybody, well that's where everybody went for their loaves and dinner rolls and such, and during hard times, you could get a whole basket of day old rolls for free, they'd just give em away. my uncle hewdie used to make kuchen—you know what kuchen is? it's like a, like a sweet roll with the cinnamon and the brown sugar and it's kinda buttery, and it just like melts in your mouth, o man it's so good. hewdie'd always bring us a sack of kuchen when he came over. he was alright hewdie was. he never married. they say he was engaged to some blind girl, went to the school for the blind over on frankfort. she had an older brother carl went there and i guess that's how they met up. carl lost his sight, yknow, in a fire when he was a little kid. he was a grown man already when i knew him. real natty dresser. tuned pianos all around town. i think he made out pretty good with that. uncle carl used to give me silver dollars and i remember his eyeballs'd kinda roll around some when he was looking at you—well i mean he wasn't looking at you cause he was blind, but you know what i'm getting at. he's dead now, carl is, he died. he's dead. my uncle hewdie, he's dead too. they're all dead, every single one of em, dead dead dead. i don't know about

the girl. she's probably dead, too. that's what happens. alright i need, i need to backtrack, i need to situate myself. let me, let me explain. see what it is, i'm a volunteer, ysee, at the thomas edison house over on washington street which is where thomas edison where he lived when he lived in louisville, which he did, he lived right here in butchertown in 1866, lots of people don't know that but it's a fact. he was working for western union as a telegraph operator at the time, and then he got fired under murky and unjust circumstances which i know what that is, i think many of us know what that is when an employer does not, does not fully appreciate who it is we are and what it is we have to offer, and lacks any kind of imagination or vision and is just a narrow-minded kinda person who can't stand to be challenged in any way and is just waiting for us to make a mistake, just one tiny slip, because they're unable, ysee, to go beyond their own tiny little view of the world and they wouldn't know a good idea if it came up and punched em in the face. i know i certainly know what that is, to be in that situation. but of course edison went on to become one of the most famous americans there ever was, and he went on to invent so many many things, the phonograph and the light bulb, the moving picture camera, and he made a fortune and was beloved by millions, and who remembers that little shit who fired him, i'll tell you who, nobody that's who. thomas edison is my personal hero.

(PETE HENZEL *retrieves objects from a gym bag, one by one as he speaks.*)

PETE HENZEL: this is his shoe. this is thomas edison's shoe. this is his fork. he used this fork to eat, i don't know what, pie. this is his shirt. this is his comb. he used this comb. i know i'm not supposed to have these things like this, but that's alright. it's not like i'm gonna abscond with them or nothing like that. i just—i guess—well i guess i just wanted—well there's something about a thing you can touch and you know this other person, this person who lived once, this person you maybe look up to or admire, they touched this same thing, and it's like they left some part of themselves, some kinda residue, and now they're dead and in the ground, but the thing's still here, it's still here. what i'm getting at, what i'm trying to get at it, ysee, at the end of his life, thomas edison, he was in the process of inventing a machine, a machine in which the dead would be able to talk to the living. he called it a thanaphone and he believed that when he was finished, we would be able to hear the dead talking to us, kinda like voices through a telephone.

(the lights begin to flicker. the thrumming of an electrical current can be heard. PETE HENZEL *begins to recede from view.)*

PETE HENZEL: and the phone would ring, and you'd hear it like this faint *ring, ring,* and you'd pick it up and on the other end would be this person you knew from a long time ago, someone who was already old when you were just a little kid, somebody who had to be dead, no way they could still be living cause if you did the math, if you worked it out in your head, they'd be way too old to be alive, but there they were, talking to you like it was no big thing, like it was the most natural thing in the world. cause the dead, ysee, they're like an electrical current or a sound wave, and all you gotta do all you gotta be able to do is plug in, and that's what i think happened, i plugged in, i was plugged in, and that's what i was thinking when i saw this thing, that i had somehow plugged in and i didn't even know, i didn't even realize.

(the sound of the electrical current grows louder. voices, static, the sound of ancient radio transmissions. a phone starts ringing. PETE HENZEL *exits. the sounds cut out.* RONNIE MARSTON *enters. she wears a windbreaker, jeans, work boots. she has a six pack of a beer in a plastic bag. she opens a bottle and drinks.)*

RONNIE MARSTON: i got a cousin pete. i nearly ran him over the other day in my truck.

(projection: ronnie marston, story avenue.)

RONNIE MARSTON: i was on story avenue up where the road curves round real sharp, down by the greenway, where the pumping station's at, and you know how the cars, how they're always taking that turn a little too fast and some of em, they go skidding and they crash straight into that house that's right there with the brick that's all messed up from the cars that keep crashing into it, but that's all beside the point cause i wasn't speeding. i never speed. i'm a good driver, i never had a ticket in my life not a one, except for some dumbass parking tickets i never shoulda gotten in the first place, and then they had the nerve to tow my truck and that made me so mad, but i didn't have nothing to do with that little a-hole falling down, i did not push him, i did not lay a hand on him, but that's a whole other story i don't want to get into on account of a pending legal action. anyway this incident i'm talking about right now, this was all my cousin pete, it was all his fault. pete's got about ten lugnuts loose in his head, no common sense none at all. my sisters, they're all like, o poor pete. poor poor pete. and i'm like, to hell with pete. pete pisses me off. cause it ain't

59

like he's slow. he ain't slow. he's just a screwup is all. always gettin himself
into some kind of trouble cause he doesn't use his head, he doesn't think.
pete volunteers now full time at the edison house over on washington.
he's some kinda tour guide or something like that. he has this thing, see,
he knows everything there is to know about thomas edison. you just ask
him whatever you want to know, and he'll tell you. pete used to work at
fischers, but then he got let go on account of some situation i don't know
the full details of. i work at fischers, too. a lot of my family do—well two
of my sisters and my brother-in-law, and his dad, and my dad, and my
dad's brother, pete's dad, and pete's brother frank—anyway there i was,
driving down story rounding that curve, and suddenly pete's right in
front of me, he's just there all of a sudden running into the middle of
the road, and thank god i got fast reflexes or i woulda run him over, so
i slam on my breaks hard and i'm outta the truck in a flash, and i grab
him and i'm up in his face shaking him and i'm like, what the hell is
wrong with you i coulda run you over i coulda killed you just now. but
pete he ain't even listening to me. he's babbling about seeing something
down by the point, down by where beargrass creek lets out into the river,
and did i know that the dead live on as particles of free-floating energy
in the atmosphere like an electrical current or a sound wave and that's
what ghosts are and do i wanna see what he's talking about, come see,
ronnie, come and see. and i'm just looking at him, and i'm thinking, this
person, i'm related to this person. i'm related to him by blood and that
just, that disturbs me. and i look at pete and he's still talking and finally
i'm just like: pete. you know what, pete. i really don't need this right now.
i just got off work and it was one of those days. the feed tube broke, then
the chlorine pump gave out, then the ammo line went tits up for three
hours, and then if that weren't bad enough, the goddamn power goes
out, some kinda short, who the hell knows. it's out all along mellwood
and frankfort, all the way over to crescent hill. 59 condemned hogs. we
dumped near five thousand pounds of meat, and now my carpal tunnel
is acting up and i don't even want to talk about the smell, you don't even
want to know about the smell. so right now, pete, it's really not a good
time for you to share with me your thoughts about the afterlife.

(*pause.* RONNIE MARSTON *drinks her beer.*)
RONNIE MARSTON: you know sometimes, sometimes i speak out of turn. i get
  impatient and angry. not just with pete. with my kids, with the guys at
  work, with just about everybody. and i ain't sayin that to make excuses.
  that's who i am, take it or leave it. cause i hear em talk, yknow, all these

years. i ain't deaf. god took him so young and it's sad, it's a sad thing. and i just wanna say to them, i don't need your pity. i don't need no one's pity. i raise my kids, i go to work, i do just fine, thank you very much. everything, everything's just fine. and now i see, i see pete he's starting to say something and that's the last thing i need. so i just tell him: pete. don't you say another word. why don't you just get in the truck. just get in the truck and i'll take you home.

(a BOY *gradually appears in the darkened space. he wears a windbreaker, corduroy pants, sneakers. he is the young* PETE HENZEL.*)*

RONNIE MARSTON: and so that's what i do. and as we're driving down the interstate, i look over at him, and i'm thinking to myself i don't understand a damn thing about anything. here's this man, this grown man, and i've known him all his life, since he was a baby, and i can hardly understand the inside of his head, and how can that be? how can that be? and i think what a beautiful little boy he was.

(a german lieder begins. it plays on the phonograph. it sounds faint and crackling, faraway.)

RONNIE MARSTON: so sweet and smart. big brown eyes and a smile that'd light up a room. he had such a light in him, he was so full of light. and i think where did that boy get to? where did he go?

(the BOY *vanishes.* RONNIE MARSTON *exits as* NORA HOLTZ *enters. the german lieder continues.)*

NORA HOLTZ: my name is nora holtz. i'm fifteen years old. i was born in louisville, kentucky january 15th, 1921.

(projection: nora holtz, school for the blind.)

NORA HOLTZ: i had scarlet fever when i was a baby and that's how i lost my sight. i have no memory of what it was to see, and so i never think what if, what could've been. i don't think like that. i go to the school for the blind on frankfort. at school, we study music and grammar and composition. we study history. every year in springtime we do a play. we do it outdoors. we have a stage and we have costumes and everybody, everybody comes to see it. this year we're doing "the tempest" by mister william shakespeare. i'm playing miranda. hewdie says i'll be a beautiful miranda. hewdie's my friend carl's brother. i think hewdie, i think he's sweet on me. but like i told him, i have things to do and so he better be alright with that cause that's how it's gotta be. i'm learning shorthand,

and i already type 72 words a minute and that's pretty good. my teacher miss miller says i can learn a skill and work downtown at an insurance office or a bank or maybe even the brown hotel, no reason why not.

(a male tenor rises above the rest.)

NORA HOLTZ: you hear that? that's my father, georg holtz. he came from germany to america in 1882. travelled inland to pittsburgh to where the allegheny and the ohio meet, then he sailed down the ohio all the way to louisville. he had the most beautiful voice you'll ever hear. you'd never think a butcher'd have such a beautiful voice. cut up hogs all day long, and still he sang like an angel. he was in the orpheus society. do you know orpheus, do you know the story of orpheus? on his wedding day, his bride, she got bit by a snake and died, and orpheus, he was so full of grief, he followed her down to the underworld, and he sang to the spirits of the dead, and his songs were so beautiful even the queen of the dead, her heart softened, and she said to him, you can have your wife back. go back to the world of the living, and your wife, she'll be right behind you, but if you turn, if you turn to look at her before you reach the sunlight, she'll vanish forever. and of course, orpheus, he does the one thing he's not supposed to do, and in that moment he lays eyes on her, he sees and he knows, all of a sudden he knows he's made a terrible mistake. and there's no going back, there's no undoing what he's done.

(the german lieder ends. the sound at the end of a record, needle scraping against the void.)

NORA HOLTZ: and he replays that moment in his mind, the moment right before she goes. and in his mind it's like an old photograph of a girl he used to know.

(a GIRL appears. she wears a white dress with beads sewn in that sparkle in the light.)

NORA HOLTZ: and she's standing on the lawn in front of the school and she's wearing a white dress with tiny beads stitched in all along the hem and the sleeves. they shimmer in the light. sun against her face. the smell of honeysuckle and clover. and she can hear the birds in the trees. and she can hear their tiny hearts racing. she can feel the rough edges of their wings against her skin. what if you could read the future? what if you could go back? what if you could change one thing? how do you go on knowing you can't? how do you bear it? he thinks these things. he thinks: i am looking into the eyes of a ghost.

(NORA HOLTZ *recedes from view. the* GIRL *runs towards the audience. she runs a great distance very fast. she is a blur of light and flesh in a field of darkness. and then she's gone. a thousand birds explode into the sky. the sound their wings make. the sound of the wings dies down. a bird song. light on* MIKE TOTTEN. *he's eating a sandwich. next to him is a shopping bag.*)

MIKE TOTTEN: i saw this thing down by the point this morning. all these birds, small like starlings, only that's not what they were. and the sound they made, it sounded kinda like voices, like human voices whispering. i never saw birds like that around here before. they flew up and out of the trees and filled the sky. hundreds of birds, thousands even. and i had this sense, i had this feeling—well i can't, i can't put it into words exactly, but it was strange. the whole thing, it was just, it was kinda strange.

(projection: mike totten, the greenway.)

MIKE TOTTEN: i work at the impound lot over by the greenway. you get all kinds of birds down there. swallow-tailed kites and red-tailed hawks, i see hawks all the time. i just sit and sketch birds all day long and nobody tells me what to do, which i appreciate. and then, you know, every so often someone comes along for their car, and i take their check and give em their keys and that's about it. it's a pretty good job as jobs go. only thing is sometimes yknow you get these people, and they got all this anger, they're all pent up and pissed off at the world and they'll just take it out on you and that just, well that just kinda sucks. there was this one woman, and she comes in raising hell about her truck and how she ain't gonna pay any dumbass parking tickets and i better give her her keys or she's gonna hurt me, and i tell her to calm down, and she says something i ain't gonna repeat here in mixed company, and then she starts pushing and shoving on me, and she's strong, too, and before i know it, i'm on the pavement staring up at the sky. i hit my head, i got a concussion. i also bruised my ulna. that's this bone right here. hurts like hell. now i'm suing her ass, you bet i am. it's my legal right as an american and i'm gonna exercise it. i'm gonna have my day in court, cause that kinda shit, that's just uncalled for.

*(*MIKE TOTTEN *retrieves a stuffed bird from the shopping bag.*)*

MIKE TOTTEN: this is a hooded merganser. i shot it, i stuffed it, and then i painted it. my friend tessa thinks that's fucked up. she can keep her opinions to herself as far as i'm concerned. that's how i gotta do it, see, otherwise i can't get up close, i can't see what i need to see to get everything, to get it all just right. to make it look alive, i gotta shoot it and stuff it. that's the paradoxical nature of the whole endeavor, see. i was inspired in my technique by john james audubon. audubon lived right here in louisville, i don't know if you knew that. he painted birds up and down beargrass creek and the river and down by the point. his painting of the carolina parakeet, he did that here, and his painting of the kingfisher, and the whipporwhill, and the oriole, he did them all right here, right here in louisville.

tessa don't give a damn. i mean i tell her all this stuff cause i think it's pretty cool and it's our history, it's like our fuckin forefathers, it's like our fuckin history, but she's just like whatever. personally, i think that way of thinking, that's just ignorant. she don't care. tessa's a painter, too. we're friends. no romance, it ain't nothing like that. i mean we make out sometimes yknow, but it's just, well it's no big thing. tessa works over at hadley pottery painting little piglets and chickens and shit on all the pitchers and the soup tureens. tessa keeps trying to paint her own original designs, like a kinda abstract expressionist effect is what she's going after. but see now every time she tries to do her own thing, tessa's mom and all the other hadley ladies, they about have a fit. they just shut her down. fear of the new, yknow what i'm saying. fear of change. that's all it is. sometimes people, they can be so close-minded. it's like their brain's wearing a girdle and it's like cutting off all the circulation. her mom got her that job at hadley pottery, and it pays pretty good but it's, well it's a job, you know what i'm saying? sometimes tessa and me, we smoke out, up on the hill by the impound lot and we laugh at all the crap we gotta deal with. my older sister mary catherine and her husband kevin, they're just over the river in indiana. they got some land up in the knobs and they grow this weed, and it's like the most intense shit you will ever partake of. this stuff, this stuff will impair you, it'll humble your ass. i smoke out and i think sometimes i'm seeing god or something. well not god cause i don't know about god, but like, like the tendrils of the universe, like the arteries and synapses and ganglia. i fuckin love that word. ganglia.

(the sound of a violin. as MIKE TOTTEN *speaks, the violin melody begins to break down and distort.)*

MIKE TOTTEN: you want an experience, i tell you what, you go up on that hill by the impound lot at sunset. you roll some of kevin's weed and you smoke out, and you look at all those cars down below, hundreds of fords and chevys and oldsmobiles in every color you can imagine, new cars and old dented up cars, every make and model and they're all there, they're all down there arrayed before you, and the sun's low in the sky, and the light's shimmering off the metal and the glass, and the cars, they're all kinda all melding together, reflecting the sky, the beautiful enormity of the sky, all fuschia and tangerine and deep deep purple, just seeping into the horizon line, and it's about the most amazing thing, it's about the most amazing thing you'll ever see, it's like the whole universe is there, it's right there in front of you, reflecting back at you, and it's everything, it's the cars and it's the sky and the trees and the creek and the river and tessa's freckles and the little scar she has above her eye, every single eyelash, and her lips, the feel of her lips, and the feel of the grass and the earth and the sound of the pump station and the river and the scent of mud and leaves and birds all those crazyass birds, so many i can't even count them all—

(the violin grows louder. if chaos were a song. light streams in through cracks in the walls. MIKE TOTTEN *disappears through a wall. music ends. a mirror is revealed in the darkness where once there had been just a solid wall. light on* MARTIN KINFLEIN.)

MARTIN KINFLEIN: my dad tells this story of how he bought this mirror from the devil.

(projection: martin kinflein, oertels brewing company.)

MARTIN KINFLEIN: the devil, as it turned out, was a gypsy woman travelling through town. i said, dad, how did you know she was the devil. and he said: son, some things you just know. see now what you gotta understand is that my dad's mom, she was church of christ, and some of her people were holy rollers, handled serpents, spoke in tongues, the whole nine yards, and some of that fire and brimstone, i guess some of it musta stuck. anyway the devil tells my dad, you can pay some now, pay the rest later. i'll be back through the following spring. my dad says, fine. so a year passes. and then another and another one after that, and before you know it, ten years have gone by, and it gets so that my dad, he forgets about the whole thing. then one day, there's a knock on the door, and it's the devil, and she says to him: mister, i'm here to collect. and my dad says: ok, now, see, this is the thing, times have gotten hard since last we spoke, i've been laid off from my job at oertels. i make beer see, that's what i do, that's all i know how to do is make beer, that's what my father and his father and his father did, and now all of a sudden drinking beer's against the law, and i gotta say i don't know what kinda country goes and makes drinking beer against the law, i think that's maybe the stupidest thing i've ever heard in my life, so now we're supposed to be making pop, 'cept see i don't make pop, i make beer, that's what i do, that's all i know how to do and i'm too old to change. that's what i told the foreman, and the foreman told me: henry. henry. you don't like it, there's the door right there. and so i walked right out that door, and i haven't been back since. to hell with them is what i say, cause i got my pride, 'cept pride don't come cheap, and now i'm down to my last nickel, and that's how it stands with me that's how it is, and so basically, basically what i'm tryin to say to you is i don't have your money. and the devil says: mister, that's a problem. how about i give back the mirror, says my dad. and the devil says, i don't want the mirror. i want my money. and my dad, he's startin to get a little nervous. he's thinkin, i'm gonna have to give up my firstborn child or my eternal soul or somethin i know it's gonna hurt to give up, and i don't want to do it, i'm afraid, he said. i'm afraid. they worked it out in the end. turns out the devil, she had a little boy. and when she learned my dad played the fiddle, they struck a deal. teach my boy to play, she said, and we'll call it even. by the end of the week, he had that little gypsy boy playing "turkey in the straw." by the end of the year, he was playing mozart. i work at the brewery where my dad used to work. i'm no master brewer like he was. i'm nothing like him really. i'm just an accountant. i do the books. i can't play the fiddle or nothing like that, not like my dad. my dad, he was something else. he lived to be a hundred and four. died on derby day 1949. said he was feeling a little tired, lay down for a nap and never woke up. just like that. peaceful. my dad was from a different time, a whole different place in time. when he came up, it was people riding around in horse and buggy. that's how old he was. he could remember the civil war. he could remember the boys coming back home with wooden legs and empty sleeves, half their faces blown away. sometimes he would talk about the riots in the summer of 1855. this was all over louisville, west side, east side. they called it bloody monday when the mobs came hunting for germans and irish and set the town on fire. that was when that irish fellah quinn died. my dad was just a little boy.

(a young BOY *becomes visible in the darkness. he wears clothes from the last century. he is* MARTIN KINFLEIN'S FATHER *as a boy.)*

MARTIN KINFLEIN: he hid in an ice cellar by the river, near where the heigold house is now far as i can figure. he hid behind a giant block of ice and he was so cold, even though it was summer. he stayed down there for a day and a night and into the next day, and then he went home. i don't know if that ice cellar, if it's even there anymore.

(the sound of a violin playing mozart.)

MARTIN KINFLEIN: i went once to look for it. i walked all through thruston park, down by the point, but i couldn't find it.

(the young GIRL in the white dress appears as a reflection in the mirror. she gradually comes into view as MARTIN KINFLEIN speaks.)

MARTIN KINFLEIN: i did see something that struck me as being, well, kinda strange. there were all these children. i didn't think much of it at the time, but then later i thought how odd it was to see all those children there like that in the middle of a school day. they musta been on a field trip or something. but there was something about the whole thing, well it was just, it was off. they were running through the trees. i could hear them laughing and shouting. they were running so fast, it was hard to see them. all i could see were glimpses of them through the leaves. Then all of a sudden one of them, this little girl, she just stopped and she stared at me from across the field. she stared at me for the longest time as if she knew who i was, as if she knew me, and then she turned and ran away.

(flash from a camera. MARTIN KINFLEIN turns and walks away. as he walks away, his image frays and dissolves. he vanishes from view. the BOY in clothes from the last century runs into the shadows. the GIRL in the white dress follows him. the sound of distant thunder. the BOY and the GIRL run through the shadows. in the space, we hear the sound children whispering facts one after the next. a susurration of historical facts underneath everything: "linden hill was built in 1815. bourbon stockyards were established in 1834. the kentucky distillery company burned to the ground august 14, 1840. the school for the blind was established in 1842. woodland gardens were opened in 1848. the german american civic school opened in 1854. the heigold house was built by christian heigold in 1865. c. f. vissman packing company was established in 1876. the home of the innocents was built in 1880. st. josephs church went up in 1883. oertels brewing company was incorporated in 1906. fischer packing was founded in 1909. the great flood occurred in january 1937. the interstate was built in 1965. mary alice hadley founded hadley pottery in 1939. it still exists today." as the facts are read, the BOY in clothes from the last century emerges from the darkness. the GIRL in the white dress follows him. they play orpheus and eurydice. the BOY walks ahead of the GIRL.)

A BOY: there used to be a man named william wells. he ran a ferry cross the river. he lived in linden hill right in the heart of butchertown. they say he married an indian maiden. sweet breeze was her name. and that she died of typhoid fever before the year was out. they say her soul left her body, and turned into a bird, and flew away.

(the sound of thunder grows closer.)
A GIRL: we used to go down when we were kids and swim in the river. the water was so cold, even in the summertime. and deep, deeper than you ever thought. the mud would give beneath your feet and you'd suddenly, you'd drop off and you'd fall and you'd fall and you'd fall and you'd fall until all you saw was green black water.

(the BOY turns around and looks at the GIRL. lightning. thunder. the GIRL vanishes. the BOY vanishes. rain. rain. rain. the walls buckle and crack. a terrible creaking sound. wood cracking. the walls explode. water comes rushing in. the song of the flood. a final thunderclap. the rain, the thunder, everything cuts out. silence. light on IDA MILLER sitting in a chair.)
IDA MILLER: in '37 we'd be underwater where we're sitting now. that's a fact.

(projection: ida miller, wesley community house.)
IDA MILLER: 52 feet and 6 inches, that's how high the river rose. it rained for forty days straight. we lived down four blocks on washington, 1500 block near where the interstate, near where it cuts through. the water was up to our backyard. my sisters and i we had a marker set out, a little stick where you could see how far the water rose. and it just rose and rose and rose. we got around by rowboat. we rowed down main street, can you believe it. we'd wave at the guardsman on the pontoon bridge. we saw all kinds of things floating by. we saw a cow on top of a roof. we saw whole houses floating downstream. we even saw a couple of nuns paddling by in a canoe. my sister hazel gotta hold of a barrel of pickles, it was just floating by, and we pried it open and we ate those pickles, we ate so many pickles, we just stuffed ourselves with pickles. i got so sick on pickles and i never ate a pickle again. that's a true story. i'm a teacher. i have been all my life. i never married. never had children of my own. me and my sisters none of us did.

we were what they used to call maiden ladies. hazel worked at the seelbach, dorothy worked at kauffman strauss, and me, i taught down at the school for the blind.

(the german lieder begins.)
IDA MILLER: there was this one girl i think about sometimes. her name was nora holtz.

(the young GIRL *in the white dress playing the young* NORA HOLTZ *comes into view.)*

IDA MILLER: i see her like i see you. she's standing on the front lawn waiting for me. it's like a photograph in my mind. it's late spring and i can the smell the honeysuckle and the clover, and the sun, the sun is so bright, it's so bright. this was june 1936. she's miranda in "the tempest" and her costume, i sewed it myself. a white dress with tiny beads stitched in that shimmered in the light. i can see her clear as i'm seeing you. just they way she was. come the flood that winter, in the panic of the first night, nora crept down into the old root cellar at her uncle's place down on quincy. she stopped her ears against the thunder and curled up on the hard earth, and fell asleep to the sound of the rain above her. no one knew to look for her, no one knew till after. but by then, it was too late. by then she was already gone.

(the german lieder gets caught in a groove. the same phrase repeats in a loop and begins to break down and disintegrate. IDA MILLER *slowly exits. the young* GIRL *playing the* NORA HOLTZ *spins. She spins faster and faster. the skirt of her dress is a blur. her face is a blur.* TESSA RHEINGOLD *enters the space as the* GIRL *vanishes. she's in the middle of packing cardboard boxes.)*

TESSA RHEINGOLD: ok here's the deal, ladies: this is my art we're talking about. this is my artistic vision. and this is the fuckin future. you're looking at the future, right here, that's me, and if you don't like it, well that's too damn bad. cause time's on my side. so you better get with the program or you gonna be fuckin obsolete. like, like fuckin eight track tapes. hell yeah. fuck yeah.

(projection: tessa rheingold, hadley pottery.)

TESSA RHEINGOLD: that's exactly what i said to them just like that. you shoulda seen their faces. my mom's been working at hadley pottery practically all her life, and she was looking at me right then like i was like devil's spawn or something, like my head was about to spin round and green gunk was gonna come shooting outta my mouth. they fired me on right on the spot. whatever. me and that job, it just wasn't meant to be. but you know what gets me, the thing that burns my ass—if she was alive, mrs. hadley, she would've totally backed me up. mary alice was hip, yknow what i'm sayin. she was cool. i seen those pictures of her with the weird little hats and the little mona lisa smile. i know she had a wild side. you can tell just lookin at her. and she woulda dug my shit. i know she woulda, too. alright, look, i know, i know i give my mom, i give her way too much grief, i know that. but see now i justify it in my mind, cause my mom was a hellraiser when she was comin up, way worse than i ever was, staying out late and drinkin and smokin and carryin on. her dad, my grandpa kinflein, she drove that poor man crazy. he was like an accountant. he worked at oertels his whole life. he passed away last year. he was walking out by thruston park down by the point, and he had a heart attack and he died. he just died there on the spot. these little kids found him. my mom was pretty torn up about it. i guess i was, too. he was sweet yknow, and kinda crazy. he was a real packrat. he had all this stuff crammed into his house. he had this big old mirror in a gilt frame. i don't know where he got that thing. i wonder.

(TESSA RHEINGOLD *begins to recede from view.*)

TESSA RHEINGOLD: he'd tell stories about his dad or the way things were back in the day, just little things. i don't remember all that much. i wish i remembered more. i wish i'd paid more attention. sometimes when i'm down at the point, i picture him walking along the railroad tracks.

(*the thrumming of an electrical current begins.*)

TESSA RHEINGOLD: it's like i can almost see him. he's walking away real slow and steady towards the horizon line. and i'm standing there watching him, and i can't move. and i know if i call out, he won't hear me, so i just stand there, watching. i watch him as he walks away, till he's just a tiny speck, so small i can hardly see. i watch till my eyes ache. i watch till there's nothing left but sky.

(*the sound of the electrical current grows and cuts out.* TESSA RHEINGOLD *vanishes. light on* FRANK HENZEL. *he smokes.*)

FRANK HENZEL: the power went out today. some kinda short. nobody knows for sure.

(*projection: frank henzel, fischer meatpacking plant.*)

FRANK HENZEL: it was out all along mellwood and up frankfort, all the way over to crescent hill. they shut down the cut floor. we had to dump near five thousand pounds of meat. it was bad, stank to high heaven. afterwards i kinda, well i kinda had it. i went for a walk down by the greenway, and ended up down at the point. i saw a guy down there taking pictures. i watched him a while. finally he looked over at me and he said: c'mere. i want to show you something. and so i went and looked into the camera, and i saw this thing. the bark of a tree but close, so close that you could see all the patterns the wood made, layer upon layer, swirled and jagged. it looked like something i can't put into words, and it was, it was beautiful. later the guy, he asked if he could take my picture and i said alright. and so he did and we got to talking. he wanted to know what i did for a livin, and i told him: mister, i kill hogs is what i do. i kill em and i cut em up. and he asked, what's that like. and i ended up telling him about this old guy i used to know, worked at the same plant i work at. we called him old man holtz. old man holtz, he knew the score. my first day i go in, i see him sittin there and i say, i'm lookin for a job. and he says to me, i never hire someone lookin for a job, I hire someone lookin for *work*. he wasn't kiddin either. kill floor, cut floor. i don't care what the hell you're doin on the line, you're gonna work. old man holtz knew. he'd been there forever and a day. he sang. i remember that. he had a beautiful voice. i heard him sing karaoke one night. you'd never guess he'd have a voice like that. cut up hogs all day long, and sang like an angel. i started on the kill floor. worked my way up from scalder to splitter to loin puller. i even worked in the order room boxing up the quick cut hams. i did just about everything. it's a system, yknow, it's a whole system. you know what a dark cut is? it's when the animal gets scared and the adrenaline gets released into its system, and it stains the meat, and you can taste it. you can taste the fear in the meat. old man holtz, he always said, talk to em soft, soft and sweet. don't be yellin and cursin. talk to em soft and gentle, as you would a child. i used to pull loins. i used to use what they call a draw knife. now i work splitting and i use a chainsaw, and it's different, well it's a different kind of thing. these days you take what you can get. i'm lucky i got a job. at least that's what they tell me. sometimes you think about things, you can't help but think about things. work here long enough, and you're gonna get messed up, ain't no way around it. i saw a man once, his hand slipped, he was working the band saw, took two fingers clean off, knuckle on down. tore the skin all along his hand. you could see underneath, you could see the muscle and bone. just takes one slip, one slip is all. you can tell a man, i think, by the scars on his hands. by the cuts and burns, and how they turn, how they turn all white and smooth, translucent-like. like you can see, like you can see straight through.

(*the* BOY *playing the young* PETE HENZEL *gradually emerges from view. he wears a windbreaker, corduroys, and sneakers. he wears a mask.*)

FRANK HENZEL: see, i wonder how you tell a stranger about yourself, who you are and what you know of the world. everything you've seen and all the people you've known. i wonder what you tell em, so that they can understand. i was driving down story avenue the other day and i thought of this thing i hadn't thought about in years. when we were kids, my brother pete and me, we used to go to this halloween party.

(*an older* BOY *playing the young* FRANK HENZEL *emerges into view. he wears a mask. he wears the same clothes as the* PHOTOGRAPHER'S OLDER SON.)

FRANK HENZEL: mrs. hadley, she used to have this halloween party for all the kids in the neighborhood all along story. powder donuts and apple cider, and all the children wore costumes, and mrs. hadley she gave a prize to the best one. and one year, i remember, me and my brother pete we went, and i didn't even have a costume, and pete, all's he had was this plastic mask the color of skin, and it was shitty costume cause you could tell, you could tell it was him. and he'd been cryin, cause somebody was makin fun of him. kids were always makin fun of him cause he was kinda strange. he's still kinda strange. i mean he's pete, and he's my brother and i love him, but yeah he's fucked up. something's broken and it ain't getting fixed, and that's just, well that's just the way it goes. so there he was, standin there with tears and snot runnin down his face, and our cousin ronnie, she came over.

(*a* GIRL *appears. she wears the same clothes as the* PHOTOGRAPHER'S DAUGHTER. *she wears a mask.*)

FRANK HENZEL: and ronnie, she always looked out for us, me and pete both, and she cracked some joke about some smartass kid we all hated, and before we knew it, we were all crackin up, we were laughin so hard, and somebody, i forget who, they took a picture. pete. and ronnie. and me. just like that. and if you look real close, you can see right there at the edge of the picture, you can see ronnie's husband jimmy. they weren't married yet. i mean they were just kids, we were all just kids. later, they'd get married and have kids of their own and jimmy, he'd enlist. one hundred and first airborne division stationed out of fort campbell. shot and killed in an ambush outside a place called hung nhon, 400 miles north of saigon, somewhere on the other side of the world. this was april 1972.

(*a woman sings a cappella. a song of eastern mountains and northern seas. a song of loved ones gone away.*)

FRANK HENZEL: i remember right before he shipped out, jimmy got glasses. he was already a grown man and he never even knew he needed them.

all those years and nobody knew. i remember he said, he put em on, and he was amazed. how everything, how it was all so clear.

(the BOY *playing the* YOUNG PETE HENZEL *takes off his mask.)*
FRANK HENZEL: he said it hurt, it hurt to see everything so sharp and clear. to be that aware, it was almost too much, it was almost too much to bear.

*(*FRANK HENZEL *vanishes. the* CHILDREN *remain. the* PHOTOGRAPHER *appears. he approaches the* CHILDREN *across a field of darkness. as he approaches the* CHILDREN, *the song fades away. the* PHOTOGRAPHER *stares into the light. the light gets brighter and brighter.)*
PHOTOGRAPHER: what do you see, i asked him. and he said, i see my wife. i see my children, i see the faces of my children. i see my mom and dad. i see the place where i grew up. i see the trees and the river and how the light, the way the light, how it sparkles on the water. and it's so beautiful, it's so beautiful, you never realize, you never even realize till it's gone—

(the YOUNG PETE HENZEL *sings a cappella the hymn "o god our help in ages past." the* PHOTOGRAPHER *recedes from view. the* YOUNG PETE HENZEL *finishes singing. the* CHILDREN *turn into birds and fly away. a blur of skin and color scattering in all directions. silence and stillness. in the stillness, you can hear the sound of louisville, kentucky at nightfall. cars passing on the street outside. and beyond the cars, the stirring of leaves. the sound of breathing. if breathing were a song. a cavernous space, a wrecked and ancient space. the sound of a light switch being turned on. a simple prop that indicates a bar. think a neon michelob sign. think a coors sign with a holographic waterfall. the sound of footsteps.* MAUDIE TOTTEN *enters the space. she has a bottle of bourbon and a shot glass. a painting of a hooded merganser hangs in the void.)*
MAUDIE TOTTEN: my stepson mike painted this. it's a kind a bird. i forget what it's called.

(projection: maudie totten, johnson's bait and beer.)
MAUDIE TOTTEN: i tell him, mike, you paint it and i'll hang it on my wall, and maybe one of these days, some patron'll come in for a nice cold beer and look up and see your painting and say: i like that. i would like to purchase that. that has not as of yet happened, but that don't mean a thing. i think he's pretty good. my husband, mike's dad, he says don't encourage him. he says mike and mary catherine, that's mike's older sister, he says they're a never-ending source of irritation and dismay. my husband and is entitled to his opinions, but this is my place and

i'm gonna do what i'm gonna do, and if i wanna hang mike's paintings on every square inch of my damn wall, then that's what i'm gonna do. my name is maudie. maudie totten. i've lived here my whole life. i own this place. i own it free and clear. it used to be called the last chance and the drovers comin through, they'd stop for a pint. totten is my married name. i've had five of em. i was an epperson, i was a kirchner, i was a krebs, i was a miller. my current husband, mike's dad, he worked over at fischers. his name's roy totten. they called him hubcap, don't ask me why. started on the kill floor, worked his way up. that's how it used to go over there. you started at the bottom, worked your way up. when we got married, roy was working the cut floor, pulling loins. that's a bracket one job. good money. hard work. you gotta be quick and strong. the speed of the rail is 300 hog an hour. you got 25 men workin the rail, that's five hogs per minute, 12 second per hog. and you gotta do it right the first time out, cause i'll tell you what, you don't get a second chance. roy had a friend named frank henzel. he worked the kill floor splitting hogs. they used chainsaws, and they didn't have the automatic brakes back then, and the saw, it got away from him, and it's on a pulley right, on a chain, and it flew up and coasted see, turned all around, turned back on him, and tore him up, it tore him to pieces. only family he had when i knew him was his brother pete. pete's a little touched i guess you would say. used to work at the plant, but then he got fired. he let out all the hogs. he just opened up the gate in the holding pen and shooed them out, and out they went, trotting down the road, and then running, hogs everywhere, in the streets blocking traffic, chasing people down the sidewalk, everybody shoutin and runnin. it was a mess. after that, pete he got fired, o you bet he did. the plant's closed down now. it's different now, it's all, well it's just different. a whole new world. nothing stays the same, and maybe that's not a bad thing. it just is. i'm still here. me and my sister both. i have a twin sister. her name is maddie. everybody used to get a kick outta that when we were comin up. maddie and maudie. maudie and maddie. o how we hated that. now we don't mind hardly so much, but then, then it was like nails on a chalkboard. maddie lives in lexington. she moved there with her husband gene. i liked gene. i met him at my wedding, my first of many. it was a church wedding. i got married over at st. joes. i had a nice white dress. and we had the kids choir, yknow, and they sang. and then we had the reception out by the old water tower. gene was from normal, illinois and i thought that was very odd. he used to take photographs, and he liked jazz, ornette coleman and dizzy gillespie, and i didn't know much about jazz, but i

learned. gene was a good teacher. he'd blast that jazz on his old phonograph and then he's show you his pictures. he'd want to know what
you saw. and i'll tell you what, they were like no pictures i'd ever seen.
gene, he had all these photos of twigs. i swear to god, i've never seen so
many damn twigs in my life. but the thing—this was the thing—gene
could make you see a twig like you had never seen a twig before. like
it was some kinda alien life form, like it was the most amazing thing
in the world. gene went through his days seeing the world like that. all
the little league games and the kids' birthday parties, all the camping
trips down in red river gorge. that was a time. that was a good time.

(darkness gradually falls. the circumference of light that MAUDIE TOTTEN *occupies gets smaller and smaller.* MAUDIE TOTTEN *is alone in a vast darkness.)*
MAUDIE TOTTEN: the last year of his life, he took pictures of all of us. he was
making a family album, he said. not like a regular family album. different. i remember he took a picture of himself and maddie. this was
right before he died. we knew he was leaving us, we knew that, and it
was hard, it was so hard. they'd come to visit one last time, and we'd
gone out to the point. we'd brought all of our kids, and it was such a
beautiful day, so clear and bright, and the kids were laughing and hors-
ing around, and the sky was so blue, and the smell of grass and earth
and new leaves. and underneath it all, you could hear the river. but the
thing i remember most, what i remember was looking across a field, and
seeing my sister and gene, these two people who loved each other and
who had built a life together, a whole entire life, and he's leaning towards
her, and he's saying something i can't hear, and as i watch them, i think
of all the things that pass between them, all the things i have no words
for, all the things alive in that precise point in time, the tiniest things.

*(*MAUDIE TOTTEN *turns and goes. she turns out the last lights remaining. darkness.)*

THE VENUS DE MILO IS ARMED

Kia Corthron

Production Notes

THE VENUS DE MILO IS ARMED was commissioned by Alabama Shakespeare Festival and produced by ASF in 2003. The subject matter was inspired by the short films focusing on land mines featured in the 1999 Human Rights Watch International Film Festival at Lincoln Center's Walter Reade Theater in New York City. The playwright became suddenly aware that despite much American corporate responsibility for land mines, we rarely thought about them because they were so far away: We had not yet felt any comparable violence within our own borders. That condition changed drastically within a few years and was reflected in the revisions that occurred prior to and during rehearsal, but we were still living in that less-complicated world when Alabama Shakes committed to producing the play on September 10, 2001.

CHARACTERS (IN ORDER OF APPEARANCE)

RIN, 28

GIRL, 10

TAL, rhymes with "gal," Rin's mother

W.J., "dubya jay," Rin's father

LARK, W.J.'s sister

FRY, Lark's husband

MARI, rhymes with "starry," daughter of Lark and Fry, twenty-eight

WALSH, Rin's brother, thirty

Act 1 occurs in two spaces: the living room connected to the garage, which has been converted into Rin's bedroom. The first scene of act 2 takes place in the garage/bedroom only; act 2, scene 2, is outside.

Rin's room: Still garage-y—bicycle, metal tool shelves and tools, cement floor, the upstage wall might be the former car door—but also a single bed, neatly made, CD collection and books on the shelves, small refrigerator, probably a throw rug over part of the floor. A shelf with several athletic trophies. A big something or other in the corner covered with a heavy-duty garbage bag. A flat map of the world with numerous thumbtacks, especially in southern Africa, but just four in the United States: Shreveport, Louisiana; Boise, Idaho; South Bend, Indiana; and Hanover, New Hampshire.

Living room: Middle-class furnished. Stereo, piano. Door to the outside upstage; an exit leading to the kitchen and another to the hall and other rooms.

The reproductions of Greek art that are indicated in Act 1:

the maniacal Medusa	the Medusa from the relief pediment of the temple of Artemis, Corfu
man lying, crawling	from Olympia, temple of Zeus, east pediment
lion	from the Mausoleum at Halikarnassos
woman with infant	Kephisodotos's Eirene holding Ploutos

I found photos of the pieces in Nigel Spivey's *Understanding Greek Sculpture: Ancient Meanings, Modern Readings* (London: Thames and Hudson, 1996; Medusa, p. 97; Venus de Milo, p. 184 [but there are better photos of the Venus elsewhere]); and in John Boardman's *Greek Sculpture: The Classical Period* (man lying, plate 20.7) and *Greek Sculpture: The Late Classical Period* (lion, plate 18.2; Eirene holding Ploutos, plate 24; London: Thames and Hudson, 1985 and 1995, respectively).

Many of the decisions regarding when characters removed prosthetics, when they used crutches and when not, and the like, were drawn from the needs of the original Alabama Shakespeare Festival cast, all of whom happened to be able-bodied.

Songs (and raps) are in italics and are always sung (or rapped) rather than simply being spoken. Sometimes songs are sung lower volume under other spoken dialogue. The verse text will be written in full though the character may not get through the entire verse. Whenever a song is sung under other dialogue, it is indicated as such in the stage directions, and the type of the lower volume lyrics is reduced in size and italicized.

All spirituals, to the playwright's knowledge, are in the public domain. The exceptionally bad rap lyrics are all the creation of the playwright.

Rin's is a gentle, easy laugh.

Act 1

(RIN, in a casual dress, in her room. She reads from typed pages. The GIRL sits on bed, listening, attentive.)

RIN: Fear. Giving in to it brings down the great, overcome it and the small grow mighty. October 10th, 1952. Without water for two days, without food for four we wait it out, wait it out. A twig snaps. I swing round and suddenly am eye-to-eye with North Korea. I expect hatred in his eyes. I see terror. And know he sees the same in mine.

(RIN stops, thinks.)

RIN: My eyes. *(Beat. Muttering:)* Mine. *(Takes a pencil, edits:)* My eyes. Mine. My eyes.

GIRL: Can I play with the cans?

(RIN nods absently. GIRL dumps onto the floor a plastic bag full of empty soda cans meant for recycling. As RIN resumes her reading, GIRL will play a game: she will roll a can from the inside of one foot to the inside of the other and back again, counting out loud each roll [interrupting her counting when she

speaks her lines], immediately followed by her jumping on the can [both feet], smashing it. she will start with three rolls, and increase by one the rolls for every can thereafter; the count for the first can is 1—2—3—SMASH, for the second 1—2—3—4 SMASH, and so on.)

RIN: *(Reading:)* Men fighting men. Two feet between us I memorize every line under his eye, every breeze-blown hair. My military foe, but I've never felt such unity, such oneness of purpose. Five minutes we stare, ten. Fifteen and in some zen synchronism we both suddenly, simultaneously step forward.

    Boom! We've stepped on the same landmine! His leg flies off one direction! mine the other!

(GIRL giggles.)
RIN: It's not a comedy!

(GIRL continues to jump and smash as she speaks.)
GIRL: Your brother never did that, face to face with somebody like that.
RIN: *Fiction!*
GIRL: Your brother was in the Gulf War, whatchu know about Korea 1952?

(Offstage a brief buzzer.)
GIRL: Microwave! Microwave! Microwave!
RIN: Always jump like it's the ice cream truck.
GIRL: Food! Starvin'! *(GIRL stops game to stare at RIN.)*
RIN: *(Reads:)* In the hospital tent we are side by side.
GIRL: This isn't how you remember me.
RIN: *(Reads:)* To the surprise of both of us, we have the same tattoo on our lower right arm, his in Korean, mine English: "Mom."

(As GIRL speaks, TAL and w.j. enter the living room from the kitchen, arranging dishes of newly microwaved hors d'oeuvres on the table.)
GIRL: How come I don't have an accent? Ain't I Angolan?
RIN: Pick up that mess.
GIRL: You said I could play.
RIN: Changed my mind.

(Picking the cans up, dropping them back in the sack:)
GIRL: *(Sulky, muttering.)* What I'm s'posed to play with?
RIN: *(Reads:)* Chapter Fourteen. A great storm wails outside—

(Doorbell. TAL *and* W.J. *stand, face the living room outside door, tense.* GIRL *continues with the cans.)*
RIN: Sh!

*(*GIRL *is still.* TAL *finally musters the courage to answer the door,* W.J. *with her.* RIN *smiles when she hears the door open. Standing outside are* LARK, FRY, *and* MARI. *[All may not be immediately visible to the audience.] They, like* W.J. *and* TAL, *are attired nicely. An awkward pause. Then:)*
RIN: What're you standing outside for?

TAL	RIN
What're you standing outside for?	Come on in!

TAL: Come on in!
LARK: Tal.
W.J.: Hey sister.
LARK: W.J.! *(They enter. Hugs.* GIRL *finishes throwing cans in sack.)*
RIN: We haven't seen each other six years. Since Africa.
GIRL: Then get your butt out there and say "hi."
RIN: Yeah so you can get into those cans forget it.
GIRL: I want somethin' to play with!
RIN: Quiet! I need to finish this part. *(Back to her pages.)*
GIRL: I wanna play!

(Without looking at her, RIN *throws a plastic or rubber ball at the* GIRL, *hard.* GIRL *plays with it, happy. Meanwhile* TAL *leads the others to the hors d'oeuvres. They sit.)*
TAL: What can I get you. *(To* FRY:*)* Beer?
FRY: Don't mind if I do.
W.J.: *(To* LARK:*)* Red wine, no doubt. We're prepared. *(*LARK *smiles.)*
TAL: Mari?
MARI: Just water thank you.

*(*TAL *exits off to the kitchen.)*
RIN: In the third draft, the hurricane blew them into the river. They drowned. This rewrite maybe they have a little more ingenuity.
W.J.: Try these, Tal whipped 'em up. *(They eat.)*
RIN: Raft! *(Writes.)*
GIRL: Your brother had better stories. If your brother woulda wrote down what he said, Pulitzer Prize.
LARK: Tasty.
RIN: Hurricane or typhoon? What's the difference? *(Thinks.)* Search engine!

(Moves to her computer to search the Web.)
W.J.: I'll go see if Tal needs some help. Tal!

(W.J. exits to the kitchen. Others quietly munch, a bit tense.)
GIRL: This isn't how you remember me! What about *this?*

(GIRL grabs her right ankle, raises it into the air.)
GIRL: You made this up, I haven't had this since I was six.
RIN: *(Still working at computer, sings:)* When Israel was in Egypt's land
      Let my people go

(Continues under dialogue:)
      Oppressed so hard they could not stand
      Let my people go
      Go down Moses
      Way down in Egypt's land
      Tell ol' Pharaoh
      Let my people go

(LARK refers to photos of RIN and RIN's brother WALSH:)
LARK: Well. They still have pictures of both their offspring, least they haven't wholly forgot him.
FRY: Don't you keep pictures a the dead?
W.J.: *(Enters.)* She's okay. Where's your niece? RIN! *(RIN still singing.)*
GIRL: I'm bored! *(Dives under RIN's bed.)*
RIN: *(Cuts off song, gathering two wrapped gifts.)* Just don't get into those recyclables again I mean it.
W.J.: *Rin!*
RIN: Okay!

(RIN ties a ribbon on one of the gifts as GIRL pulls out a disk object from under the bed. It is a landmine though this need not be telegraphed to the audience.)
GIRL: Ooooh shiny!

(GIRL starts lightly kicking the disk between HER feet and counting, heading offstage. At the last moment, RIN looks up: horror. Stands:)
RIN: Hey!
W.J.: *(At RIN's door.)* Hey.

(RIN, *startled, turns to* W.J. *Then turns back to* GIRL *but* GIRL *is gone.* W.J. *never notices* GIRL.)
W.J.: They're here.

(RIN, *still shaken, stares after the* GIRL.)
W.J.: Come on!

(RIN *follows* W.J. *into the living room as* TAL *enters from kitchen with a tray of drinks.*)
LARK: Godchild!
FRY: Rinnie Rin!
RIN: *(Hugs, hands out gifts:)* Hi Aunt Lark. Hi Uncle Fry.
LARK: What's this?
FRY: Look at the wrappin'.
TAL: Homemade.
LARK: You made it? *(RIN smiles.)* Look at you.
FRY: Course she made it, didn't she always.

(RIN *turns to* MARI. MARI *is tense: this is her normal state of being, always compounded around* RIN.)
RIN: Hi Mari.
MARI: Hi, Rin.
RIN: Open!

(LARK *gingerly opens the gift, trying not to tear the paper.*)
LARK: Ah!

(*A handcrafted bird in a cage.*)
RIN: Real feathers, I gathered 'em in the park, dyed 'em. Just went to the art
    supply store and got these wires to make the cage, nothin' big.
LARK: Beautiful.
RIN: I know this doesn't look exactly like Chipper but . . .
FRY: I wanted to buy another *no.* She never got over that 'keet flyin' off, never
    wanted to replace him.
LARK: My fault. Who's dumb enough, forget, leave the cage door open and
    cage by the window? She came back. Year and a half later, I'm windexing
    and looky there, who on the tree branch inches from my nose. I'd *just*
    finally taken the cage to the basement, but no matter. Why she wanna
    be in jail after eighteen months' flying free? I'd like to think she didn't

feel like it was jail when she was in it, I'd like to think before she tasted freedom she appreciated the ignorance-is-bliss guarantee of regular meals, free maid service. We had nice conversation awhile, then she off again. Not too much a pipedream to hope for another visit, some parakeets live to thirteen. I'd like to think her lap of luxury early life strengthened her longevity.

RIN: Open yours.

FRY: *(Opening.)* You know, right?

W.J.: All news to us. But guess we shouldn't be surprised. Rin and her gifts.

TAL: I had an inkling. You slept through it, the clang clanging Rin up all night working on them.

RIN: These I made before I left. Last night was something else.

(The gift: a little handcrafted pool table. The balls are marbles.)
FRY: Ain't that cute.

(FRY picks up the black one, peers through it.)
FRY: Eight ball.

RIN: I thought about getting solid colors to be realistic but I dunno. Something magical, these see-throughs. In Seattle, there's this place off Queen Anne, *steep* hill, steeper than the hill out Murray Road I used to run every morning, high school.

LARK: I bet. Cross-country. How many trophies you bring home?

RIN: On this hill there's a public telescope, but away from the main touristy area so relatively serene, attracts no more than ten, twenty an evening even high season, and it's clear twilight, the Space Needle and skyline on the left, Sound on the right, and somewhere in the middle's the mountain, Rainier's the biggest thing around but in the distance it's a ghost, floating in the air you can see right through it. Sometimes even in the cloudless blue it'll completely disappear, Seattlites starting the morning with "Is the mountain out today?" Tonight, dusk, it's there, and I eavesdrop on the dozen others blah blah "Mariners" blah blah "Pike Street" no one but me sees the mountain. Everything *but* the mountain, and I feel a part of something magical cuz I *do* see it, privileged, and guilty about it, I want to point it out to them but I'm a coward cuz *one*, if for some strange reason they're unimpressed I couldn't deal with the devastation, the sudden reevaluation of my own mesmerizement, *two*, I'm superstitious, like if I help them see it I'll lose *my* magic. So I just silently observe and think hey: this must mean something. Biggest thing there but unless you're looking to see it, you don't.

FRY: Seattle? That parta your U.S. tour? Heard you on a adventure, cross-country drivin'.

RIN: More like criss-cross-country, Washington and southern Cal, Texas, Florida, Maine, Michigan, five weeks I covered a pretty representative range of the forty-eight contiguous.

LARK: Surprised me when I got wind of it. *(To* TAL *and* W.J.*:)* Driving. Herself.

W.J.: If you mean the stuff that's been happening lately, the news, the stuff that's been happening lately's been happening the last two weeks, Rin left five weeks ago.

TAL: Luckily she was long out of those states by the time—

LARK: I don't mean the stuff that's been happening lately I mean driving. Herself.

TAL and W.J.: Try and stop her!

FRY: When you get back? Recent, right? Couple weeks?

RIN: Day before yesterday.

FRY and LARK: *Day before yesterday?*

LARK: But how . . . ? We found out about this get-together week and a half ago.

RIN: Idea came to me while I was planning my trip. Made the gifts, e-mailed Mari on the road. How could you say no? I figured. Six years.

FRY: Six years.

RIN: Traveling is breathing! Don't you think? Hadn't been on a trip in a while, soon's I started all I thought: Look what I've been missing!

(Silence.)

RIN: I know you've done plenty of other trips, Mari. Since Africa.

MARI: No.

FRY: Still gotcher hand in it, huh. Crafts.

RIN: See my office!

*(*RIN *runs off into the garage. The others stare after her, silent.* RIN, *in the garage, looks behind, puzzled that no one followed her.)*

FRY: Runnin'?

(Pause.)

LARK: Her *office?*

W.J.: Come on.

(They follow W.J. *into the garage.)*

RIN: Where were you?

LARK: Oh my.

FRY: I remember this place just a tool shed. Wow. Livable. Comf'table. *(Now notices* RIN's *computer, is drawn to it.)*

RIN: Guess "office" isn't quite accurate. Better "workshop slash boudoir." *(Laughs.)*

LARK: Tools still here.

W.J.: Her work.

LARK: There he goes Don't you sit down playing, Fry!

FRY: I'm not sittin' and it's not playin'. Just lookin'. *(To* RIN:) Hey! Dot com. Which one a the computer wizzes sought the other out first? Set this little reunitin' up.

LARK: Look who's talking, can't get him off the thing get so tired, pick up the phone trying to make a call and all I hear's static "Fry! Get off that damn computer!" Scuze me, W.J.

FRY: I just wonder which e-mail correspondent had the original initiative to glue the family back together after . . . *(Beat: Doesn't complete his thought.)*

MARI: Rin's idea. Rin came to me.

*(*TAL's *eyes have been stuck on the large object in the corner covered in a heavy-duty garbage bag. Now she notices* RIN *looking at her. As the conversation continues and when* LARK *isn't looking,* FRY *will fiddle with the computer mouse.)*

TAL: I didn't ask! Some masterpiece, all secretive she won't tell me a thing. Once or twice I must admit, my curiosity, think hard of peeking *never!* Whole time you were gone. I'm worth your trust.

RIN: I know.

LARK: Fridge. Hot plate. You ever get mad at your landlords, guess you just slam your door, camp out here. Self-sufficient.

RIN: Still need the bathroom. *(Laughs.)*

LARK: *(To* W.J.:) Hey. What happens you get mad now? I recall this was your sulking place.

W.J.: Few times I made the mistake, head out here 'til she remind me: her room.

RIN: Knew you'd see this first.

*(*MARI *is startled that* RIN *has addressed her.* MARI *is gingerly touching an elaborately built and furnished dollhouse.)*

LARK: Oh my Lord. Sorry, W.J.

RIN: *(To* LARK:) Never saw it before? College. Worked on it Christmas breaks, summer.

LARK: *Built* it? *(*RIN *nods.)* Stairs! Running water!

RIN: Mari came over and played with me. *(Taking in* MARI:*)* Suddenly we were seven. *(*MARI *smiles, shy.)*

W.J.: *(Who'd wandered over.)* Piano! Pool!

RIN: We kept building on the serial drama, the new adventures of the Morgans the good ol' bourgey Morgans.

LARK: Beautiful.

*(*LARK *refers to a half-painted newly built wooden toy wagon.)*

TAL: All Rin's business. People special order a pull wagon, straw Christmas wreath, she provides the meticulously worked product.

W.J.: Charges a fair fee too. Her skill. Creativity.

TAL: Hey. Where's your statues?

FRY: Right here. *(He has wandered over to the trophies.)* Softball. Volleyball. Track. Cross-country, runnin', that your specialty, right?

W.J.: Long distance *and* the sprint. First place States'. Regionals, could've gotten a scholarship just based on athletics but her academics even bypassed that. Didn't they say it, high school grad: "Best All Around"?

TAL: I meant the *other* statues.

RIN: She means my sculptures. Put 'em away. Things getting a little cluttered.

TAL: Put something else away! My favorite sight in here was your Play-Doh masterpieces. *(*RIN *pulling a box out. To* LARK *and* FRY:*)* These *not* for sale.

*(*RIN *takes out several hardened Play-Doh reproductions of ancient Greek sculptures. Each is a different Play-Doh color [one solid color per statuette] and represents the condition in which the original was found: armless, legless. No figure has all its limbs.* FRY *holds up a relief of a maniacal woman. She has no hands or lower legs.)*

FRY: Look at that.

RIN: *(Fun:)* She's crazy! Don't you think? Medusa, she's a lunatic that's why I like her. Or some doll came alive on a horror movie, got her hands cut off now on a revenge spree.

LARK: *(Picks up lying man, ribs showing through his flesh, seeming to drag his body.)* Never seen 'em like this. On their bellies.

RIN: I know. Hunger. Humanness.

FRY: You made these?

RIN: Copied 'em.

FRY: Rin the artist, 'member we used to say it? Mari the Scientist, Rin the Artist. Or Preacher. Well guess that's a kinda art too.

LARK: What's this? Lion? *(Lion with no feet.* RIN *nods.)*

85

FRY: *(More to himself.)* Scientist, artist. Ain't it opposite.

TAL: Here's my favorite. But Baby Jesus lost an arm.

RIN: It's not Madonna and Child. Eirene holding Ploutos. Eirene means "peace," Ploutos "wealth." Why'd she name him that? I used to think, "wealth" and "peace": don't they conflict?

FRY: I think you confusin' "wealth" with "*greed.*"

LARK: I know her.

FRY: Nothin' wrong with a little extra.

RIN: Aphrodite. Peasant found her on the island of Melos, 1820, though it's generally thought she was created elsewhere, second century B.C. Turk government stole her from the peasant, French stole her from the Turks and beat the Turk they stole her from, French named her "Venus de Milo," kept her. Louis the Eighteenth had French sculptors give her arms that held apples, arms that held clothing, a lamp, pointing arms 'til finally Louis said stop she's beautiful as is. Started the new thinking: leave art like you found it.

(RIN's stomach growls.)

RIN: *(Giggles.)* Sorry!

TAL: Ask why she's hungry.

(LARK and FRY look at each other, confused.)

LARK: Why—?

TAL: Fasting. Ask why she's fasting.

RIN: Not in a big way I don't want this to be some pretentious self-righteous thing but in a little way, in a small way. Two-day fast. Just a tiny insight into what it's like. Starving.

LARK: And why're you looking for such insight?

RIN: See how it feels!

(Silence. Eventually RIN breaks the tension with a little laugh.)

RIN: Artist. Too bad all my "talent" doesn't quite add up to pay the rent. Twenty-eight, still temping, still living with Mommy and Daddy.

TAL: You contribute. Rent *and* plenty of beautiful pieces decorating this house *and* fix-it woman don't belittle that, *great* help. Not having to run to the plumber the electrician your classes. Engineering. *(FRY has gone to try out the couch.)*

RIN: Engineering major art major music major writing major all adds up to this: BA General Studies. But my flakiness does come in handy around here.

TAL: Just don't say you don't contribute to this household, your contribution to this household's infinite.

RIN: My brother sure caught hell, flaking around—

TAL: *Hey.*

(Beat.)

FRY: *(Couch:)* Not bad.

RIN: Goodwill.

LARK: Know what it needs? Throw cover. Big crocheted thing, recall the sweater I made for you? You were three. Baby blanket. You kept it for your dollies.

RIN: Still have it. Basement. Somewhere.

LARK: Tell me the colors you like I do a two-tone pattern.

RIN: Sounds like a lot of—

LARK: No trouble doing what you love you know that. Craftswoman.

RIN: *(Thinks.)* Blue. Royal blue. Black trim.

(During FRY's monologue MARI, who'd wandered over to the statues with the others, will move back to the dollhouse.)

FRY: Ain't we lucky people! We didn't have much but our kids. Choosin' the right neighborhood, public school got the excellence of a private. Good foresight cuz though we have the supplemental, college scholarships to our well-applied offspring mean we barely touch the nest egg. Cum laudes. Computers.

LARK: We had plenty you underestimate the real richness: family.

FRY: We got money!

LARK: Talk like we're filthy rich.

FRY: Enough for jazz legends the concert hall, enough for a second honeymoon Caribbean adventure year ago.

W.J.: Little expendable income don't hurt. Nothing to be ashamed.

LARK: Nothing to be proud.

W.J.: Isn't *money* that's the root. *Love* of.

FRY: I *am* proud why the hell not? Pregnant teens, crackhead teens, bullets Never kidded myself: difference between us and them's just a number after the dollar sign. Good upbringing? Number after the dollar sign make good upbringing a lot easier all I'm sayin's plenty a people in the world spends plenty a time worryin' on the gas bill, groceries whether their kid's shot on the way to the playground ain't we lucky we ain't got to worry.

(Beat.)

FRY: About that. 'Course other . . . other worries . . .

(FRY glancing at TAL and W.J.)

FRY: Sorry.

MARI: SORRY! SORRY! SORRY! SORRY! SORRY! SORRY! SORRY! SORRY! SORRY!

(MARI had dropped a miniature standing full-length mirror from the dollhouse. all stunned to silence by her outburst. RIN walks over, picks up the mirror, examines it. A piece of the wood frame has broken off.)

RIN: It's okay, Mari. Just needs a little Super Glue.

(RIN gets some Super Glue, starts fixing the miniature mirror.)

TAL: Rin Rin Rin can't tell I'm the proud parent. But proud aunt too, I heard
    a rumor somebody's been raking in the promotions.

FRY: Sure has.

TAL: How many years you been there now?

(TAL is looking at MARI. MARI looks at TAL, at others, panicked, speechless. RIN doesn't look up from her work on the mirror. Finally:)

RIN: *There is a balm in Gilead*

RIN	W.J.
To make the wounded whole	She can't work in the silence.
There is a balm in Gilead	
To heal the sin-sick soul	

(RIN stops singing when TAL starts talking.)

TAL: Last week we introduced ourselves to this new family in church and they
    asked me what we do. I said I'm a high school counselor, W.J. says he's
    a musicologist. *"Oh,"* says the couple, *so* impressed with W.J.

W.J.: How you know me? They had a teenage son, I'm sure when you said
    "high school counselor"—

TAL: *So* impressed with W.J. Their fourteen-year-old son looks confused,
    then says "My uncle's a doctor too." The couple laughs, then W.J. says,
    "Well, colleagues, I might know him." The couple stops laughing: maybe
    "musicologist" *is* doctor?

W.J.: *Is.* P H doctor.

LARK: *(Laughing.)* W.J. *(Beat.)* Missed you.

(FRY looking at books on shelves built into the wall.)

FRY: Dalai Lama. *Zen and Motorcycle Maintenance.* Bhagavad Gita you got a nice selection a spiritual texts, your various Bible translations plus thinkin' beyond the Judeo-Christian.

RIN: *(Laughs.)* I *do* have other stuff not *just* a religious freak. The typical: *Beloved. Malcolm X* as told to Alex Haley. Okay.

("Okay" meaning the mirror is repaired. All smile. Then LARK *goes to* MARI *and* RIN, *puts her arms around them.)*

LARK: My girls my girls. My twenty-eight-year-old girls.

(Beat.)

TAL: *(Moving toward the living room.)* No one gonna say I threw a dinner party, kept the guests in the garage—*(*LARK *and* W.J. *are following.)*

LARK: "Guests." *Family.*

TAL: Family, family.

FRY: Boise. South Bend.

(All stop to stare at FRY. *He is looking at the world map, the four thumbtacked places. Now* FRY *turns to* RIN.)*

FRY: Hanover, New Hampshire. Shreveport, Louisiana.

(Pause.)

RIN: I'm keeping track! no one else around here's talking about it. I gotta . . . talk I gotta . . . Went back to my novel! War novel I know Walsh was never in Korea, his landmine business was the Gulf War, but I like the setting I like history.

LARK: This isn't fiction this isn't history. Landmines popping *this* country. Now.

FRY: Lark—

LARK: You write, Rin, you keep writing good girl. *(To* W.J. *and* TAL:*)* I know what you lost but can't just go on pretending—

FRY: Lark!

MARI: I have to go to the bathroom!

*(*MARI *rushes out of the garage, through the living room and off the exit to the hallway. Silence.)*

TAL: Hors d'oeuvres getting cold. *(Exits to living room.)*

RIN: Wanna see slides from my trip?

FRY: Love ta.

W.J.: *(Looking after* TAL.*)* Bring 'em into the living room. *(Exits to living room.)*

LARK: Rinnie. We have a little something for you too. *(Reaches into her purse.)*

TAL: Where are they?

W.J.: *(Puzzled, calls:)* Lark? Fry?

LARK: Just a minute! *(Pulls out six little wrapped gifts.* RIN *surprised.)* Nothing much. Perfume, a doll from our New Orleans weekend, itty book about how every day is joy joy joy.

FRY: Six birthdays we missed. Just makin' up.

RIN: But I'm grown now. You don't have to give presents to an adult niece.

FRY: All them overnights at our place, ain't we closer than the average father's sister and spouse?

(The three hug.)

W.J.: Lark!

RIN: Lemme put the slides in order, be there in a minute.

(LARK and FRY enter the living room as RIN starts preparing the slides.)

LARK: Here we are.

FRY: Just needed a little hug time with our niece.

LARK: Look at that! Doesn't it water my mouth.

TAL: Vegetarian shish kabobs you have to try!

FRY: Everything vegetarian today?

LARK: Oh eat it.

W.J.: Believe me, I was a skeptic myself. Wait 'til you taste.

(They do.)

LARK: Mmmmm!

TAL: It's the seasoning. And the charbroil flavor, grill in the basement.

FRY: You right, though a little hog fat be the perfect added touch.

LARK: Look at this spread. Hummus, grape leaves. Brie.

TAL: I started hostessing a few years back, took a few gourmet classes.

LARK: Hostessing?

TAL: Teas.

(Beat.)

TAL: Charities. I provide the scones and petit fours, everyone else comes with their wallets.

W.J.: Before the night's over ours opened too.

LARK: Charities?

TAL: Black college funds, food for starving African children, food for starving U.S. children.

FRY: *(More to himself.)* Ain't we lucky people.

(As they munch, GIRL *enters the garage, hopping in a potato sack as if in a race.)*
GIRL: That wasn't how you remembered me, this is how you remembered me.

*(*GIRL *hops closer to* RIN.*)*
TAL: You try this humus, Fry. *(He does. Frowns.)*
FRY: Nice.

*(*GIRL *drops the sack. One leg has been amputated below the knee. For the remainder of the play, she'll appear this way.)*
GIRL: Before you remembered me one leg too many.

*(*GIRL *hops offstage as* LARK *speaks.)*
LARK: God 'at's good! Scuze me, W.J.
W.J.: Stop saying that!
LARK: *(Not quite genuine.)* Well, didn't want you to take offense—
W.J.: *You*'re offended I'm a lay minister now.
LARK: I am not—
W.J.: Testing me.
LARK: Nope.
W.J.: You are! Stop it. Speak as you like, I'm no preacher. Just go where they ask. Somebody in the hospice needs a body to pray with. Talking with the youth about music.
FRY: My best friend since eight years old, don't worry, W.J., I'm not changin' for ya. Can't speak for your sister.
LARK: I'm not changing either.
FRY: Always was there though. Why else your dissertation be spirituals when all your buddies dissectin' jazz?
W.J.: Not just my buddies I know jazz.
FRY: Rin in your footsteps, took after you before you knew what you were yourself.
W.J.: I know jazz.
FRY: Hey. What happened to Rin the Preacher?
TAL: *(Shrugs.)* Seem to give it up.
FRY: *Or.* Maybe like her daddy, *lay* preacher. I remember all that volunteerin' she used to do. Battered women, prison literacy. We got good daughters.
W.J.: No lie.
FRY: We blessed.
TAL: Proud.
LARK: How come our success story twenty-eight-year-old daughters still at home?

(Beat.)

LARK: Never said marriage! Fine with me they don't get caught up with some
　　　clown but . . . funny. Both us, our only daughters I mean, don't they
　　　seem young to you? I mean, younger than twenty-eight? Like we're six
　　　adults but feels like four adults, two kids?

(Silence.)

LARK: Mari the best daughter! no complaints. And Rin. Nice. Nice girls.

FRY: Lark—

LARK: I can't wait 'til Mari gets over bein' so sad!

*(RIN enters with packets of newly developed photos and slides. Pulls from a
cabinet a slide projector, starts arranging slides in the cart.)*

RIN: Sometimes I can be a slob. Take a pack out, look at 'em, throw 'em in the
　　　drawer. Take a pack out, look at 'em, throw 'em in the drawer. *(Looks
　　　around.)* Where's Mari?

LARK: She still in the bathroom? That girl loves the bathroom *Mari!*

FRY: Rin. You still do your volunteering? Battered women? Prison literacy?

(RIN continues activity, shakes her head no without looking up.)

W.J.: I know jazz so what? no shortage of scholars there. I was interested in the
　　　roots: spirituals led to the blues, blues led to jazz. Jazz and gospel led to
　　　rock 'n' roll, soul. Without spirituals would have been no ragtime, gospel.
　　　Spirituals the foundation. This country. Any further back you're in Africa.

RIN: *(Still arranging slides.)* Soul led to funk, funk led to hip hop. *(Chuckles
　　　to herself.)*

W.J.: She says this because she knows the glaring absence in all my studies.

RIN: He can't stand hip hop.

W.J.: Sure exposed to it around here! *(Others laugh.)* Enough to formulate a few
　　　theories. African roots. You and Walsh. *(Others stop laughing.)* Good
　　　kids except for that "music." *(Fingers the quote marks.)*

*(By now, MARI has returned. RIN sets up a screen next to the outside door. TAL
holds up an hors d'oeuvre.)*

TAL: *(To RIN:)* Before the show, eat. *(RIN hesitates.)* Rin!

RIN: Okay! Just have to get something first. *(Moves toward kitchen.)*

FRY: While you out there you wanna see any chips on hand? Salt and vinegar?

RIN: Okay. *(RIN gone.)*

TAL: Bring a bowl!

LARK: Fry! What you talkin' about, chips?

FRY: What?

TAL: It's okay—

LARK: *Not* okay you see how hard she worked on this food, you ask for chips—

W.J.: Lark, if that's what Fry wants to eat,

W.J. *(Cont'd.)*	FRY	LARK	TAL
then he should	Wait a minute.		It's really
be able to eat		He can act like	okay, Lark.
it.	If Tal wants me	an *adult*.	
	to eat the hummus,		
Lark, what do you	I'll eat the		I am *not*
think we have the	hummus. I'm		dictating to a
chips for?	sorry if I was	Then he should	grown man
It's not a—	rude to you—	*act* like a	what he can
		grown—	or can't—

(RIN *enters with a bag of chips, a bowl and an individual can of grape juice. she trips, very briefly losing her balance, as if her leg got stuck.* RIN: *a little gasp. Silence. All stare at her.*)

RIN: No salt and vinegar. Barbecue?

(TAL *motions for* RIN *to bring the chips and bowl to her.* RIN *takes a slice of white bread out of the bowl, which puzzles* TAL.)

TAL: What's the bread for?

RIN: Break my fast. Go to my room—

TAL: What, you living on bread and water now? juice?

RIN: Why? Think I turned anorexic?

TAL: I think you might decide to *really* see how it feels, starvation.

RIN: That's not it.

TAL: What *is* it?

(RIN *is embarrassed. Finally:*)

RIN: "This is my body which is given for you: this do in remembrance of me."

(*Stuffs the bread [a healthy chunk] in her mouth, gobbles it down.*)

RIN: "This cup is the new testament in my blood, which is shed for you."

(*Big gulp of the juice.*)

TAL: (*Embarrassed.*) Sorry.

W.J.: Except . . . that's what Christ did *before* his fast, not after. (TAL *puts chips into bowl.*)

RIN: I know I just feel like . . . I can't break my fast without something, *some* kind of ceremony. Mark the experience by. I don't forget.

LARK: Why'dju give it up? *(RIN looks at LARK.)* Preacher.

RIN: *(Beat.)* Didn't have the sensitivity.

LARK: I don't believe that.

RIN: College sophomore, the women's shelter. There was somebody, Trish, twenty-one, I was twenty, she had three little ones on her face. All cut up. On and on "what a bastard," me cheerleading her every word, but then I'd come another day and she's gone, back to him. Then at the shelter again, she comes in, arm in a cast "Never going back!" I'm relieved, encouraging. Then back to him again. I walk in one day, she's filling out her readmittance, baby in the arm without the cast, two- and three-year-olds looking at me, eyes wide, wild. They're getting ready to hop her and her bleeding face into an ambulance and she sees me, happy to see me, arms around me but I guess I don't trust her, guess my arms around her not so warm, tight "You've never been me! Twenty years you missed don't think you can jump in the last second see me!" Then she's gone. I volunteer the rest of the semester but she doesn't come back, I pray it's cuz she found another shelter. 'Course I got along well with the women who left their men for good. Some preacher. Hanging with the converted.

(Pause.)

RIN: *(To LARK:)* I saw something you like. In the kitchen.

TAL: Rin!

RIN: Was it a surprise? I didn't know!

LARK: M&Ms? *Peanut* M&Ms? *(TAL nods.)* Well bring 'em on out here! No! No I'll eat the whole damn bag let's hold off. Least 'til after the pictures.

(Simultaneously RIN clicks on projector as TAL turns off the light. RIN describes the projection on the screen.)

RIN: Crookedest street in the world!

FRY: San Francisco, I heard tell a that.

(A moment of blackness before the next slide. There is always a moment of blackness between slides.)

LARK: Coal minin'?

RIN: Exhibit. Science and Industry. Chicago. And this. *(Slide:)* Michigan Avenue. Fancy. Fur coats like Fifth Avenue, Manhattan.

TAL: *(Slide:)* The Arch, that's what I've always wanted to see. One of these days gonna finally make it to Louie.

RIN: Six hundred thirty feet, tallest monument in the U.S.

LARK: *(Slide:)* Times Square! How you get around, New York? Not the subway, didja.

RIN: *(A vague irritation.)* Sure.

LARK: *Did*ja? Dirty thing. Scary.

RIN: Not scary, easiest. Cheapest *not accessible!* People with wheelchairs stuck taking buses all day, or have to be helped up steps—*(Frustrated grunt.)*

W.J.: *(Slide:)* Wow.

RIN: Pueblo Indian Village, Acoma, New Mexico. Oldest continually operating city in the U.S.

LARK: *(Slide: The HOLLYWOOD letters.)* Look just like in the movies!

W.J.: *(Slide:)* Civil Rights Museum.

LARK: Birmingham! we been there!

TAL: *(Slide:)* Horses!

RIN: Spring drive near the Gallatin. Montana.

W.J.: *(Slide:)* That the Library of Congress? Inside?

RIN: *(Nods.)* The Great Hall.

TAL: Gorgeous.

RIN: In the Main Reading Room eight statues above the marble columns representing law, poetry, religion et al. Under commerce: "We taste the spices of Arabia yet never feel the scorching sun which brings them forth."

LARK: *(Slide:)* Ooooh pretty!

RIN: Blue Swallow. Over two hundred fifty bird species are found in Malolotja, this is one of the rarest.

(Pause.)

LARK: Malolotja?

RIN: *(Slide:)* Mhlangamphepha Falls.

W.J.: We were looking at pictures from your America trip.

LARK: This is Africa.

FRY: I thought you were showin' us the Grand Canyon, Statue a Liberty.

RIN: Six years ago but we never got together to share 'em.

LARK: Six years ago this is old. *(Walks toward the piano.)*

RIN: *(Slide of whales:)* Mari took this. *(To MARI:)* Remember? Dolphin's Point.

LARK: Hey W.J., name this spiritual. *(Plays a tune.)*

RIN: *(Slide:)* Sobuza II was a popular Swaziland king. This is his monument and mausoleum.

W.J.: "Roll Jordan Roll" we've seen these, Rin, I'm sure Mari's shown them her pictures.

FRY: No. She hasn't.

LARK: This one? *(Plays another tune.)*

RIN: *(Slide:)* Some kind of tool, pulled out of a river in the Lubombo Mountains, Mlawula. Million years old.

TAL: Anybody knows "Battle Hymn of the Republic."

LARK: *(Sings:)* John *Brown's body lies a-mould'ring in the grave*

(Continues under other dialogue:)

> *John Brown's body lies a-mould'ring in the grave*
> *John Brown's body lies a-mould'ring in the grave*
> *But his soul's marching on*
>
> *Glory, glory Hallelujah*
> *Glory, glory Hallelujah*
> *Glory, glory Hallelujah*
> *His soul's marching on*

RIN: *(Slide:)* Mantenga Cultural Village. Everything's traditional, representing life in the 1850s, poles, grass, cow dung.

LARK: Hey Rin, here's your favorite. *They crucified my savior and nailed him to the cross*

(Continues under other dialogue:)

> *They crucified my savior and nailed him to the cross*
> *They crucified my savior and nailed him to the cross*
> *And the Lord will bear*
> *My spirit home*
>
> *And Joseph begged his body and laid him in the tomb*
> *And Joseph begged his body and laid him in the tomb*
> *And Joseph begged his body and laid him in the tomb*
> *And the Lord will bear*
> *My spirit home*

RIN: Sixteen huts, each for its own purpose. Spaces for cattle and goats. These fences block the wind.

LARK: Such a pretty tune. Sing it with me, Rin. *(Picks up song where she left off.)*

(After the blackness, a slide of a woman with one leg, a baby on her back.)

RIN: Angola.

W.J.: This is just what I didn't want to see.

(W.J. *moves away.* RIN *continues showing slides of civilian amputees as dialogue continues, the pictures snapping quickly:*)

RIN: Why? If we don't see 'em they're not there?

TAL: Nobody said that, Rin, how much money we send each month? Food for starving African children,—

RIN: She didn't lose her leg from hunger.

LARK: Can't ya sing me just a verse, Rinnie? *(Still singing and playing.)*

RIN: Every twenty-two minutes some man, woman or child gets it. Lost arm, or leg. Or life! Every twenty-two minutes!

TAL: Well what are we supposed to do?

(Slide: The GIRL *with one leg [from* RIN's *room] in Angola. This slide should be held a beat longer than the others.)*

TAL: Answer me!

RIN: Just see it! Just think about it. Once in awhile.

W.J.: Okay we have. That's enough now.

LARK: Rin!

W.J.: You can turn the projector off now. *(Pictures keep snapping.)*

RIN and LARK	TAL
He rose	
He rose	
He rose from the dead	
He rose	
He rose	
He rose from the dead	Rin, turn off the projector.
He rose	
He rose	
He rose from the dead	

TAL: OFF!

(The song stops. After the momentary blackness, an empty space in the slide crate leaves the screen lit and white. Standing in the whiteness, amputated below one knee and on crutches, is a filthy, tattered HOMELESS MAN *who'd apparently entered in the brief blackness through the outside door.)*

HOMELESS MAN: Arguably the survival of spirituals to this day is attributable to the concert tours of the Fisk Jubilee Singers 1871 to 1878. Struggling in its early years, the university was rescued by income generated from its choir's performances across the U.S. and Europe, bringing the musical genre to an audience outside of the Black community. Black faces on the stage before an all-white patronage prefigured the Cotton Club:

opinion varies whether the decision to share our tradition was visionary or whether we were just Stepin Fetchit.

(RIN *is smiling.*)
RIN: Hi Walsh.
WALSH (HOMELESS MAN): Hi Rin. *(Beat.)* Hi Dad.

(Silence.)
WALSH: Hi Mom.

(Silence.)
WALSH: Hi Aunt Lark. Uncle Fry.
LARK: Hi Walsh.
FRY: Walsh.
WALSH: Hi Mari.

(Silence.)
WALSH: *(Mostly to* TAL:*)* I know you're surprised I showed up and filthy to boot. Nobody's fault but mine, 5:30 A.M. to seven, very restrictive, very limited time for the church showers and I knew the restrictions, I take full responsibility, knew I had a crack of dawn reveille and *still* up half the night resulting in my oversleeping this morning. And sound sleep an anomaly for a person on the street, car alarm going off, cop kicking your feet, somebody violently hostile to the extreme poor come anytime with a gas can and match yet like a rock I slept 'til 7:15 after up like a fool 'til five with that crossword, every day I'm at the library, fifteen-cent investment to Xerox the British *Times* puzzle, and this time a clue stumped me.
FRY: "Stumped me."

*(*FRY *chuckles.* LARK, TAL *and* W.J. *look at* FRY, *tense.*)*
FRY: Joke! *(Beat.)* Wa'n't it?
WALSH: Finally, five A.M., I get it and sleep. One hundred go together.

(All stare.)
WALSH: "Cleave."

(All stare.)
WALSH: One hundred: C. *(Beat.)* Roman numerals. Go: leave. Put 'em together: Cleave.

(All stare.)

RIN, LARK and FRY: *Oh.*

TAL: You wanna take a shower, Walsh?

WALSH: Bad enough I haven't bathed in awhile but now the sweat. Humidity clouding over, think it's gonna storm. I'll wild guess everybody'd appreciate I freshen up a little. *(Chuckles.)*

(Silence.)

WALSH: My sister invited me.

TAL: We figured that out. You know the way.

WALSH: I wasn't sure things were still on, under the circumstances. *(Pause.)* The news.

(Silence.)

WALSH: Boise.

W.J.: We know.

WALSH: Maybe we should turn it on, any more developments—

TAL: Towels still in the hall closet.

(WALSH nods, exits down the hall. Silence until shower water is heard. TAL stares at RIN several seconds, then exits into the kitchen. RIN looks at the others, who stare back at her.)

RIN: *(Shrugs.)* Family reunion.

W.J.: *What!*

RIN: He's my brother.

(W.J. swiftly moves toward the garage.)

RIN: My room.

(W.J. groans.)

W.J.: Basement.

(W.J. exits through the kitchen.)

LARK: Maybe you were too little to remember when he first came back. Or maybe don't wanna. My well-behaved gentleman nephew returned from the service one leg less and all this . . . *(Gestures indicating rage.)* Suddenly everything defying gravity, plates flying, knives. A love seat once.

RIN: We're two years apart. I wasn't little.

(TAL enters rapidly, puts down bowl of M&Ms on the table and immediately turns back toward kitchen as she speaks:)

TAL: Sometimes you act eight 'stead of twenty-eight.

RIN: I didn't—

TAL: I PLANNED SIX FOR DINNER NOT SEVEN!

(Stillness. Then TAL exits into the kitchen passing W.J. entering from the kitchen.)

W.J.: This town not so big of course I looked for him *found* him, found him sometimes when I wasn't looking *no!* No he wouldn't come home *my* son. My—

(W.J. stops himself. Silence. Then exits back into kitchen as the shower water is turned off.)

WALSH: *(Off:)* Dad!

(W.J. instantly enters from the kitchen moving toward the hall exit.)

W.J.: Probably that new trick with the hot water valve YES?

(As W.J. exits, TAL enters.)

TAL: Town isn't that big. So how come I never saw him? Searching, searching, giving to every homeless I see, five dollars. Then one day I give and the panhandler says "Mom" and my heart stops, breathe hard fast I move away, move away. Down the other side of the street, catch my breath. Wait. Turn around. He's white. I know he said "Mom" but . . . Ages since I looked into the face of whom I was giving it to, 'f you'd asked me I'd've said this and believed it myself: too afraid of another disappointment, not Walsh. But truth is. Too terrified maybe it *is* Walsh. *(Beat.)* Just cuz I no more give on the street doesn't mean I don't give, I give bigger. Checks. Partnership for the Homeless. Homeless Advocacy Project. National Coalition for the Homeless. Resources for the Homeless. Covenant House. Homes for the Homeless.

W.J.: *(Enters.)* Middle of the shower he realizes he doesn't have any clean clothes. Aren't there a few of his suits lying around somewhere? All given away, right? *(TAL nods.)* Guess I'll loan him one of my robes. Guess I'll run to the mall for underwear.

RIN: I'll go.

W.J.	TAL
No!	No! you stay here entertain your new dinner guest *I*'ll go.

W.J.: I'll get the robe.

TAL: Where's my damn car keys.

(W.J. exits down the hall, TAL exits into the kitchen. Both will return during RIN's speech [TAL in sweater with purse], stop to listen. Later in the speech, the shower cuts off.)

RIN: I was in the park reading *Zen in the Art of Archery* when I notice this man standing before me. This was two years ago. "Have you gotten to the part with the Master and student in the dark?" I say No. "Okay" and he moves away from my picnic table, and only now do I see he has an amputated leg. A week later I'm in the same seat, *The Tao of Physics.* He's there again, he says "I'm noticing a trend." Time and life, he's read it, understood it, travel eighty percent the speed of light you live one point seven times normal, travel ninety-nine percent speed of light live seven times normal, instead of seventy, four hundred ninety! But you can't tell the difference, only your observers can. And he finds that funny, chuckles and it's the laugh . . . "Walsh." He smiles. 'Til then. He was a stranger.

(WALSH's first words are off; he enters speaking. Shirt, slacks. Very clean, preppie. Moves [with crutches] toward a chair.)

WALSH: Picked up your old habits, Dad, find an empty church, wander in. This white church, weekday afternoon. After awhile the organist enters, smiles, practices. A few Europeans, then "Swing Low." I know he's doing this for my benefit, he looks at me and makes assumptions about my music preferences, he smiles, I smile but I'm trying not to laugh it's a nice song but Lord, do white people think it's the only one we know? Then "Balm in Gilead," "Lord I Wanna Be a Christian" and by now I'm put in the mood to hum. Sing. He smiles, then gets serious: "Mighty Fortress." I continue singing and he's obviously surprised I know that one, I know that one *and* its author, the Protest, start of congregational singing in the white church he doesn't know my father's a musicologist, aunt teaches piano. *For still our ancient foe.* I ask the organist,

(WALSH puts his hands behind his head, leans back.)

WALSH: Did you know it's probable that Martin Luther's true reference was not to the Devil but to the Pope?

(All staring at WALSH. It takes all a few seconds to realize they are focused on the hideous sores and bruises on the backs of his forearms near the elbows. He brings his arms down, embarrassed.)

WALSH: Crutches. They rub.

LARK: How'd you get all the way out here, 'burbs, Walsh? Not walk?

WALSH: Going to. My sister offered to drive me out but no. Wasn't quite sure how the folks respond, me suddenly show up, then hang around hours before dinner.

TAL: Much better to heart-attack surprise us.

WALSH: Then she gonna spot me a taxi, I say if I miss the morning church showers no cab's gonna want smelly me in the back. Finally resolved: Rin picked me up this morning, drove me to the supermarket. Spring having finally sprung, I spent the time on the outside bench watching the people, writing in my journal. Then only a mile . . . walk . . .

(WALSH trails off, noticing TAL in sweater with purse.)

TAL: *(Awkward, indicating her sweater.)* I know you said humid but it's not quite summer yet, still best to have—

WALSH: Where you going?

(TAL, embarrassed, whispers in WALSH's ear.)

WALSH: Why would I shower then put back on filthy things? *(Looks at W.J.:)* Dirty *clothes*, I never said dirty *under*clothes. I have five sets, shorts, socks, wash 'em out when they're soiled. Might be a bit raggedy, but clean.

TAL: *(Heading for the door.)* Then you need some new ones *not* raggedy.

WALSH: *Now?*

(Pause.)

TAL: No. Not now.

RIN: Walsh. Watch.

(RIN goes to a switch on the wall, turns on the overhead chandelier. WALSH, LARK, and FRY marvel.)

LARK: That chandelier never worked.

FRY: Rin the electrician. Build anything, fix anything. Cantcha.

WALSH: Speaking of electric. How's your work, Mari? Still the same place?

MARI: *Yes.*

(Silence.)

TAL: Walsh. I'll sew a piece. Pads, something. Make your crutches more comfortable.

WALSH: Thanks, Mom. 'S okay.

TAL: No! Buy new ones where you get 'em? We'll get you some well padded—
WALSH: 'S okay.
TAL: Why didn't you wrap it right? Could've gotten a prosthesis, could've—
RIN: *(Eyes on* WALSH.*)* I have something for you.

*(*RIN *moves toward her room.* WALSH *reaches for his crutches.)*
TAL: Why can't you bring it in here, Rin—?
RIN: I can't it's in there.
WALSH: I'm fine.

*(*RIN *exits to the garage,* WALSH *behind.* TAL *sighs, falls in with others following* WALSH. *In the garage:)*
RIN: Don't sit.

*(*WALSH, *who almost did, is puzzled.* RIN *rolls the covered item toward him.)*
WALSH: *(Guessing what it is.)* No.

*(*RIN *smiles. Unveils a wheelchair.)*
RIN: I used rod bearings instead of ball. You'll have to work a little harder
   but they'll last longer.

(Silence.)
TAL: You . . . *made*—?
RIN: Ralf Hotchkiss off the Internet. Paraplegic from a motorbike crash, his
   brainchild: Third World amputees build their own 'chairs, amputees
   design their own 'chairs, who else? Who knows their needs better?
FRY: I don't believe it.
LARK: Rinnie!
TAL: *Walsh! (All turn to her. Awkward:)* I'm sure this is better than any store-
   bought thing but if you needed . . . never had to wait—
WALSH: Worth the wait.
LARK: *(To* W.J.:*)* Ain't she a genius? *(*W.J. *silent.* TAL *exits to other rooms.)*
WALSH: She took my measurements one day, said she's shopping for new
   clothes, my birthday. Birthday came and went I said nothing when
   instead she gave me a little tape player and recordings of my old CDs.
   I preferred it.
RIN: Too wide it'll be hard to push.
WALSH: But . . . my butt, that's the measurement you wanted!
RIN: Try it!

(WALSH *eases himself into the wheelchair. Moves around a bit.*)
WALSH: Feels good. Feels good. (RIN *claps, delighted.*)
RIN: Lemme adjust the footrest.

(RIN *quickly does, steps back.* WALSH *moves around the room.*)
WALSH: That's it.

(TAL *returns with a pillow.*)
TAL: Here.

(WALSH, *surprised, raises his bottom up. Sits on pillow.*)
TAL: (*Touching him affectionately.*) Better? (WALSH *smiles at her.*)
W.J.: *You think we forgot?!*

(*Silence.*)
W.J.: Waltz right back in, what you did to the family, broke it up, broke it . . .

(*Pause.*)
WALSH: Doesn't look broken up.
W.J.: DON'T YOU—
WALSH: I didn't mean it smartass! I'm happy all's intact, I didn't, I didn't—
TAL: He was a good boy, w.j.
WALSH: I didn't come back to disrupt! I just wanted to show you I'm not . . .
   I'm okay now!
TAL: Before it all, he was a good—
W.J.: Why was he there? He wasn't there for being a good boy, all rebellion—
WALSH: Decision! You wanted me to make a decision—
W.J.: Not *that* one! You knew—Sign up, didn't ask *any*body—
TAL: He was an adult—
W.J.: Worse kind! If you'd defied me to my face, we'd had a few explosive
   matches would've been upfront! honest! No you Yes Daddy Yes Daddy
   I'll pick a major I'll stop flitting smile smile next thing you come home
   enlisted! Didn't plan on a war, didja? Didja?
WALSH: I didn't mean to—
W.J.: Didn't plan on stepping on some . . . some—
RIN: I flitted, Walsh.
TAL: (*To* RIN:) Stay out.
W.J.: Didn't plan on a war, DIDJA?
WALSH: NO!
RIN: I flitted but they let me do whatever I wanted.

TAL: Rin!

RIN: Encouraged it.

W.J.: QUIET!

RIN: Guess I benefited from you going first guess they were afraid I'd join up, get *my* leg blown off. *(Silence.)* Ironically.

(Sudden great flash of lightning and booming thunder. It terrifies W.J., TAL, LARK, FRY, *and* WALSH. *Now quiet except for the pouring rain.)*

TAL: Foolishness! Now we jump every time a car backfires? This is paranoia not me! *I'm* keeping a firm grip on sanity. Not me.

LARK: Remember how nine-eleven shook the world? *our* world? Tragedy in Washington, catastrophe New York, so far away but still stunned us: enemy our own grounds. Well no one dead from this thing yet, four—

*(*LARK *stops herself.* WALSH *glances at his stump.)*

WALSH: Four maimed.

LARK: Yes. Compared to thousands killed on one day 2001, all we got now is four hurt so why I find this eerier?

FRY: Cuz it ain't enemy. Not what the TV call "enemy," somebody other side a the world, somebody *dark* other side a the world cuz *white* foreigners the TV news likes. But this. Somebody among us, American.

LARK: Sure. Way it keeps happening? Nine-eleven confined to one day.

W.J.: Boom, boom. We think it's over, three days later boom again.

FRY: Don't seem so outta reach cuz where it pop next? Anywhere!

LARK: And not just the big cities. Boise? South Bend?

W.J.: Hanover, New Hampshire.

FRY: College town. Ain't it?

LARK: Shreveport! Our backyard.

TAL: Damn mines!

WALSH: *Dumb* mines. As opposed to the new smart ones, self-destruct in forty-eight I don't believe it. I don't believe it but these definitely the old-fashioned Dumb mines got the patience, the heartiness of Methuselah Decades they'll wait for a false step Vietnamese still getting limbs blown off from what we laid sixties, seventies. Blast. Not fragmentation, frags kill. Blast mines designed to maim but keep the victim alive, send the victim hopping home cuz enemy morale much more affected, somebody screaming searching frantic for his leg bit more disconcerting than just some dead bodies lying around. Quiet.

RIN: What about when the enemy just thought it was a kick toy for her and her dolly?

(Pause.)

RIN: *(To* WALSH:*)* What happened to you . . . *ugly. Cowardly* but . . . least men fighting men *soldiers. Not* civilians which is eighty percent of who gets it, what kind of war strategy is that? *(Beat.)* Yours tragedy, too! I don't mean to say it's not.

WALSH: I know.

RIN: Just . . . what I saw there, *(Glancing at* MARI*)* what *we* . . . *Why* they starving? Not lack of food *fear!* Don't know what's in the fields, keep them from tending their fields, tending their crops boom! Little boy out to play come back no arms boom! Mommy walked out to get water for baby come back crawling *desperate people!* A sign warning it's a minefield they'll steal for fuel! this . . . *(Shaping her fingers like a mine disk:)* this little thing, all the terror for this little plastic thing. Know how many American parts in 'em?

MARI: I work in research for one of the largest corporations in the world, I work in research and have been part of the development of various technical medical products, many life-saving apparatuses. In addition to diagnostic imaging equipment which saves lives, our diverse line of products includes items related to lighting, industrial automation, nuclear power, commercial and military aircraft, computer-related information services, and we are probably best known for our various major appliances. Through our acquisition of a major television network, our services have expanded to include the operation of commercial television stations as well as cable and Internet programming. My part as a minute cog in a leviathan wheel has been to actively participate in the development of devices that enhance the earliest detection of cancer, saving lives. Our revenues for the past three months exceeded thirty-two billion, our CEO alone took home forty-six million last year. I can't say I like or know every pie my company has its fingers in, I can say my part has saved countless lives and with so much going on it's difficult to imagine all the activities that contribute to the ultimate good or even why my company's mind-boggling diversity of products could still be thought of simply as *general*-ly *electric.*

(Stove buzzer.)

TAL: Duck's ready.

FRY: Me too.

WALSH: Most the countries in the world signed the mine-ban treaty but not the U.S. Course not the U.S. Too many corporations need the business, right? *(Eyes on* MARI.*)*

W.J.: Walsh—

WALSH: They make the parts and sell 'em to the army to put together then claim innocent, "We don't make the mines we just make the *parts* for the mines."

LARK: That isn't what Mari does—

WALSH: Who CARES!

(WALSH's outburst is not directed at MARI but rather a more general philosophical question. A brief silence, then RIN answers:)

RIN: People care. Americans. Just don't usually think about it. Something happening far away. 'Til now.

TAL: *People care* what can we do? Besides go insane *Look at it!*

(TAL indicates the zillions of thumbtacks on RIN's map, particularly in southern Africa. All quiet.)

TAL: Come to the table.

(TAL exits, through the living room and to the kitchen. W.J. and LARK exit through the living room and out via the hall. FRY in the rear turns around just before exiting.)

FRY: Come on, Mari.

WALSH: I know it's not just your company. Alliant, Raytheon, Thiokol, Lockheed-Martin I didn't mean to attack you. Sorry probably didn't even know—

MARI: I did.

(FRY and WALSH stare at MARI. TAL enters the living room from the kitchen with roast duck on a platter and exits down the hall. FRY exits the garage, through the living room and down the hall. WALSH looks at RIN. Then follows the path of the others through the living room and off the hall exit, leaving RIN and MARI alone in the garage. RIN flops down supine on her bed.)

MARI: Okay?

(Beat.)

RIN: Yeah. Just kind of tired.

(RIN rests a few moments, then gets up, heads for the door to the living room.)

MARI: What about "vengeance is mine"? *(RIN, confused, stops, looks at MARI.)* Says the Lord.

RIN: Oh. *(Chuckles.)* I'm not worried about that this isn't vengeance. This is about building this country's character, I think it'll be good for the U.S. to walk a mile in Angola's shoes. *(Beat.)* Thank you. The information. Supplies.

MARI: I had to sneak, figure ways to . . . get past security my company . . .

(Pause.)

MARI: Just parts anyway parts could have been used for anything.

(Pause. MARI refers to the map.)

MARI: Where else you lay 'em?

RIN: Observation deck of the St. Louis Arch. Under a beam, Golden Gate Bridge. Coal mine display, Chicago Science and Industry Museum, and inside a mailbox, Michigan Avenue. First L in Hollywood. Corner in the big tunnel stroll 1 train to Port Authority under Times Square—

(Sob from MARI.)

RIN: Not every place! Some places I didn't go to for work, some places just for me. Not the Civil Rights Museum. Not George Washington Carver National Monument. Diamond, Missouri.

MARI: *My. Fault.*

RIN: Me? *(Shakes her head.)* What were you supposed to do? Cross the mine save me, get yourself blown up? We all stir crazy all agreed to a nature walk. Checked it out a hundred times, asked *everyone*, people'd walked *through there* before. Everyone sure AAAAAAAAH!

(RIN stumbles as she had earlier with the potato chips, this time causing severe pain.)

MARI: *Okay?!*

(RIN flops down on the bed again.)

RIN: Yeah. Yeah just . . . little cramp.

(From under her pant leg, RIN removes an artificial leg.)

MARI: Better?

(RIN nods, clearly in pain but less.)

MARI: What hurts?

RIN: My foot.

(MARI *confused.* RIN *laughs.*)

RIN: Weird, right? No foot but the nerves. Still active talk to my brain burning. Shooting *aaaah!*

(*Silence.*)

RIN: Just cuz you can't see the pain. Doesn't mean it's not there.

Act 2

Scene 1

(*Six weeks later.* RIN's *room [the garage].* GIRL *enters downstage, crossing from one end of stage to the other on her uneven crutches, chatting to no one in particular:*)

GIRL: When I got *my* leg blowed off, I cried and cried. Then amputatin' in the hospital *hate* the hospital! they don't have stuff. Food. Anesthesia. My daddy goes "Praise God you lived. Look around, this is not abnormal. Look around. Happens every day."

(GIRL *off.*)

LARK: What happen to your brother's wheelchair?

(RIN *is working on a wheelchair part. Walsh's wheelchair is in the room.* FRY *on the computer chair, typing away.* LARK *sits on* RIN's *couch crocheting a huge afghan, royal blue with black trim, which rests across her lap and falls to the floor over her legs. On the map behind, four more straight pins are stuck in Kentucky, North Dakota, Los Angeles, and New York City.*)

RIN: Had to replace the front wheels someone stole 'em.

FRY: Besides the obvious addiction issue, problem with card games on the screen is ya never wanna go back to the riffle and smack a conventional Solitaire. Too long to deal. Piles never get computer neat.

LARK: You got that old sad mad rainy day look "I wanna go out and play!" Listen, I was a lot wilder than you or Walsh or Mari. Wouldn'ta told you before, 'fraid you follow my example, but now s'pose you old enough. Drinkin'. Smokin'. Time or two the reefer. Once, fifteen, I didn't get home 'til four, my bedroom off the kitchen and I try slippin' quiet through my winda, hopin' they upstairs, gone to bed, I musta been looney, easin' in backwards, touch my toes to the floor, slowly slow pull down my winda and instant it touch I jump cuz Daddy in the dark behind "WHAT TIME IS IT?" In these situations you wanna thinka anything to say but the truth yet know what's the point? Get the switch *and* a groundin' month! I survived it, my confinement. You'll survive yours.

(Silence.)

LARK: Guess you wonder what I was doin' out 'til four, age fifteen.

RIN: First-grade arithmetic I could subtract your March wedding from Mari's September birth.

LARK: Three years later! *(Beat.)* Well. We been together, may as well been married—

RIN: *I'm twenty-eight!*

TAL: *(Enters.)* Where's W.J.?

(Pause: RIN, LARK, and FRY stare at TAL, confused.)

TAL: It's time for that program. It's time for that music-video program he's at the TV W.J.! *(Exits.)*

LARK: Our first date, walkin' we see this boy givin' girl a bouquet. So Fry take me to my door, our front yard uncut, he collects a bouquet for me: dandelions. I wa'n't quite sure how to take that: cheapskate. Then he blows 'em, slow, gentle. My face. *(FRY smiles to himself.)* This became our private thing. On good days my heart touched, tear my eye. Bad days he tender blow at me, I hard blow the damn things right back at him ain't he sneezin'!

RIN: *(Chuckles.)* "Ain't."

LARK: Don't think I'm co-optin' somethin' weren't mine, grew up talkin' regular. Too much education, it stopped feelin' comf'table but lately . . . all the changes . . .

RIN: Twenty-eight-year-old grown woman. How'd I get grounded? AAAAAAAH!

(RIN has stood to look for a bolt or screw, and the standing has caused her agony.)

LARK: What!

RIN: Bad day. *(An exaggerated limp.)*

LARK: Why?

RIN: Just happens I don't know, physical or psychological. Some days good, some days bad. *(More to herself:)* Nothing but the latter lately.

(TAL enters again. One of her fingers is missing. The audience may not have noticed before. A bandage covers the nub.)

TAL: I feel like a bad hostess I didn't know you were coming, in the middle of the laundry, down to the basement up you know if I'd known you were coming I would have delayed it another day. I put a cake in the oven. You know I usually make it from scratch if Rin had told me you were coming I would have been prepared but fortunately this mix is good, angel food, fluffy. Sorry I'm in and out but between checking on the cake and making sure the rinse cycle doesn't get by me without the adding of the fabric softener, plus you both seem busy I wouldn't want to disturb anybody's work—

LARK: Not disturbin' anybody, if you wanna do your laundry do it, why you always gotta be worryin' 'bout the Good Housekeepin' award? *(TAL: weak smile.)* You find W.J.? *(TAL nods.)*

TAL: Lemonade?

LARK: Delicious, thank you.

TAL: *(Not looking at anyone.)* Anybody else?

(RIN gives FRY a look: smirk. He looks back, not a smirk.)

TAL: One glass. *(To LARK:)* You're staying for lunch I hope.

LARK: You didn't plan on me for lunch and I'm not invitin' myself, have you scramblin' to add to your menu, I *know* you ain't goin' out grocery shoppin'—

TAL: If I needed more I could just have it delivered. I don't. Stew, Lark! simple. Just chop up a few extra vegetables.

LARK: Careful with the choppin' knife.

(TAL looks at her nub, embarrassed. Now hip hop music is heard, getting louder: female voices. W.J. enters carrying a big boom box, notebook and pencil, a small CD carrying case. He wears a suit but it is very wrinkled, sloppy. His speech is as before except when he is doing a rap song, in which case he may imitate rappers' inflections. The music is blasting. TAL yells at W.J. but cannot be heard over the boom box.)

W.J.: HUH?

TAL: TURN IT DOWN!

(W.J. turns it off.)

W.J.: I figured it out! *(Reads from the notebook, rapping:)*
> Fee fi fo fum fo fi fee yaw
> My sister's a whore and my mama OD'd yaw
> My babysittin' uncle tried to put it in me yaw
> Ya think I'm still blind but now I do see

I thought they were saying "My babysittin' uncle tried puddyin' me," if you only knew the many ways my mind was defining "puddying." *(Chuckles.)* Hear the "Amazing Grace"? Not a spiritual but its rich history in the black music canon have raised it to similar stature. And the redundance

of the "yaw" at the end of each line immediately brings to my mind a
hundred examples, among them

On my journey now Mount Zion
On my journey now Mount Zion
Well I wouldn't take nothin' Mount Zion
For my journey now Mount Zion

*(w.j. turns the boom box on very loud again for a few moments. Perhaps be-
cause the words are yelled and/or fast and/or inarticulated, it is impossible to
understand what is said. w.j. turns the box off.)*
W.J.: Hear that?

*(FRY, who had turned to w.j. when w.j. entered, now laughs, turns back to the
computer.)*
TAL: Nobody can understand anything, W.J.—

(w.j. blasts the box again.)
W.J.: *(All yelled over the music:)* YOU COME AND GO JUST STOP FOR PUSSY
        DON'T THINK I'M JUST YOUR DOORMAT WUSSY
        CUZ A NEW DAY'S COMIN' AND YOU BETTER FEAR IT
        DROP THE BOMB, BOY, EVERY TIME I FEEL THE SPIRIT
        BESIDES THE TITLE COMPLETELY SPELLED OUT IN THE LAST LINE, THE
        "NEW DAY" THEME IS RIGHT OUT OF "MY LORD WHAT A MORNING," "IN
        THAT GREAT, GETTIN' UP MORNING,"—
TAL: TURN IT OFF!

(w.j. does.)
RIN: I'm out! why I gotta stay here? Twenty-eight ground me? Quarantine
        me? You don't have the authority!

(TAL gives RIN a look.)
RIN: Oh, your house your—
TAL: What kind of fool'd walk around after what happened?
RIN: What, think they mined our front yard?
TAL: *Bomb exploded this town!*

(Beat.)
LARK: Why he mine *this* town? Well. Guess it wa'n't the only borin' place had
        a bomb exploded recently, few middle a nowheres Kentucky. Dakota.
        Ya wonder how many more there could be, every time we come close to

breathin' easy another one somewhere pops. *(To* RIN:*)* There's a business for ya, custom wheelchair designer!

RIN: Not true. Not every time you turn around one goes off, there were those first four, then a while 'til Kentucky. Then a long silence 'til Hollywood. And then . . . New York—

LARK: That poor little boy.

TAL: Snatched out of his daddy's hand. Went to some kiddie play now on their way home, Harlem, and he spies something shiny, runs to get it.

LARK: Six years old? *(TAL nods.)* No arm. Wonder it didn't kill him.

RIN: Blast mines maim don't kill!

(Silence: they stare at her.)

RIN: 'Specially in the U.S. Good medical treatment. U.S.

LARK: *(Glancing at* RIN's *map.)* How many now? Ten?

RIN: *Eight!*

TAL: Tired of this subject, *(To* W.J.:*)* you want some lemonade?

W.J.: Mmmm yes, icy, cold, pulpy. *(Starts flipping through the CD carrying case.)* Anybody seen my Puff Daddy?

RIN: *(Glancing at her own leg.)* People survive maimed. All the time.

(TAL turns to exit.)

RIN: HEY! *(TAL turns to* RIN. *Meaning* LARK:*) She* came over! How you think she got here, fly?

TAL: I didn't know she was coming over!

LARK: Hasn't been two bombs the same town, Tal.

TAL: *Yet!* Maybe nobody found the second.

RIN: *(Mutters as she brings the wheelchair part to* LARK:*)* No two bombs the same town.

TAL: How would you know!

RIN: Anyway! *(Lifts pant leg to show prosthetic.)* I wouldn't get hit. Lightning doesn't strike the same place twice.

(LARK has removed the afghan. She has no legs and is in a wheelchair. RIN *adjusts the part to the wheelchair.)*

LARK: That's my theory.

(LARK tries out the wheelchair, now complete.)

FRY: *(Confidentially to* RIN:*)* Told her now I just get easier access. *(RIN giggles.)*

TAL: What's so funny?

RIN and FRY: Nothing.

LARK: Pretty good.

RIN: I mounted the rear hubs farther back. Otherwise, no legs, uphill traveling you could tip backwards.

LARK: Ain't she thoughtful? Ain't she the artist?

W.J.: *(Grins.)* Artist.

LARK: I was beginnin' to feel like Mari's the ventriloquist, me the dummy. Started when Fry sick in bed, Mari stuck carryin' me 'round to my errands, the hairdresser's, dry cleaners. The car to here. Day I started makin' Howdy Doody noises she breaks: Be quiet Shut up Be quiet Shut up.

FRY: Bad day.

LARK: I was the goader I guess. Needed someone to flip out fifty-three years old! Suddenly no toilet visits without assistance.

(FRY stands, a little closer to LARK.)

FRY: No more transportation dependencies. Goin' places.

LARK: Goin' places! I got the means!

TAL: Fastest recovery I ever seen, not miss a beat. Why'dju refuse the hospital wheelchair?

LARK: Walsh happy with his. My mama and daddy made me my legs, guess I needed family gimme my wheels.

(Knock on RIN's door.)

TAL: Must be Mari.

(As TAL answers the door, LARK moves about the room:)

LARK: Gonna be drive-travelin' like my niecey! Move the break, gas pedal to hand controls easy custom-made. We got money!

(WALSH, filthy, enters with crutches.)

TAL: It's Walsh. Hi Walsh.

WALSH: Hi Mom.

TAL: Well. Haven't seen you since your *last* pleasant surprise.

LARK: *(Rolling around.)* Look at me! Look at me!

FRY: You didn't tell Tal again?

RIN: No I didn't tell Tal again it's *my* place I invite who I want.

(WALSH is examining LARK's wheelchair.)

WALSH: Ooooh, beaut.

LARK: *(To TAL:)* She's fixin' his 'chair. Front wheels stole.

TAL: He doesn't need an invitation to come home.

(TAL *now sees that* WALSH *has taken notice of her nub, staring at it. she hides it, embarrassed.*)

TAL: Cooking accident.

W.J.: *(Grinning.)* Hi son.

WALSH: *(Startled.)* Hi Dad.

W.J.: Look at this.

(W.J. *shows* WALSH *the liner notes on one of the CDs he had been looking at. As* LARK *speaks,* GIRL *will enter with her uneven crutches, sit at the computer and start tapping zillions of keys.*)

LARK: Round around around. Mercedes Benzin' the sidewalk, no more some carry doll, I got wheels! Drive-travelin'! Vancouver, been wantin' to visit that big Chinese garden, *El Castillo!* Twelve hundred miles southeast a the Rio Grande I'ma see that Mayan pyramid! gonna walk through the past. Better time.

FRY: *(To* GIRL:*)* Hey! Get away from there!

GIRL: Make me.

(FRY *picks* GIRL *up, playfully turning her upside down or tickling her. She's all giggles.*)

LARK: *(To* TAL:*)* You don't think I recovered *too* fast? Losin' my husband?

FRY: *(Still funning with* GIRL.*)* Ask *me!*

TAL: No. Everybody has their own clock. Grief.

LARK: That's what I think. I think Fry'd understand, Fry knows how I feel.

TAL: Fry understands.

LARK: *(Suddenly upset.) That damn rainbow!*

W.J.: New station one oh five twenty-four hour hip hop! *(Turns boom-box radio on.)*

RADIO VOICE: . . . Chicago's Michigan Avenue. The mine, placed in a mailbox, exploded at eight twenty-three during the morning rush—

W.J.: *(Turning stations.)* Music! Twenty-four hour does *not* mean news breaks!

(*Others silent as* W.J. *channel surfs, finally finds hip hop.*)

W.J.: That's it! That's it!

(W.J. *sits close to the boom box, starts taking notes. By this point,* WALSH *had given the liner notes back to* W.J. *Eventually* TAL *walks over, clicks the box off.*)

W.J.: Hey!

TAL: Not everyone wants to hear it, W.J., take it to the basement. *Attic!* sound rises like warmth, basement noise'll come up through the floor.

W.J.: *(Laughs.)* Okay okay, the data gathering could be a disturbance to some people I know. You'll read about it soon enough, my published treatise: *From Michael Row Your Boat Ashore to Tupak Shakur. (Exits with his stuff.)*

RIN: Did you already know? *(Silence.)* Michigan Avenue did you already know? I didn't.

(TAL and LARK gravely nod. So do FRY and GIRL, but RIN isn't looking at THEM.)

TAL: Guess this ends your little theory: mines maim, don't kill.

RIN: Somebody *died*?

LARK: I haven't heard yet. You?

TAL: Chicago? Lotta people in a small space, sure some dead.

RIN: That's what you heard or that's what you guess?

LARK: L.A.'s a city, nobody dead.

TAL: Well who goes up to the Hollywood letters except some teenagers, do whatever they do?

LARK: *Holy*wood. *(Giggles, to RIN:)* Other "L" blasted to the moon!

TAL: And right arm of that boy, he the sole casualty.

LARK: He wasn't a casualty.

TAL: Arm blown off.

LARK: He wasn't a casualty he lived.

TAL: So? "Casualty" is dead or wounded.

LARK: Thought "casualty" was just dead.

TAL: Sometimes. Sometimes not.

RIN: *That's what you heard or that's what you guess? (They look at her.)* Chicago! Dead?

TAL: Lotta people in a small space. Think about it.

LARK: Wouldn't be the first loss a life anyway you count Fry. *(Puzzled:)* You count Fry?

RIN: *No!* (FRY *looks at* RIN. RIN *notices this without looking directly back.)*

TAL: He be dead you hadn't had your legs blown off? Never heard of any heart trouble before. Casualty.

(Beat.)

LARK: Miracle Mari got that job huh. Good job. Bills ain't disappeared just cuz my legs and husband have.

(Hip hop music comes up through the floor.)

TAL: He went to the basement. He went to the basement!

(TAL *swiftly exits.* RIN *groans in pain.* WALSH *and* LARK *quickly turn to her.* RIN *massages her stump area. At some point in the following dialogue, the music goes out.)*

RIN: On and off today. Shooting needles. My ankle aaaaaah!

LARK: I get that! *(WALSH nods.)* Pain in my calves, feet. *(Giggles.)* Where it come from?

RIN: I dunno.

LARK: Bad?

(RIN *removes her prosthetic leg and is relieved.)*

RIN: Better.

LARK: Now what? Hop one foot?

RIN: Crutches. Lemme see that thing.

(RIN *takes the wheelchair from* WALSH, *rolls it into her work corner, begins work. Eventually she will go to the closet for her crutches.)*

LARK: *(To* WALSH:) Rear hubs farther back. See? Otherwise, no legs, uphill I woulda fell flat my back.

(*They watch* RIN *working in the silence a few moments. Then* RIN *sings, belting it out, startling* WALSH *and* LARK.)

RIN: *Ride on, King Jesus!*
> *No man can a-hinder me.*
> *Ride on, King Jesus! Ride on*
> *No man can a-hinder me.*

RIN: *(Continuing under other dialogue:)* For he is king of kings,
> He is lord of lords,
> Jesus Christ, the first and last
> No man works like him.

GIRL: I'm bored.

FRY: Yeah. Care for some ice cream?

GIRL: Yes!

(FRY *and* GIRL *exit.* TAL *returns with pitcher and glasses. When she speaks,* RIN *stops singing.)*

TAL: I already gave a glass to W.J., brought enough for *(Glancing at* RIN) *everybody* here in case *everybody* decides they want a glass after all.

WALSH: I met a sapper today.

(Beat.)

WALSH: Breakfast at the shelter, this guy comes up to me "hey." This obviously
　　　not *his* dining establishment. Somebody'd pointed me out: landmine.
　　　He wants to talk to me. Enlisted, he recently completed the training:
　　　detection. Clearance. He has the knowledge. Blast mine, dumb mine.
　　　And knows the procedure:

*(WALSH gets close to the floor, mimes the actions [especially awkward with
one leg]:)*
WALSH: take a garden trowel and paintbrush, carefully slowly scrape the earth
　　　away, brush it away. You see the plastic disk. A part of the whole, it's a
　　　little bigger than a quarter, the pressure plate. Don't touch it.

*(WALSH slowly lies down on his stomach. his eyes very close to the "mine."
Nothing moves but his fingers. he carefully dusts around the "mine" more,
more, then takes a breath, carefully lifts "it," just an inch or two out of the
"dirt." others gasp, silently as possible, eyes on the "mine." From here on out,
the sense that WALSH could blow up at any moment, clear enough before,
increases tenfold.)*
WALSH: Two halves across from each other on the pressure plate *don't touch
　　　it*. Pray the holes haven't filled with dirt, make your life a lot easier.

(Carefully, eyes always on the "mine," WALSH picks up something nearhim.)
WALSH: Wire. Guide it through the holes *slow*.

(Silence as he works.)
WALSH: It's through to the other side. The pressure pad is locked. Can't move.

(Others breathe a hair easier.)
WALSH: Unscrew the body.

(Silence as he does.)
WALSH: In the top half's the detonator, unscrew it *careful*. Heat from your
　　　fingers could ignite it.

*(More tense silence as WALSH unscrews the "mine." he drops the "little piece
of explosive" into his hand, holds it up as well as the "disk half" in the other
hand.)*
WALSH: Safe.

(WALSH, *no longer the sapper and exhausted from the physical exertion of the demonstration, finds a chair, sits. he pants quietly, catching his breath. Eventually:*)

LARK: Walsh always could tell a good story. Get down and act it right out.

(W.J. *enters as the discussion continues, goes straight to* RIN's *CD shelf, looking through the music.*)

RIN: I'm gonna put that in my story. Novel. Sapper, you mind I steal that?

WALSH: It's not a story.

RIN: I know but—

WALSH: Your novel's not very good. *(Beat.)* You asked. Honest opinion—

RIN: *Why?*

WALSH: Melodramatic. *(Beat.)* What, you thought cuz I'm your brother I'd four-star review it?

RIN: *Constructive* criticism, you can't just say "melodramatic" where? How?

WALSH: Everywhere.

RIN: Meaningless! Mean! "Honest opinion," couldn't have anything to do with it. I've finished a novel almost, you couldn't even finish college.

(*Without missing a beat,* WALSH *goes to* RIN's *manuscript, pulls out an arbitrary page, reads:*)

WALSH: "After eighteen hours of tending our farm co-op, Kim and I fell into deep sleeps. At that time, I had the recurring dream that I was to have an operation in which I would get my leg back, but when I woke up after the surgery, it was Kim's leg sewn onto me. Much later Kim told me he had the same recurring dream, except vice versa. We would walk down the street limping into each other because we each had my long leg on the outside, Kim's short on the in—"

(W.J. *rolls in laughter.*)

W.J.: That's funny, Rin. That's gonna be a funny book you gonna be a *New York Times* Bestseller.

RIN: *What are you doing?*

(W.J. *confused.*)

W.J.: You told me I could borrow. You said if I took care of 'em.

(*Pause.*)

W.J.: One?

(RIN, *sad, nods.* W.J. *is happy to have been granted permission but now, looking from one to the other of the several CDs he has already pulled, he becomes quickly bewildered.*)

RIN: Take 'em all, Daddy.

W.J.: *(Relieved.)* Thank you! Each has its own merits, a quick choice I could not have made.

(W.J. *chuckles, exits with* RIN's *CDs.* RIN *goes to* WALSH, *takes the paper and tears it up into little pieces.*)

LARK: I thought it was good, Rinnie.

TAL: He's your brother course he's the critic, when'd you start taking him seriously?

WALSH: Never! Else she wouldn't've been over there why were you?

(RIN *confused.* WALSH *snatches his stump leg.*)

WALSH: Looking for understanding? Got a shitload of that didn't you *dumb.*

RIN: The field wasn't marked! Other people walked through it *I asked*, they said it was safe thought it was safe.

WALSH: Trudging through those places mine-infested Mozambique, Zimbabwe, *Angola*—

RIN: They said it was safe!

(*As* WALSH *speaks,* GIRL *and* FRY *return licking ice cream cones.*)

WALSH: Why were you there? You didn't know what you were getting into! Lotsa places you could've gone to southern Africa pretty places those nature reserves? *They* were nice giraffes and monkeys and . . . elephants once I rode an elephant! In a carnival I went with Laura, remember my girlfriend Laura? So high up scary! Your legs spread, you look down, moving I was scared to wave! Scared to wave at Laura you don't think it's so high . . .

(*Pause:* WALSH *frightened by his outburst.*)

RIN: You know why I was there. I was writing on landmines. You know why I had a special interest.

(WALSH *looks away.*)

WALSH: I need . . . I gotta wash up. Little bit.

(WALSH *gathers* HIS *crutches, slowly moves toward the exit to the living room, gone.*)

GIRL: He said you didn't know what you were gettin' into.

TAL: He used to do that when he was a little boy. As a rule calm, keep it under wraps, but once in a great while it slip, bubble to the surface: fear. Then he'd start fast talking fast talking about everything in the world. But what scares him.

GIRL: Did you know what you were gettin' into?

(WALSH *will return toward the end of* RIN's *monologue, standing just outside the entrance, noticed only by* RIN.)

RIN: (*Not looking at* GIRL.) I knew what I was getting into. From 1964 until independence was gained from Portugal in 1974 Frelimo, the leading guerilla organization in Mozambique ruled, at times brutally. Renamo, a creation of Rhodesia later transferred to South Africa, became Frelimo's primary opposition and was notorious for its particular barbarity, cutting off ears, noses, and sexual organs of civilian men, women, and children. All parties involved laid land mines, resulting in ten thousand known amputees, a thousand since the '92 Peace Accord. The former Rhodesians boasted that by 1979 their border mine fields were the "second largest man-made obstacle in the world," surpassed only by the Great Wall of China. Angola's oil and diamonds attracted outside interests, the Soviet Union supporting the resistance, South Africa and the U.S. supporting the resistance to the resistance, the two hundred fifty million covert U.S. dollars exceeded only by U.S. aid to the Afghan mujahidin. Southern Africa is the most landmined area of the world and Angola the most landmined area of southern Africa and mines continue to be laid, seventy thousand amputees in a nation of nine million and each antipersonnel mine costs three dollars to build and a thousand to remove, and poachers have even used mines to decimate the elephant population—

(*Pause.*)

RIN: Well. That's the gist.

FRY: You makin' a mess!

(*Ice cream all over* GIRL's *hands. She licks her fingers.*)

FRY: Come on. (FRY *and* GIRL *exit.*)

WALSH: (*To* TAL:) Where're my books?

(TAL *initially startled by* WALSH. HE *is still dirty except for his just-washed face and hands.*)

TAL: What books?

WALSH: All of 'em. I know you guest-roomed my room but I just wonder—

TAL: The basement. Or attic I don't know. Attic probably less chance of mildew. Boxes. Someplace.

WALSH: I just want to go through 'em take a couple. My college dictionary I miss most, that I'll keep, but also . . . Now that I come home sometimes . . . It can be like a library my own private library I'll borrow some books I've been meaning to reread, then return 'em, trade for more. Or pass 'em through Rin so you won't have to have smelly me always trekking through your living room *(Laughs)*, then we can—

TAL: Rin's not leaving this house.

WALSH: Well—

TAL: You shouldn't be walking around all carefree either.

WALSH: I don't—

TAL: And don't call yourself "smelly." And I told you I don't know exactly where those books are and I have lunch and cake no time to look.

WALSH: I'll look!

TAL: Well unfortunately as I said they're in the attic or basement and as you know this house is not wheelchair accessible.

(All stare at TAL. She looks between WALSH, RIN, and LARK.)

TAL: Jesus. I'm the minority.

W.J.: *(Enters with boom box [turned off].)* There's a mouse in the attic.

TAL: WHAT? *(RIN goes back to fixing the wheelchair.)*

W.J.: There's a mouse in the attic.

LARK: Get a cat! Mice'll smell it and scram!

W.J.: I don't mind sleeping with her I named her Barbara. I just thought you might like to know before she make a venture downstairs.

LARK: Keep a cat on the second floor contain 'em in the attic.

WALSH: *(To W.J., glancing at TAL:)* Sleeping in the attic?

TAL: His choice!

W.J.: *(To LARK:)* Remember Granpa's attic? That big wicker basket. We hid in it?

LARK: Sure.

W.J.: We got a chest just like it! I hide in it. Sleep in it.

TAL: *(More upset than surprised.)* You sleep in the *chest?* I made you a bed!

W.J.: I like the chest.

TAL: You don't fit in the chest!

W.J.: Do if I bend my knees.

(W.J. lies on the floor on his back, knees to his chest.)

W.J.: Close it. All dark, dark.

TAL: *(At a loss.)* I'll get the cake. *(Moves to exit.)*

W.J.: For school?

TAL: I haven't been to school in six weeks, W.J.—

W.J.: *(To the others:)* She bring treats. The kids. They love her, seek her out. Guidance.

(TAL exits.)

RIN: This tool box I put together, never buy one already arranged I know exactly the grip I need on my screwdriver, which hammer weights work best. And Mr. Ivey behind the counter look at me all amazed, cuz I'm a girl or cuz I'm a cripple?

(Later in WALSH's speech, W.J. will look to the ceiling. No one notices.)

WALSH: Cuz he's a moron. I remember every time Dad and I'd need nails or a light bulb, Mr. Ivey call Dad "Walsh," me "W.J., ," and Dad "No. I was the junior all my life, my father 'Walsh Senior.' My son just 'Walsh.'" "I just can't get it straight," says Mr. Ivey the hundred fiftieth time. "'Walsh' sounds like the father, 'W.J.' sounds like the child."

W.J.: Hear it? Hear it? *(All puzzled, look up.)* Barbara. My mouse. Waiting for me.

(W.J. giggles, exits with boom box. A quiet moment. Then RIN goes back to her work.)

LARK: Why you didn't fix it yourself, Walsh? Just screw on a couple wheels. Right?

WALSH: Maybe just an excuse. See my family. *(Beat.)* But what's with this family, leprosy? Losing limbs contagious? How'd my mother lose a finger?

LARK: *(Looking after where W.J. exited.)* More concerned with what your daddy lost. *(Beat.)* These'd be the perfect things for the lazy amputee if only the toilet and flush built in.

(LARK starts moving toward the living room.)

WALSH: Ooooooh lemme—

LARK: No help no help I can go myself, I gotta learn, gotta AAAAAAAAH!

(LARK has hit a bump. WALSH and RIN rush to her side but she harshly waves them away. Pants, pants. Eventually:)

LARK: When's the pain stop?

RIN: It's not constant. Sometimes seems like it, going on for twenty minutes, more, but eventually—

LARK: WHEN'S THE PAIN STOP?
WALSH: *(Glaring at* RIN.) Never.

(Pause.)
LARK: You probably thought that little bump scare the pee outa me. *(Chuckles, exiting.)* Not all of it.

*(*LARK *gone.* RIN *and* WALSH *staring where she exited.)*
RIN: She'll be okay, she . . . Daddy be fine too, just . . . time, he . . . Quiet after Aunt Lark, what happened to Aunt Lark but still one piece Daddy still one piece 'til Uncle . . . 'til Uncle Fry—

*(*RIN *suddenly aware of* WALSH's *eyes hard on her.)*
RIN: What?
WALSH: Here's what I got from your novel: you have a landmine. You can build 'em. You can lay 'em. *(Beat.)* Burn it.

*(*RIN *startled.* WALSH *turns to leave on his crutches.)*
RIN: *(Suddenly:)* Turn me in! That's what you want, call the FBI bet the number's in the book. Call the SWAT team call the network news I did it! I did it what do you want? I built 'em I buried 'em my idea, I did it it's *done* what do you want? What am I supposed to do? Now?
WALSH: Asking me? You the one with the ideas.

*(*WALSH *exits.* RIN *goes back to work on* WALSH's *wheelchair a few moments.)*
RIN: *Soon I will be done with the troubles of the world*
Troubles of the world
Troub—

*(*RIN *suddenly screams and throws her tools. Knock at the door.* RIN *answers.)*
RIN: Hi.

*(*MARI *stands outside. Silence.)*
RIN: Come on in.

*(*MARI *does, carrying a shopping bag from a hardware store. Stands, stares at* RIN. MARI *no longer seems tense.* RIN *does.)*
RIN: We missed each other before, when you dropped Aunt Lark off. Literally. *(Chuckles.)* Guess I was in the bathroom. Something.

(*Silence.*)

RIN: Aunt Lark's in the bathroom speaking of which. Went by herself. I finished her 'chair! Pretty fast.

(*Silence.*)

RIN: Oh this isn't it! This isn't fixed yet this Walsh's 'chair I'm repairing. Walsh is here, everybody—

(*Silence.*)

RIN: Is that the basket? Were you able to get the basket?

(*No answer.* RIN *hesitantly steps toward* MARI, *carefully takes the bag [without any indication of an offering from* MARI] *and peers in.*)

RIN: Yes! This'll be perfect. Well, we'll see. Should fit we'll try it when she comes back. It'll take a little while for her to get used to it, the 'chair, she was doing great then had a slight mishap, bump, but I think it'll work fine for her. Any problems, you know where the manufacturer lives, bring it back. (*Chuckles.*) Lifetime guarantee. (*Chuckles.*) Are you thirsty? Mom just stirred up some lemonade. And cake in the oven, angel food I think. And you know you're welcome to stay to lunch, beef stew hey! Why don't we hang out this afternoon? We could chat, catch up and you could stay to supper, would you like to stay to supper?

MARI: What are you Rebecca of Sunnybrook Farm?

RIN: Who knew? You! *Accomplice!*

MARI: And who'd you ask for help? Somebody nothing else to think about last six years but her guilty conscience who knew how to play that? *Manipulate* that?

RIN: Never tied you up. Miss Timid. Never forced you to do anything, Miss Angel.

MARI: If you're naming me name me Miss Stupid trusting you! *This* town? You never told me you laid 'em this town!

RIN: You never asked! Helped me with the specifics of construction and materials you get easy from work—

MARI: *Not* easy.

RIN: Then never another word like see-no-evil-hear-no-evil guess you're innocent. Like your *corporation.*

MARI: No, you're the innocent. Poor yittle shing so upset 'bout her foot blowed off she so mischievous just yaying her yittle mines grow up!

RIN: Grow up? You can't even hold an adult conversation "Oh poor little Mari sitting in the corner, *so* quiet, *so* sad—"

MARI: Take responsibility for your actions! Oh I guess that's a lot to ask you can't even take responsibility for your rent.

RIN: I'm an artist! Sorry I haven't bought that condo yet *I* don't have filthy corporate money padding my paycheck.

MARI: What art this week? Toy-maker? Novelist? Singer? Preacher?

RIN: *You* take responsibility! I own up to *my* brainchild but *you.* Just a helpless pawn in my hand, huh? Mindless, brainless pawn—

MARI: I didn't—

RIN: "*This* town? You never told me you laid 'em *this* town" good to know you were cool with all the others.

MARI: I never said—

RIN: Of course you never said you never *say* anything. Just *do* well that's all I needed.

MARI: *God* I should call the cops.

RIN: Yeah turn me in then they should look real favorably at you, life sentence 'stead of death.

MARI: Whew! bases covered. What a criminal mastermind. Didn't *you* pull the "Get out of jail free" card. That little boy in New York would be so happy for you.

RIN: *(Beat.)* That little—That little boy—

MARI: Rin the Preacher "Oh those poor kids in Angola!" What about the poor kid in Harlem?

RIN: I didn't want that! I—hoped—

MARI: Rin the Hypocrite.

RIN: Well then I'm in good company, salary through the roof but bet never crossed your mind send a damn nickel to the Landmine Survivors Network. (MARI: *an incredulous laugh or sigh.*) You're dead.

MARI: I'm dead.

RIN: Dead six years ago ever since walk around like *Night of the Zombie.*

MARI: Well you oughta know. Making people dead's your specialty.

RIN: No one died!

MARI: *MY FATHER!*

RIN: That wasn't . . . That wasn't—

MARI: That wasn't *planned* it just *happened.*

RIN: Deaf to you. This logic no logic.

MARI: What about all the people you maimed? *(No answer.)* That's not an issue?

RIN: I didn't say—

MARI: What about my mother?

RIN: I think about that! I think about . . . There's meaning in this, you know? The odds, my family—

MARI: *Answer the question* trying to say my dead father didn't count how about my paraplegic mother?

RIN: YES! With much gratitude to you for supplying the vital bomb parts.

MARI: Hate you! Going to Africa with you biggest mistake *my life!*

RIN: *(Indicating her stump.) Your* life? *Your* life?

MARI: Who asked you to traipse through the goddamn field anyway *idiot!*

RIN: You did cuz you were traipsing right behind me but of course *you're lucky.*

MARI: No we both are cuz after all your FLITting you finally committed to something finally found your forté: maiming and killing!

(RIN snatches her prosthetic leg and whacks MARI with it, hard. MARI yells, snatches the leg, goes to the outside door and heaves it.)

RIN: OUT OF YOUR MIND? You know how much one of those things costs?

MARI: Crawl.

(RIN glares at MARI, then hops out the door. MARI slams the door behind RIN.)

TAL: *(Off:)* Rin!

(TAL and WALSH rush in to the garage.)

TAL: Mari!

WALSH: When'd you get here?

TAL: We heard shouting.

WALSH: Where's Rin?

(MARI stares back at them. Finally:)

MARI: *(Gentle, genuine.)* What happened to your finger, Aunt Tal?

(As TAL covers her hand, RIN enters holding leg.)

TAL: Rin!

WALSH: What are you doing?

RIN: Nothing. *(RIN goes back to working on the wheelchair.)*

WALSH: Where are your crutches?

TAL: Must be mad. When she's mad she won't use 'em, rather hop around one foot. The hard way. *(RIN glares at TAL. Off, a buzzer:)* Cake! *(Exits.)*

RIN: *(To MARI:)* There's a reason for everything that's what *I* think. Just trying to figure the odds you know, odds of all the people in this town, odds it happen to my family—

MARI: *My.* Family.

RIN: Those strangers! *People* don't mean to discount them but . . . meaning, my family, just trying—

MARI: *My family.*

RIN: Nightmare! You remember it, world upside down, what kind of place *is* this? *(LARK enters, unnoticed by RIN.)* Angola. Everywhere you look people hobbling on one leg *children!* What kind of place half its children maimed, *(FRY and GIRL enter)* what kind of bad water you people drinking Angola fucking Angola! And I'm sitting, and feel my legs moving look down, this little girl with one leg moving my two legs back and forth she wants to see how two legs work! *(GIRL smiles.)* She smiles and I smile and I hear something, her mother's there her mother snatches her away! Mother holding her, Mother glares at me: "Maybe America should see what it feels like. I'd like America to see what it feels like!"

LARK: I saw this show once, Africa, this legless woman goes flyin' 'round on her hands, agile look like a bug, faster'n I ever was on two feet. *(To RIN and WALSH:)* You ever see anything like that?

GIRL: Sure.

LARK: I wanna be it! I don't wanna get so comfortable now I got wheels that I ain't a demon without. I could be better'n with legs. I *wan*na be!

(TAL enters, laundry bag slung over her shoulder, carrying a half-sliced loaf cake and a big knife on a tray. W.J. follows.)

W.J.: Cake!

LARK and GIRL: Cake!

TAL: *(Dropping laundry bag.)* Hope you don't mind my rude economy, killing two birds. Heard the dryer shut off, picked up the load. *(GIRL looks to FRY.)*

FRY: Go on.

(LARK in wheelchair, WALSH with crutches, hopping RIN [pulled along by WALSH], and GIRL with crutches line up, single file, for cake. W.J. giggles, hops on one foot to get behind GIRL, making no indication of necessarily seeing her.)

FRY: Two sweets in a row bit much for me.

(TAL is serving the line.)

LARK: Mmmm!

W.J.: Airy.

LARK: When mix tastes this good, kinda discourages ya ever pickin' up the bakin' powder and flour.

TAL: *(Sitting to fold clothes.)* Flatterer. Don't encourage my laziness.

WALSH: Nothing touches your homemade but this. Not bad.
RIN: Mom!
TAL: What!

(TAL *confused. Gradually all, including* TAL, *see. Spots of blood on the clothes she's folded. Now noticeable: another finger [the other hand] cut deep, and band-aided. The moment* W.J. *notices, he lets out a panicked groan and quickly pulls headphones out of his pocket, connects them to the boom box and to his head, then happily bounces to the silent hip hop, periodically writing in his notebook.)*
TAL: I thought I . . . Another accident thought I . . . peroxide and bandaid, I
     taped it, thought I taped it tight . . .

(RIN *snatches* TAL's *hand, examines it.)*
RIN: Calling the doctor.
TAL: NO! not that deep! not that deep!
RIN: Taking you in the bathroom. Come on clean it up.
TAL: I can do it.
RIN: What happened, change your mind halfway?
TAL: I CAN DO IT! *(Exits quickly.)*
WALSH: She went straight to the bathroom?
RIN: Looks like it.
WALSH: No detours to the kitchen? knives? (RIN *shakes her head no.)*
GIRL: I'm bored I wanna watch TV.
FRY: Forget it you watched cartoons all mornin'.
GIRL: Bored!

(FRY *has walked over to* W.J.'s *boom box, opened a section, and pulled out* FRY's *pool table gift from* RIN. *Shows it to* GIRL.*)*
GIRL: Hey. How that get there?

(GIRL *is delighted. She and* FRY *sit on the floor to play.)*
WALSH: What's in the bathroom? Scissors? Razor?!

(RIN *turns, about to make her move to find* TAL, *when* TAL *enters with gauze, medical scissors and tape.)*
TAL: You do it.

(TAL *hands stuff to* RIN, *who proceeds to dress the wound.)*
LARK: Flittin' with my new getabout, forget my own work. *(Going back to
     work on afghan.)*

TAL: Beautiful, Lark.

LARK: Thank you.

(Pause. Before speaking, LARK *stares at* W.J. *bouncing happily. He, in his own world, doesn't notice.)*

LARK: Rin. Walsh. You see a mushroom cloud?

(Pause.)

WALSH and GIRL: Yes.

RIN: I don't remember.

*(*FRY *is distracted from the pool game by* LARK'S *words.)*

LARK: The picnic grounds almost empty cuz been drizzlin' all mornin' what? They reschedule my birthday cuza rain? no. *I'*da been all for it, complainin' through the corn on the cob complainin' through the potato salad, the ribs, across from me's Fry, raincoat and hood, "Isn't this a beautiful day?" *(*FRY *chuckles.)* Gives me a little wrapped box. I already got the new washer and dryer I wanted, I figure this somethin' less practical. Open: dandelion. Fry wipes the rain from his nose "I'n't this gorgeous, day my baby was born" and on that cue: downpour. Race for the tree. "Yeah, gorgeous," say I, and Mari lets out this giggle. Now when's the last time we heard *that?* How many years? I giggle, Fry giggles and Mari gigglin' bigger, watchin' the pork 'n' green beans drown, flowers on the cake all run together we just can't stop laughing. Then. The sun. It's let up but still a light shower and the sun and we're all waitin' for it. Mari sees it first, formin.' *Lovely,* sun through the drizzle red, orange, yellow. See Mari? See Mari, Fry? So happy. Mari so happy the rainbow, she walks out and I'm right behind *Look* at it! Strollin' through the wet grass who cares? red, orange, yellow I'm followin' red, orange, yel AAAAAAAAH!

(The scream should be bigger than any before. Pool game over. LARK *looking up:)*

LARK: Mushroom cloud? Black mushroom cloud? *(Looks down:)* Where's my legs?

*(*W.J. *removes the headphones.)*

W.J.	LARK
(Reads, raps:)	*(Spinning frantically:)*
I'm gonna tell this tale from the <u>start</u>	WHERE'S MY LEGS?! WHERE'S
It's about a family got blown <u>apart</u>	LEGS?! WHERE'S MY LEGS?!
Walsh's war hey didn't we <u>win it?</u>	WHERE'S MY LEGS?!

But there flies his boot and his foot
still in it
Rin travelin' back to the Mother Nation
Left a foot, token her 'preciation
TAL: Turn it off, W.J.
W.J.: *One leg's such a lacka symmetry*

(Simultaneous: TAL moves to W.J.'s boom box, clicking buttons as if they will turn him off; while W.J. hops into LARK's wheelchair—cross-legged or on his knees [concealing legs below the knee]. He spins around:)

W.J.	TAL
So Lark: "Look at me! Look at me!	*(Clicking:) Off! Off! Off! Off! Off!*
Look at me!"	

W.J.: *And Tal's crazy knife sayin' "When in Rome"*
(Silence.)
W.J.: Can't figure out that next line. Comb? Dome? Foam? Home?
RIN: I loved hiking! Remember? Running and climbing and flipping the monkey bars I was a jock. Remember? And hiking, *loved* the woods, up a mountain I didn't care, nothing stopped me! Strong legs, I hiked through Africa! Strong legs, jock legs *(To MARI without pause:)* Who did it? America! Angolan mother said it: "America"!
MARI: And what is it makes you so different from America?
LARK: Never seen one so big, long, all across the sky, red, orange, yellow, green, blue Mari all wonder *so* happy. *(To MARI:)* Weren't you? Weren't you?
RIN: I *did*, Aunt Lark, I *did* see a mushroom cloud! but I forgot about it. I don't think about that stuff anymore, that day Running through the field, laughing . . . poof. And in the hospital, *How can anybody do this to someone else?* Weeks in the hospital that's all I could think. But then, released, I forgot about it. Isn't that weird? All I could think. *Then.* All I could think.

Scene 2

(Pretty place in a park. WALSH in his wheelchair, clean, and MARI sit, have lunch. Sandwiches, drinks, a big package of Oreos between them. RIN sits near but doesn't eat. Folded arms on her raised knees and her face buried in her arms, a piece of paper in her hand. GIRL and FRY moving around, looking around, touching the ground.)
GIRL: We're close!
FRY: *(To RIN:)* She says we're close. She was with ya, she ought to know.
MARI: You gotta eat sometime, Rin. It'll still be there you can't starve.

WALSH: Here. *(Holds out a sandwich toward* RIN.*)* Keep your mind sharp.

GIRL: You started layin' enda winter, now toppa summer. Things just look a little different's all.

FRY: You kept good maps we'll find 'em.

*(*RIN *raises her head a little, not looking at anyone.)*

RIN: If I kept good maps—

(Frustrated, buries her face again.)

GIRL: Don't give up. *(Looking at* RIN.*)* Don't give up! *(To* FRY:*)* She ain't givin' up?

WALSH: No point beatin' yourself.

GIRL: We'll find it! *(Looking and looking.)*

MARI: We'll find it. So what, we searched this place all day, search it all day tomorrow. It's here.

FRY: What you had was a system, a key, and cuz you didn't want your paperwork to be lyin' around, evidence, you kept the key in your head.

WALSH: I can't believe they didn't fight it. How'd it happen?

MARI: I've said it a hundred times.

WALSH: I can't believe it.

FRY: What you figure you need to do is remember the key. So you sit there, thinkin' and thinkin' tryin' to remember. *(*RIN, *still buried face, nods vehemently.* WALSH *and* MARI *don't notice.)*

MARI: I explained it, real calm, I explained in detail and they looked sad but didn't seem shocked. Mom nodded. Aunt Tal cried. Not a lot.

WALSH: *(Scared to hear:)* What Dad do? *(Beat.)* You never said if he was there.

MARI: He was there. Just grinn'ed. Looked like he was thinking about something else. A song.

WALSH: Oh.

FRY: When you first entered this area, you tell them to move back, and you stompin' and stompin,' their eyes goin' wild lookin' atchu! *(Chuckles.)* Butcha couldn't find it couldja. Surprise. Guess you didn't wanna die after all.

*(*RIN *looks at* FRY.*)*

WALSH: I came cuz she's my sister. Why'd you?

FRY: Responsibility! Feel bad ya want but you ain't no help to nobody dead, *Rehabilitate!* Stop thinkin' stop tryin' and tryin' to remember that key you're scared. A livin'. Let go a the fear, you'll remember.

MARI: Sitting at my desk, work, one day I'm thinking. We did it, U.S., not all

of it but enough and now. *Everywhere.* Too late. And Rin. And *me.* Too
late. I go back to my work. Then, suddenly, this thought: Never too late.
RIN: I remember.

(MARI *and* WALSH *look at* RIN. RIN *looks at her paper, the map, immediately
turns to a particular spot in the earth, a little hill. Goes to it, carefully, carefully
touches it. This is it, and* RIN *is relieved, elated, terrified.* MARI *and* WALSH
have cautiously followed at a distance.)
GIRL: She's doin' it?
FRY: She's doin' it.
GIRL: *(Elated, laughing, clapping, jumping on her one foot.)* She's doin' it! She's
doin' it! She's doin' it!
RIN: Move back.

(MARI *and* WALSH *are unsure, not wanting to leave* RIN *alone.*)
RIN: *Move back.*

(*They take a step back.* RIN *pulls out of he bag a garden trowel and paintbrush.
Starts brushing and scraping the earth away. Eventually:*)
RIN: Wade in the water
           Wade in the water
           (Pause: RIN *motionless.)* I can't sing and work. This work. I can't
    work in the quiet.
MARI: *(Immediately picking up where* RIN *left off:)*
           children, Wade in the wa—
                      got in my car, and just before I turned on the ignition, here
    comes Uncle W.J. out the house, waving, grinning.

(MARI *and* WALSH, *stiff, move nothing but their mouths, speaking carefully,
eyes always on* RIN's *work.* RIN *had resumed her brushing and scraping as soon
as* MARI *started singing/speaking.*)
WALSH: What'd he say?
MARI: The Oreos? From him, gave it to me then, for our trip. Then started
    talking about holy wars, quoting war scripture from the Bible, I said
    Uncle W.J., this journey we're trying to study war no more.

(RIN *gets down on her stomach [a bit awkward with her prosthetic leg], her eyes
very close to the mine, continues scraping and brushing. Noticing this,* MARI
had ceased speaking. After a few moments:)
RIN: Talk.

MARI: Then he said the riverside the slave was laying his sword and shield by, across that river was freedom. Could have been heaven, could have been the North, could have been Liberia, could have been Africa, home. "Uh huh uh huh," say I, glancing at the dashboard clock. "Too much, they could've just threw up their hands," he goes on. "But never did."

(RIN, *who had been dusting with her fingers, is now gingerly lifting something out of the earth.*)
GIRL: Here it comes.

(*The disk: mine.* RIN *lifts it no more than a couple of inches above ground.*)
GIRL: See? Found it found it! We gonna do it!
RIN: Too many people.

(WALSH *and* MARI *glance at each other, confused.*)
WALSH: What?

(RIN, *barely moving, shakes* HER *head no. All eyes still on the mine.*)
FRY: Think she wants us to go.

(GIRL *confused.*)
GIRL: She wants us to go?!

(RIN, *ever so subtly, nods.*)
GIRL: *Forever?*

(*A long pause. Then* RIN, *ever so subtly, nods.*)
GIRL: *(Sad.)* Okay.
FRY: *(Holding* GIRL's *hand, walking.)* Good luck, Rinnie. You get outa this alive, one down. Just thirty-three to go.

(GIRL *and* FRY *are gone.* RIN *takes from the bag two small pieces of wire. Carefully moves the mine around looking for the tiny holes.* MARI *lets out a little involuntary cry.*)
RIN: *Talk.*
WALSH: *Lord, I keep so busy praising my Jesus*
        Ain't got time to die.

(WALSH *and* MARI, *eyes still on* RIN's *work, giggle nervously.* RIN *has found the holes and now gingerly pushes the wire in. All are holding theirR breaths.*)

Slowly RIN *guides the wire out the other side.* RIN *suddenly starts breathing nervously, silent, shaky.)*

MARI: You want us to talk, Rin?

(A silence. Then RIN *starts crying, as quietly as possible, trying not to move.)*

MARI: Rin. *(No answer.)* Rin. *(No answer.)* What can we do? help? *(No answer.)* What can *I* do? I don't know the method but . . . My fault, too. My fault, too!

RIN: I can't.

WALSH: Yeah. You can.

RIN: Can't I can't.

WALSH: *(Very quiet, gentle.) They crucified my savior*
> *And nailed him to the cross*
> *They crucified my savior*
> *And nailed him to the cross*
> *They crucified my savior*
> *And nailed him to the cross*
> *And the Lord will bear*
> *My spirit home.*

WALSH and MARI: *(Continued gently.) Sister Mary she come a-runnin'*
> *A-lookin' for my Lord*
> *Sister Mary she come a-runnin'*
> *A-lookin' for my Lord*
> *Sister Mary she come a-runnin'*
> *A-lookin' for my Lord*
> *And the Lord will bear*
> *My spirit home.*

(As they commence the refrain, RIN, *who has gradually calmed, slowly unscrews the disk.* WALSH *and* MARI *stare, very tense.)*

WALSH and MARI: *(Continue gently.) He rose*
> *He rose*
> *He rose from the dead*
> *He rose*
> *He rose*
> *He rose from the dead*
> *He rose*
> *He rose*
> *He rose from the dead*
> *And the Lord will bear*

WALSH: *(Suddenly terrified.)* Why that song, Rin! just a calvary song just a calvary we know *lots* of calvaries why *that* song what it give ya?

(MARI, *eyes still on the mine as are* WALSH's, *is terrified by* WALSH's *sudden outburst. He is shaken himself, as much by his lost control as by the fear that resulted in him losing it in the first place. At this moment* RIN *calmly takes apart the two disk halves.* MARI *and* WALSH *quietly gasp.* RIN *carefully puts one of the halves on the ground, removes the tiny explosive from the other half. The mine does not explode.)*
RIN: Hope.

BACK OF THE THROAT

Yussef El Guindi

Production Notes

BACK OF THE THROAT was winner of the 2004 Northwest Playwrights' Competition held by Theater Schmeater. It won *L.A. Weekly*'s Excellence in Playwriting Award for 2006. It was also nominated for the 2006 American Theater Critics Association's Steinberg/ATCA New Play Award and was voted Best New Play of 2005 by the *Seattle Times*. It was most recently staged in London at the Old Red Lion Theatre (2008). *Back of the Throat* is also published by Dramatists Play Service.

CHARACTERS

KHALED

BARTLETT

CARL

ASFOOR

SHELLY

BETH

JEAN

Note: SHELLY, BETH, and JEAN are to be played by the same actor.

(The setting is KHALED'S *apartment. Some time after the attacks. The play is performed without intermission.)*

*(*KHALED'S *studio. Futon on floor. Assorted objects, furniture.* BARTLETT *stands opposite* KHALED. CARL *is flipping through a book. He will continue to methodically inspect other books, papers, as well as clothes.)*

BARTLETT: We appreciate this.

KHALED: Whatever you need, please.

BARTLETT: This is informal, so—

KHALED: I understand.

BARTLETT: Casual. As casual as a visit like this can be.

KHALED: Either way. Make it formal if you want. I want to help. I've been
    looking for a way to help.

BARTLETT: Thanks.

KHALED: Horrible.

BARTLETT: Yes.

KHALED: Horrible.

BARTLETT: Nice space.

KHALED: Yes.—A little claustrophobic. But it's cheap.

BARTLETT: Live simply they say.

KHALED: I'd live extravagantly if I could afford it.

BARTLETT: What's this say?

(BARTLETT picks up a picture frame from a table.)

KHALED: A present from my mother. . . . It says, er, "God."

BARTLETT: "God"?

KHALED: Yes.

BARTLETT: It's pretty.

KHALED: It is. . . . I'm not religious myself.

BARTLETT: I've always been impressed with this . . . *(Makes a motion over the writing with his finger.)*

KHALED: Calligraphy?

BARTLETT: Very artistic. Why the emphasis on—calligraphy? I see it all the time.

KHALED: Well—frankly—I'm not sure it's—. I know in general that the religion tends to favor abstraction to, er, human representation. The idea being to avoid worship, or, too much distraction with the, um, human form. . . . In truth I don't know a whole lot about it.

BARTLETT: No television?

KHALED: No. Too addictive. It's easier to remove the temptation.

BARTLETT: *(Picking up a book.)* You didn't see the images?

KHALED: Oh yes. God, yes. How could I not. I wish I hadn't.

(The tinkling of a tune is heard. KHALED and BARTLETT turn in the direction of CARL, who is standing holding a music box.)

(A beat as they all stand and listen to the tune.)

CARL: "Oklahoma"?

KHALED: I've never been able to identify the tune.

BARTLETT: *(Referring to the book.)* And what's this about?

(CARL closes the music box and places it next to another object he's selected. He resumes his search.)

KHALED: It's the, um—Koran.

BARTLETT: Huh. So this is it.

KHALED: Another present from my mother. Her idea of a subtle hint.

BARTLETT: *(Flips through book.)* You're not religious, you say?

KHALED: No. She is.

BARTLETT: Didn't rub off.

KHALED: Unfortunately not.

BARTLETT: Why "unfortunately"?

KHALED: Well—because I hear it's a comfort.

BARTLETT: And if you had to sum up the message of this book in a couple of lines.

KHALED: Er. The usual. Be good. Or else.

BARTLETT: Sounds like good advice to me. How come you're not religious?

(KHALED looks over at what CARL is rifling through.)

KHALED: I was never comfortable with the "or else" part.

BARTLETT: Nobody likes the punishment part.

KHALED: I'd like to think God isn't as small-minded as we are.

BARTLETT: I guess the point is there are consequences for our actions. Funny, huh. How a book can have such an impact.

KHALED: Yes. I was just reading about Martin Luther and the Reformation and how the whole—

BARTLETT: *(Interrupting.)* Am I pronouncing that correctly? "Kaled"?

KHALED: Close enough. *(To CARL.)* Is there anything in particular you're looking for?

BARTLETT: Don't mind him. He's just going to do his thing.

KHALED: But if there's anything—

BARTLETT: *(Interrupting.)* With your permission, if we still have that.

KHALED: Go ahead, but if there's something—

BARTLETT: *(Interrupting.)* "Kaled"?

KHALED: Er, Khaled.

BARTLETT: "Haled"?

KHALED: More Khaled.

BARTLETT: "Kaled."

KHALED: That's good.

BARTLETT: But not exactly.

KHALED: It doesn't matter.

CARL: Khaled.

KHALED: That's it.

BARTLETT: It's that back of the throat thing.

KHALED: Right.

BARTLETT: Carl spent some time in the Mid-East.

KHALED: Oh yes?

BARTLETT: So how do you stay informed then? with no TV. Newspapers? the Internet?

KHALED: Both.

BARTLETT: And when you want to kick back, you—?

KHALED: *(Not getting what he means.)* When I—?

BARTLETT: How do you relax?

KHALED: Well . . .

BARTLETT: How do you spend your free time?

KHALED: Really?—That's relevant?

(BARTLETT stares at him.)

      Er, sure, okay. I read, mostly.

BARTLETT: Uh-huh.

KHALED: That's my big thing, reading.

BARTLETT: And when you want to amuse yourself, you do what?

KHALED: *(Referring to the books.)* Actually I find that stuff amusing.

BARTLETT: *(Holding up a periodical.)* This stuff?

KHALED: Some of it.

BARTLETT: *(Reading the cover.)* "Wheat Production and the Politics of Hunger"?

KHALED: A real page turner.

BARTLETT: *(Pointing to the computer.)* Can we look at that, by the way?

KHALED: It's kind of private.

(Slight beat.)

      It's—kind of private.

(CARL and BARTLETT are looking at KHALED.)

      Will you be taking it away?

BARTLETT: I doubt we'll need to look at it.

KHALED: If you want to.

BARTLETT: I'm actually more curious about how you kick back. What you do when you want to relax. Break your routine. Spice things up.

KHALED: Can I ask how that helps you? Knowing how I amuse myself?

BARTLETT: The questions will seem a little intrusive, unfortunately. There's no avoiding that.

KHALED: I understand. I just don't have that exciting a life. Did I mention I'm a citizen, by the way. I can show you my—

(CARL *holds up* KHALED's *passport.*)
> Right. Just so you know.

(CARL *puts it among two or three other items. This pile will gradually grow.*)

BARTLETT: Here's the thing. We know you're bending over backwards, and I sense we're going to be out of your way shortly.

CARL: Be done in five.

BARTLETT: And we know you didn't have to let us do this.

KHALED: Are you looking for—anything in particular? Maybe I can just point you to it.

BARTLETT: He's just going to poke around. It's a random thing.

KHALED: Are you sure? The strange thing is I was going to call you. A friend of mine said he would, which made me think I should, too.

BARTLETT: Who?

KHALED: Er—a friend?

BARTLETT: Right; and that friend's name?

KHALED: *(Hesitates.)* Hisham. He wouldn't mind me telling you.

BARTLETT: Hisham what?

KHALED: Darmush. He was thinking of calling you, too.

BARTLETT: I look forward to hearing from him.

KHALED: I thought maybe I should, just to let you know I'm—here, you know. I am who I am and—just so you're not wondering—in case my name comes across your desk, which it obviously has. I wish you'd tell me who gave you my name.

BARTLETT: Also know that anything you say here will be held in strict confidence.

KHALED: *(Continuing.)* Because then maybe I could address the concerns head on; so you don't waste your time. I imagine you're getting a lot of calls. People with scores to settle. Or skittish neighbors. Was it George? He seems a little too curious about where I'm from. He doesn't seem to understand my connections with my country of birth are long gone. Was it—Beth? We had a falling out. It's very strange not being able to address whatever accusations have been made against me. It's like battling ghosts.

BARTLETT: I didn't say anything about accusations.

KHALED: There haven't been?

(BARTLETT *stares at him; slight beat.*)
> Er, amuse myself? Let's see, I go to movies, I read. I like eating out; I sit in cafes. I like to go for long walks. I feel like I'm writing a personals

ad. I wish there was more to tell. You'll leave here thinking, gee, what a lame life this guy leads.

BARTLETT: That's the other thing: If you have nothing to worry about, then you have nothing to worry about. I know a visit from us can be unsettling. It's an awkward part of this job that when we come around people aren't necessarily happy to see us. We've held meetings to see if we can't fix that, but I guess there's no avoiding the fact that this is what it is. I'm a government official, uninvited, and you've been yanked out of your routine.

KHALED: You're more than welcome, I assure you.

BARTLETT: And we appreciate that.

KHALED: I've wanted to help.

BARTLETT: What I'm saying is we know we've put you on the spot.

KHALED: Well—.

BARTLETT: *(Continuing.)* It would be natural to be ill at ease, regardless of whether you want us here or not.

KHALED: Sure.

BARTLETT: *(Continuing.)* Don't waste time *trying* to appear innocent if you are. If you're innocent, you're innocent. You don't have to work at it.

CARL: *(Turning around, to* KHALED.*)* "Karafa."

KHALED: What?

BARTLETT: So relax.

KHALED: I'm trying.

BARTLETT: We're not here to get you for jay-walking. Don't worry about us finding small stuff. We all have small stuff we'd rather not have people see.

KHALED: Not even that. That's what I'm saying, I'm not even hiding any interesting, nonpolitical stuff.

BARTLETT: Stuff like this.

(From under a pile of magazines, BARTLETT *picks out a porn magazine.)*
      Don't worry about this stuff.

KHALED: OK. That.

BARTLETT: It's not a big deal.

KHALED: It's—sure.

BARTLETT: *(Flipping through magazine.)* Not a huge one, anyway.

KHALED: It's legal.

BARTLETT: It's porn. Not good. But it's still okay.

KHALED: They haven't outlawed it yet.

BARTLETT: No, but that doesn't make it all right.

KHALED: It's—it's a debate, but sure.

BARTLETT: A debate?

KHALED: Er, yeah.

BARTLETT: A debate how?

KHALED: About—you know—the place of erotica in society.

BARTLETT: Uh-huh. . . . You think this is healthy?

(Shows KHALED *a picture.)*
        With cows?

KHALED: I don't much care for the farm theme, no.

BARTLETT: You think this should have a place in society?

KHALED: It already does have a place in society.

BARTLETT: So does murder. Doesn't make it okay.

KHALED: I'm not sure I'd equate that with murder.

BARTLETT: You go for this stuff? On the kinky side?

KHALED: What's kinky? She's draped over a cow. It's actually meant to be an antileather kind of thing. If you read the blurb. A cow wearing a human. A reverse sort of—vegetarian's point of view of sex and fashion. It's a stretch. But someone in that magazine is obviously an animal-rights person. Or is pretending to be for the sake of something different.

BARTLETT: The woman doesn't seem to fare too well.

KHALED: No, but—. What does this have to do with anything? It's one magazine?

*(*CARL *holds up four or five more porn magazines.)*
        Yes. I'm allowed.

BARTLETT: Careful there. You don't want to get caught in little lies over nothing.

KHALED: What lie? I thought you didn't care about the small stuff.

BARTLETT: I don't. It's just a pet issue I have.

CARL: *(To* KHALED.*)* "Hany-hany."

KHALED: I'm sorry: am I supposed to understand that?

BARTLETT: You don't speak Arabic?

KHALED: No. That's why I didn't call. I knew you were looking for Arabic speakers.

*(*CARL *holds up two books in Arabic.)*
        Yes. I keep telling myself I should learn it. Look, I hope you're not going to pick apart every little thing because I'm sure you could come to all sorts of conclusions by what I have. As you would with anyone's

home. Come to a bunch of false conclusions by what someone has. Which may mean nothing more than, you know, like a Rorschach test. Without taking anything away from your training; but still: a porn magazine; Arabic books? So what?

BARTLETT: Uh-huh.

KHALED: It's my business.—I don't have to apologize for it. Do I?

BARTLETT: No, you don't. Or any of these titles.

(CARL *hands him a few of the books he selected.*)
"Getting Your Government's Attention through Unconventional Means," "A Manual for the Oppressed," "Theater of the Oppressed," "Covering Islam," "Militant Islam." *(Holds up a little red book:)* "Quotations from Chairman Mao Tsetung"?

KHALED: I'd heard so much about it.

BARTLETT: Do you feel that oppressed?

KHALED: I was a lit major; I read everything.

BARTLETT: And so on.

(BARTLETT *throws the rest of the titles on the futon.*)
It's not what we care about.

KHALED: Good because on the face of it I know—

BARTLETT: *(Interrupting.)* On the other hand, a person is reflected by what he owns. It'd be silly to deny that. If you walked into my home, or Carl's, you'd find us. In what we did and didn't have. Just as you are here in all this.

KHALED: But—context is everything. Otherwise, yes, some of this I know looks suspicious. I've played this game myself: walked into my studio and wondered what it might say about me; seeing if something would make me out to be something I'm not.

BARTLETT: You're surrounded by the things that interest you.

KHALED: I have a book on assassins, what does that mean? I bet you've seen it, and a red flag's gone up.

BARTLETT: What *does* it mean?

KHALED: Nothing. If I found that book in your home, what would *that* mean?

BARTLETT: It would mean in my line of work it would make sense to study the topic. What does it mean for you?

KHALED: I'm a writer; I read lots of things, for just in case—in case a plot line requires an assassin. I have a book on guns which I'm sure you've selected. *(Seeing it.)* Yes, you have. I actually hate guns but finding that you might think gee, OK, here we go.

BARTLETT: Why *do* you have a book on guns?

KHALED: I told you, I'm a *writer*. I need any number of reference books on different subjects. *That's* the context.

BARTLETT: Okay. Now we know. That's why we have to ask. We have no way of knowing unless we ask. Which means throwing our net pretty wide. Please try not to get worked up in the process.

KHALED: I'm not.

BARTLETT: We're not here to unravel your personal life beyond what we need to know.

KHALED: It just feels this isn't as casual as you make it out to be. You're here for something specific, obviously, something brought you to my door. My name came across your desk, and I wish you'd tell me why? If you allowed me to clear that up, maybe you could get on with finding the people you really want.

(BARTLETT *and* CARL *stare at him.*)

    I mean I appreciate the effort you're making, but I just sense something's being left unsaid, and I would really like to address whatever that is. It's like this itch you've brought in that I wish I could just scratch, for all our sakes.

BARTLETT: Huh. Itch.

CARL: *(Removes his jacket.)* Can I use your bathroom?

KHALED: It's right through there.

CARL: "Shukran."

(CARL *exits.*)

BARTLETT: No, right, it's probably not as casual as I'd like it to be. Though we have begun training sessions on that very subject, strangely, even for old timers like me. "How to put people at ease." I didn't do too bad at it.

KHALED: No, you're—I am at ease.

BARTLETT: Thank you. In fact:

(Takes out a form from his pocket.)

    If I can have you fill this out at the end of this, I'd appreciate it. It's an evaluation form. And then just mail it in. We're trying to get direct feedback from the public. Especially from our target audience.

KHALED: I'd be happy to.

BARTLETT: And if you could use a number 2 pencil.

KHALED: Sure.

BARTLETT: So yes, we try, but at the end of the day, there's no getting around the intrusiveness of all this: What am I doing here? A government official, in your home, going through your stuff and asking you questions.

KHALED: I'd love to know that myself.

BARTLETT: And that's what we'll find out. But in the meantime there's no avoiding the fact that that's who I am. Engaged in trying to find out who *you* are.

KHALED: I wish there was a way of showing you that I'm nobody interesting enough to have you waste your time.

BARTLETT: And you might not be.

KHALED: I'm not; how can I show you that?

BARTLETT: Well that's the thing. How can you show me that?

KHALED: Is there anything in particular you want to know?

BARTLETT: Is there anything you'd like to tell me?

KHALED: If you told me what brought you here—

BARTLETT: *(Interrupting.)* How about the computer? Anything I might want to see?

KHALED: No. Unless you want to look at a bunch of half-finished stories.

BARTLETT: Half-finished?

KHALED: Most of them.

BARTLETT: Why?

KHALED: "Why?"

BARTLETT: Writer's block?

KHALED: Sometimes.

BARTLETT: How come?

KHALED: It's an occupational hazard. It happens.

BARTLETT: Something going on to make you lose focus?

KHALED: Apart from the world going to hell?

BARTLETT: That inspires some people.

KHALED: Not me.

BARTLETT: It inspires *me* to do the best I can.

KHALED: Well, good.

BARTLETT: What inspires you, if I can ask?

KHALED: I never know ahead of time, that's why it's an inspiration.

BARTLETT: We know some of your interests, right, politics, sex.

KHALED: Not even that. But then, doesn't that cover most people's interests?

BARTLETT: I wouldn't say that. No. You wouldn't find these books in my house.

KHALED: Still, they're pretty basic, whether you have a direct interest in them or not.

146

BARTLETT: They're basic if you consider them important, otherwise they're not.

KHALED: To be an active, informed citizen? And to have a healthy interest in, in—sex; that's not normal?

BARTLETT: No. No, this isn't normal. I have to tell you, Khaled, none of this is normal. Right about now I would place you a few feet outside of that category.

(KHALED *looks dumbfounded.*)

To be honest, you are shaping up to be a very unnormal individual. I am frankly amazed at just how abnormal everything is in your apartment. I have actually been growing quite alarmed by what we've been finding. More: I'm getting that uncomfortable feeling that there's more to you than meets the eye and not in a good way. I wouldn't be surprised if we were to turn on that computer and find plans for tunneling under the White House. Or if Carl was to walk out that door having found something very incriminating indeed.

KHALED: You're—joking.

BARTLETT: I try not to joke before drawing a conclusion. It takes away from the gravity of the impression I'm trying to make.

(*The toilet flushes.*)

Carl. Are you done in there?

CARL: Just washing my hands.

BARTLETT: Can you hurry up, please.

CARL: I'll be right out.

KHALED: What happened to being casual?

BARTLETT: Oh, we're done with that. Could you turn on your computer, please.

KHALED: I—I think I'd like to, er . . . speak to a lawyer.

BARTLETT: Ah. Uh-huh.

KHALED: I—don't know what's going on anymore.

BARTLETT: I think you do is my hunch.

KHALED: Yuh. Okay. I think I'd like to speak to a lawyer if you don't mind.

BARTLETT: I do mind.

KHALED: I have the right.

BARTLETT: Not necessarily.

KHALED: Yes, I believe do.

BARTLETT: I'd have to disagree.

KHALED: I know my rights.

BARTLETT: What you do have is the right to cooperate with your intelligence and do the right thing and asking for a lawyer is a dumb move because it alerts me to a guilt you may be trying to hide. Which further suggests that I need to switch gears and become more forthright in my questioning; which usually means I become unpleasant. Which *further* irritates me because I'm a sensitive enough guy who doesn't like putting the screws on people, and *that* makes me start to build up a resentment towards you for making me behave in ways I don't like. . . . I am perhaps saying more than I should, but you should know where this is heading.

KHALED: *(Taken aback.)* I'd . . . I'd like you to leave, please.

BARTLETT: I'm sorry you feel that way.

KHALED: I'm sorry too, but I—I think that's advisable. If there's something specific you want me to address, then fine. But. And in that case I would like to have a lawyer present. But I no longer wish to be subjected to this—whatever is going on here, so please. *(He gestures towards the door.)* I'd appreciate it if you—and then if you want me to come in, I'll do so willingly with a lawyer.

BARTLETT: Er, Khaled, you can't have a lawyer.

KHALED: Yes, I can, I know my rights.

BARTLETT: No, you don't, you've been misinformed. Could you switch on your computer, please?KHALED: I don't have to do that.

BARTLETT: Yes, you do, because I'm asking nicely.

KHALED: *(Moves towards the phone.)* I'm—I'm calling a lawyer.

BARTLETT: Is it smut you're trying to hide?

KHALED: *No.*

BARTLETT: Weird fantasies? Child porn?

KHALED: No!

BARTLETT: Child porn with domestic pets involved?

KHALED: *What?*

BARTLETT: So then it must be something to do with, what? dicey politics? military info? blueprints? communiqués with the wrong people?

KHALED: *(Overlapping.)* No. What are you—? None of that. No; that's—

BARTLETT: I mean we've already established you're a left-leaning subversive with Maoist tendencies who has a thing for bestiality and militant Islam. Throw in your research on guns and assassins, and I could have you inside a jail cell reading about yourself on the front page of every newspaper before the week is out.

KHALED: Is this—? What—? Are you trying to intimidate me?

(BARTLETT *stares at him.*)
>   *No.*—Look, I—No.

(KHALED *goes to the phone and starts dialing.*)
>   I don't know if this—if you're kidding me or—but. This isn't—

BARTLETT: Khaled.

KHALED: I don't know what's going on anymore. Something isn't . . .

BARTLETT: Put the phone down.

KHALED: I don't even know now if you're who you say you are. You could be a couple of con artists who walked off the street for all I know.

BARTLETT: Would you like to call our office instead?

KHALED: I would like you to leave.

BARTLETT: Okay, but put the phone down first.

KHALED: I'm going to call my friend who'll know who I should—

BARTLETT: *(Interrupting.)* PUT THE PHONE DOWN!

(KHALED *puts the phone down. Slight beat.*)

KHALED: *(Quiet.)* I have rights.

(Slight beat.)
>   I do have rights. This is still—. . . .
>   I don't have to show you anything if I don't want to unless you have a—. . . . Which doesn't mean I'm trying to hide anything, it just means I care enough about what makes this country—you know—to exercise the right to say no. There is *nothing* on that computer that would interest you, I promise you. And even if there were, I still have the right to—. . . .

(BARTLETT *continues to stare at him.*)
>   They're stories, OK, I told you. Still in progress. I'd rather not have people go poking around something that's still very private. It would be like opening a dark room while the photos are still developing. It would be a horrible violation for me. That may be—

BARTLETT: *(Interrupting, holds up his finger.)* Sorry: Khaled? Hold that thought.

(BARTLETT *goes to bathroom door.*)
>   Carl. Could you stop whatever it is you're doing and come out please. (The door opens, and Carl emerges wearing a fatigue jacket and a baseball cap.)
>   Ah. Ah-ha.

CARL: I was searching the pipes.

BARTLETT: *(Re: the clothes.)* Well. There we go.

CARL: *(Re: the clothes.)* In the laundry basket, at the bottom.

BARTLETT: Really. Oh, well.

CARL: *(Holds up bottom of jacket.)* Evidence of nasty right here.

BARTLETT: *(Feels bottom of jacket.)* Yuck.

CARL: Smell it.

BARTLETT: I'll take your word for it.

CARL: Also: *(Takes out a swizzle stick.)*

BARTLETT: A swizzle stick.

CARL: And: *(Takes out a small piece of paper.)*

        BARTLETT: A receipt. From. *(Reads it.)*

        CARL: Guess where.

BARTLETT: Oh; wow.

CARL: Look at the date.

(BARTLETT looks.)

        Same date.

BARTLETT: Wow.

CARL: Proof positive.

BARTLETT: Looks like it.

CARL: He's our man.

BARTLETT: Uh-oh.

KHALED: What?

BARTLETT: Uh-oh.

KHALED: Why are you saying that?

BARTLETT: You were where you shouldn't have been, Khaled; in a place you shouldn't have gone to. Bad news. Very bad news.

KHALED: What is—? What does that—*(Re: the receipt.)* I don't even remember what that is.

(KHALED moves to look at it, but BARTLETT gives the receipt back to CARL, who pockets it.)

BARTLETT: As we shift a little here *(BARTLETT takes off his jacket)*, I want to assure you of a few things: we will not overstep certain lines. We will not violate you or your boundaries in any way. Though we might appear pissed off, you are not to take it personally or feel this is directed at you per se. And though we may resort to slurs and swear words, the aggression is not focused on you so much as it is an attempt to create an atmosphere where you might feel more willing to offer up information.

(Over the above speech, CARL has taken a chair and placed it in various spots— as if to see where they might best place KHALED.)

CARL: Here?

BARTLETT: Anywhere. *(Turns back to KHALED.)*

KHALED: What are you doing?

BARTLETT: One more thing: at no time should you think this is an ethnic thing. Your ethnicity has nothing to do with it other than the fact that your background happens to be the place where most of this crap is coming from. So naturally the focus is going to be on you. It's not pro-filing, it's deduction. You're a Muslim and an Arab. Those are the bad asses currently making life a living hell, and so we'll gravitate towards you and your ilk until other bad asses from other races make a nuisance of themselves. Right? Yesterday the Irish and the Poles, today it's you. Tomorrow it might be the Dutch.

KHALED: Okay.—Okay, look, look: You need to tell me what the hell is going on.

BARTLETT: We'll get to that. We're doing this as efficiently as we can.

KHALED: Because. I think. Actually, you know.

(KHALED moves to the door,)

· You need to leave. I'm sorry, but—er. I don't have to do this. And I, er, yeah. You need to go.

(KHALED opens door.)

BARTLETT: Khaled.

KHALED: You need to go.

BARTLETT: Don't be a party pooper.

KHALED: I would be happy do this with a lawyer.

BARTLETT: Close the door.

(CARL moves towards KHALED and the door.)

KHALED: You know what? I need to see your badges again because I'm not even sure anymore.

(CARL takes hold of the door and closes it.)

Can I see your badges again please? Because. Whatever this is, this doesn't feel like it's, er, procedure. This is more like, you know, I mean, you're acting like a couple of, er, thugs, frankly. And I realize intimi-dation is part of the process, but this is—*(A nervous laugh perhaps)* speaking of boundaries.

BARTLETT: Anything you don't like, you write it down on the evaluation form.

CARL: You gave that to him already? (CARL *searches his pockets for the form.*)

BARTLETT: I understand your getting nervous. I don't care for this part myself. We're switching from being civil and congenial to being hard-nosed and focused. It will have the effect of taking away from your humanity, and it doesn't do much for ours. Plus we're trying new approaches. It's all new territory for us. Which is why we're handing out these forms.

CARL: Here we go.

(CARL *hands form to* KHALED.)

BARTLETT: You don't like something, write it down. Even if we haul you into permanent lockup, we're still going to pay attention to your feedback. We might get things wrong in the short term, overdo things, with the interrogation, et cetera, but our image, honestly, how we come across, that can't be our main priority right now.

KHALED: Interrogate me about what?

BARTLETT: Our image can't be more important than questions of safety.

CARL: We don't give a rat's ass.

BARTLETT: We *do* give a rat's ass. But is it more important?

CARL: (*Half to himself.*) No, obviously we give a rat's ass.

BARTLETT: You care about this country? Yes? You want it safe?

KHALED: But I haven't done anything, and you're acting like I have, what have I done?

BARTLETT: What is more important: inconveniencing you with accusations of having broken the law or ensuring the safety of everyone?

KHALED: But how am I a threat to that, I haven't broken the law!

BARTLETT: I'm speaking about in principle.

KHALED: Even in principle!

BARTLETT: I'm trying to be clear about this. I want the process to be transparent.

KHALED: I'm more confused than ever.

CARL: (*To* KHALED.) You look like you need to sit down. You're beginning to wobble.

KHALED: What?

BARTLETT: Would you like a glass of water before we start?

KHALED: Am I under arrest?

(Neither CARL nor BARTLETT *answer.*)

Am I under arrest? Because if I'm not and you're not taking me in, then you need to—this is over.

BARTLETT: Khaled.

KHALED: You need to go. *(KHALED goes to the door.)* I know my rights. This is over. *(KHALED opens door.)*

BARTLETT: Khaled.

KHALED: You bet I'll fill in those forms. This is—this is way over the line. Acting like some—cut-out pair of thugs playing tag to try and intimidate me. This is my country, too, you know. This is my country! It's my fucking country!

BARTLETT: Khaled, the neighbors.

KHALED: I don't care if they hear it, let them hear it!

CARL: Not if you're guilty.

KHALED: I'm not guilty!

CARL: Then sit down and tell us about it.

KHALED: Tell you what? You haven't told me what I've been accused of!

CARL: Shut the door, and we'll tell you.

KHALED: I'm not going to tell you anything until I have a lawyer present! This is still America, and I will not be treated this way!

(BARTLETT quickly walks over to KHALED, grabs him by the arm, and drags him into a corner of the room—away from the door, which CARL shuts. BARTLETT pushes KHALED into a corner and stands inches from him. While being dragged to the corner, KHALED says:)

    What—? What are you doing? Let go of me. Let go of me.

BARTLETT: First thing: Shut up.

KHALED: No, I—

BARTLETT: *(Interrupting.)* Second thing, shut up.

KHALED: No, I won't, I—

BARTLETT: *(Interrupting.)* If I have to tell you what the third thing is, I will shut you up myself.

(KHALED opens his mouth but is interrupted.)

    I will shut you up myself.

CARL: *(Walks over to BARTLETT and KHALED.)* Listen to the man.

BARTLETT: And if I hear you say "this is still America" one more time, I am going to throw up. I will open your mouth and hurl a projectile of my burger down your scrawny traitorous throat. Do you understand me?

KHALED: I'm not a traitor.

BARTLETT: *Do you understand me?*

CARL: Come on, man. Be cooperative.

BARTLETT: *(To KHALED.)* If I hear another immigrant spew back to me shit about rights, *I will fucking vomit. . . .* You come here with shit, from shit countries, knowing nothing about anything, and you have the nerve to quote the fucking law at me? Come at me with something you know nothing about?

CARL: *(To* BARTLETT.*)* Easy, man.

BARTLETT: It pisses me off! . . . "It's my country." This is your fucking country. Right here, right now, in this room with us. You left the U.S. when you crossed the line, you piece of shit.

CARL: *(To* BARTLETT, *quietly.)* Hey, hey.

BARTLETT: America is out there, and it wants nothing to do with you.

CARL: Hey, Bart.

BARTLETT: *It's galling.*—Sticks in my craw. To hear these people who got here *two hours ago* quote back to me Thomas Jefferson and the founding fathers. They're not his fucking fathers.

CARL: They become his fathers. That's what makes this country special, man.

BARTLETT: I *understand;* but it's like they wave it at you like they're giving you the finger. *(Sing-song:)* "You can't touch me, I have the Constitution."

CARL: They do have the Constitution.

BARTLETT: I *know* that, Carl. I'm just *saying* it's galling to hear it from people who don't give a shit about it.

KHALED: I do give a shit about it.

BARTLETT: No, you don't.

KHALED: I do, very much.

BARTLETT: Don't lie to me.

KHALED: It's why I became a citizen.

BARTLETT: You became a citizen so you could indulge in your perverted little fantasies, you sick little prick. Come here, wrap the flag around you and whack off. *(He picks up a porn magazine.)* Well, I don't particularly want your cum over everything I hold dear!

CARL: Hey, Bart. (CARL *takes* BARTLETT *aside.)*

BARTLETT: *(To* CARL.*)* I don't!

CARL: I know, it's okay.

BARTLETT: Jesus. *God damn it.*

CARL: I know.

BARTLETT: It's plain to see, and we dance around it. We tip-toe, and we apologize, and we have to kiss their asses.

CARL: Don't blow it.

BARTLETT: I'm not; but sometimes it has to be said.

CARL: Okay, but let's stay on topic.

BARTLETT: This *is* the topic.

CARL: The point of the topic.

BARTLETT: *(Beat; to* KHALED.*)* And I have nothing against immigrants. Let me make that clear.

CARL: *(Takes porn mag from* BARTLETT.*)* Hear hear.

BARTLETT: The more the merrier. God bless immigrants. My great-grandfather was an immigrant.

CARL: Mine, too. Both sides.

*(*CARL *will start leafing through the porn magazine.)*

BARTLETT: This country wouldn't be anything without them. God bless every fucking one of them. My family worked damn hard to make this country the place it is. And if you came here to do the same, I will personally roll out the red carpet for you. But if you've come here to piss on us. To take from us. Pick all the good things this country has to offer and give nothing back and then *dump* on us? . . . then I don't think you're making a contribution, not at all.

KHALED: I am making a contribution.

BARTLETT: You're *unemployed.* You're on *welfare.*

KHALED: I have grants

BARTLETT: That's *taking.*

KHALED: It's a prize.

BARTLETT: For what?

KHALED: For my stories.

BARTLETT: You haven't finished one.

KHALED: For past stories.

BARTLETT: You're blocked, you aren't writing, that means all you're doing is taking from the system.

CARL: *(Still leafing through the magazine.)* Leeching.

KHALED: I *am* writing, I'm just stressed out.

BARTLETT: You're involved in something you shouldn't be, that's why you're blocked. It's hard being creative when all you're thinking about is plotting destruction.

KHALED: I'm not, why are you saying that? *What are you accusing me of?*

CARL: The point is he doesn't have anything against immigrants. Let's be clear about that.

BARTLETT: *(To* KHALED.*)* I'm *dating* an immigrant.

CARL: She gave you her number?

BARTLETT: *(To* KHALED.*)* This is not why I'm pressing down on you. Apart from the reservations I just spoke about, the best thing going for you now is that you *are* fresh off the boat.

CARL: *(Re: the girlfriend.)* You lucky bastard.

BARTLETT: If it turns out you're not involved in any of this shit, I will person-ally apologize and invite you out somewhere. *(To* CARL.*)* In the mean-time, why don't you show Khaled why he's neck deep in doo-doo.

CARL: Love to.

KHALED: What?

CARL: *(Searches his pockets; to* BARTLETT.*)* Hey, you know I met Miss September.

(Referring to the porn magazine.)

BARTLETT: Who?

CARL: When I was helping the guys out on vice. Miss September. Just the nicest person. Devastated the attacks came on her month and ruined what could have been her big breakthrough. Was ready to quit until some guys wrote in saying how her body helped them through their darkest hours.

BARTLETT: *(Not amused.)* Great.

CARL: *(Reaches for his jacket.)* Now she only does spreads for special occasions. Usually to do with law enforcement.

BARTLETT: I don't really need to hear this.

CARL: *(Searches his jacket pocket.)* I'm just saying, funny, huh? You never know what gets some people through the night. For some it's like, you know, the Church. For others—

(Finds what he's looking for.)
    it's a place like this.

(CARL shows KHALED a photo.)
    Ever been to this strip club?

(KHALED tries to focus on the photo.)
    Well, we know you did because here you are in this photo.

(CARL shows KHALED another photo.)
    Hidden in this hat and jacket I'm wearing, but: now that I'm wearing it, we can pretty much say it's you. You can make out your jaw under the hat, and the earlobe is always a distinguishing feature. It's you, right?

(KHALED looks but doesn't answer.)

BARTLETT: Khaled.

CARL: Plus we have your receipt from the club and a bunch of other stuff that places you there.

KHALED: Why are you—? Why was this—?

CARL: So it *is* you.

(KHALED *hesitates.*)

    I would acknowledge the obvious so you can quickly move ahead and establish your innocence, if that's the case. Which is *not* obvious.

BARTLETT: It's far from obvious.

CARL: I'd use this opportunity to clear up your name, if I was you.

(KHALED *is about to speak but is interrupted; sotto voce:*)

    And look, man, don't be embarrassed about going to these joints. I've frequented these places myself. I'm not as hung up about this as Bart here is.

BARTLETT: I'm not hung up about them.

CARL: What I'm saying is someone in this room understands.

BARTLETT: I *understand*. It was the cow that put me off.

CARL: Personally, you can whack off all you want. You can take your johnson and do what you want with it, as long as it's legal. We're not here to judge you for what you do with your dick. What's that expression in Arabic they use? About a fool and his schlong? Anyway. If you're just embarrassed to admit you go to strip joints, don't be. I love a good lap dance myself. That ass waving in your face. The thighs working up a sweat.

(CARL *shows him the photo again.*)

    You, right?

KHALED: Look I . . . I don't know where you're heading with this. I'm not going to incriminate myself when I don't even know what I'm being accused of. You asked if you had my permission to come in here and everything, well, you don't anymore, I'm sorry.

BARTLETT: We're so past that, my friend. Right now you're standing on our permission not to be disappeared into little atom-sized pieces of nothingness and then shoved up the crack of the fat ass you'll be sharing a cell with. The best thing you can do for yourself is to identify yourself right now, and I mean right now.

(CARL *sticks the photo in front of* KHALED'*s face.*)

KHALED: *You can't tell anything. It's too dark. It's a silhouette for chrissakes.*

BARTLETT: Then maybe we shed some light. Would that be helpful?

CARL: Shedding light is always a good idea.

BARTLETT: *(To* KHALED.*)* This is going to be like pulling teeth, isn't it. Carl.
CARL: I'm ahead of you.

*(*CARL *goes over to the closet doors as he takes off the baseball hat and jacket.)*
BARTLETT: Exhibit number one:

*(*BARTLETT *shows* KHALED *another photo.)*
    Have you seen this guy?

*(*CARL *slides open one of the doors, revealing* ASFOOR: *erect, still. Perhaps a spotlight from within the closet is shone on him. Also helpful if a sound effect of some sort accompanies the opening of the door.)*
    Of course you have, he's been in all the papers. "Terribilis Carnifex," bringer of chaos, exemplar of horror and ghoulish behavior, and very committed. And dead of course. Dying at the conclusion of his mad little goal. As a writer do you often wonder what might have been going through his mind at that instant he knew he'd accomplished his goal? Do you? I do. I wonder what he saw—just before he stopped seeing. What he thought, before he accomplished seizing everyone's mind and focusing it on him and his odious little ways. I admire him, you know. If I was an evil little shit, I'd want to be him. That's commitment for you. Dedication.

(To ASFOOR.*)*
    What *did* you see, by the way?
ASFOOR: Nothing.
BARTLETT: What did you think?
ASFOOR: Nothing.
BARTLETT: Unfortunately, I can't get into his mind. But he did do a lot of typing.

*(*ASFOOR *goes over to* KHALED's *computer.* ASFOOR *will start typing.)*
    Quite the wordsmith. If a little cryptic. We've been able to trace most of his e-mails. Worked out of a library not too far from here. The librarian remembered him. Said he was like a dark cloud that changed the mood the moment he walked in. But said she felt sorry for him nonetheless. Reminded her of Pigpen, she said.

*(*CARL *slides open the other closet panel revealing* SHELLY, *wearing glasses.)*
SHELLY: Like in "Peanuts."

BARTLETT: Ah.

SHELLY: (SHELLY *enters studio.*) You know, the way he always had this cloud of dirt around him.

BARTLETT: I see.

SHELLY: That way. I thought it might be sadness at first and felt the urge to say something to him. Cheer him up.

(To ASFOOR.*)*

    It's a wonderful day. We haven't had this much sun in weeks.

(ASFOOR *turns to her without saying anything.*)

    Have a nice day.

(To BARTLETT.*)*

    Didn't say much in return. No, I can't say he did. Barely smiled. His eyes were so . . . (SHELLY *can't find the words.*)

BARTLETT: Yes?

SHELLY: Piercingly nondescript. As if I was looking at a description of a pair of eyes and not the eyes themselves. Of course all these impressions may be hindsight.

BARTLETT: What do you mean?

SHELLY: You know, how new information about a person suddenly makes you see that person in a different light. I'm sure if you'd told me he'd saved the lives of a family from a burning house I'd be remembering him differently.—Though probably not.

BARTLETT: Anything else?

SHELLY: Well . . .

(SHELLY *hesitates.*)

    He may have misread my attempts to be nice. Because one day he followed me into the room where we archive rare maps. And, well, made a pass at me. Didn't know he was there until I felt his hands. I screamed, of course. Pushed him away. I even had to use one of the rolled up maps to ward him off. I kept thinking, I hope it doesn't come to anything violent because this is the only existing map of a county in eighteenth century Pennsylvania.

BARTLETT: Why didn't you report the assault?

SHELLY: I don't know why I didn't.—I didn't want to give it—importance. Perhaps if I had, you would've caught him, and none of this would have happened. I'm sorry. How do you recognize evil?

BARTLETT: We appreciate the information you're giving now.

SHELLY: All I saw was an awful sadness. I had no idea his hurt had no end.

BARTLETT: Thank you, Ms. Shelly. If we have any follow-up questions, we'll contact you.

SHELLY: I wish . . .

(To ASFOOR.*)*

I wish you hadn't done that. I wish there had been a way to get to you earlier, before things turned; before your mind went away. Because it has to go away to do that, doesn't it? Become so narrowed that nothing else matters.—I wish I could talk to you.—I would even let you . . . touch me, again. If it would open you up. If I could talk to you one more time and find out more about you. Every day I walk into a building filled with more knowledge than I could ever hope to digest. But none of the books can explain to me why you did what you did or who you are. . . . I wonder if you'd even be able to tell me.

BARTLETT: Thank you, Ms. Shelley. Carl will show you out.

(With one last look at ASFOOR, SHELLY *heads for the front door.* CARL *opens the door and exits with her.)*

BARTLETT: I don't suppose you've ever seen this man up close?

*(*BARTLETT *briefly picks up a library book.)*

KHALED: Because we used the same *library*?

BARTLETT: Locked eyes across a library table?

KHALED: That's the connection? It's the only library for miles, *everyone uses it.*

BARTLETT: *(Continuing.)* Rubbed shoulders in the book shelves. Shared books? E-mails?

KHALED: *(Overlapping.)* That's what brought you here? You don't think I wouldn't have come forward if I'd seen him, if I'd have had *any* information about him.

BARTLETT: Perhaps you did and didn't know it; look at him again.

*(*BARTLETT *shown* KHALED *the photo. At this point, if not before,* ASFOOR *is on his feet.)*

KHALED: I know what he looks like. I would've remembered.

BARTLETT: Look at him again.

ASFOOR: Khaled.

KHALED: You're not going to pin this on me just because I went into the same *building.*

ASFOOR: I'm bleeding into you, and there's nothing you can do about it.

BARTLETT: Pin what?

KHALED: Jesus Christ, I've been *wanting to help.*

BARTLETT: *(Overlapping.)* Pin what? You may have seen him, that's all.

KHALED: I *wept for this country.*

ASFOOR: So did I.

BARTLETT: I'm trying to jog your memory, you may have forgotten something, seen him at the computer.

KHALED: I know what you're doing, and I'm not going to be screwed by something this flimsy. I will not be dragged in by association of having used the same space!

BARTLETT: Khaled: calm down; you aren't being accused of anything yet.

ASFOOR: We're all in this together.

BARTLETT: Perhaps you have some insight into this e-mail he sent; it's translated:

ASFOOR/BARTLETT: "Nothing the matter today. On Wednesday, I cut myself opening a can of tuna. Don't worry about that. Do you know Luxor? It's worth seeing."

BARTLETT: Or:

ASFOOR: "Tattoos, yes. Do it where the skin folds so you can hide it if you change your mind."

ASFOOR/BARTLETT: "I have a list for you."

BARTLETT: Is "Luxor" part of your e-mail address or how you sign off?

KHALED: *No. "Luxor"?*

(KHALED *points to the computer.*)

   Check it. This is like twenty degrees of separation. Then everyone in that library is a suspect. I use books, for chrissakes, I'm a writer.

BARTLETT: So you keep telling me.

ASFOOR: You're blocked, I can help.

BARTLETT: Ms. Shelly can't be definite she saw you two together, all the same she did say—

KHALED: *(Interrupting.)* How would she know who I am?

(ASFOOR *picks up a book.*)

BARTLETT: I showed her your photo.

KHALED: Where'd you get that?

BARTLETT: Your ex-girlfriend.

KHALED: *(Digests the information.)* How many people have you talked to exactly? What did Beth say?

BARTLETT: *(Consulting his notebook.)* But Ms. Shelly does think she saw him nearby when you came to ask for a book one time.

ASFOOR: *(Reads title of book.)* "Caravans of God and Commerce."

BARTLETT: Remembers it because you kicked up a fuss when they didn't have it.

ASFOOR: *(Reading from book.)* "The road to Mecca was perilous, and not only because of the dangers of the desert."

BARTLETT: Says he stood a few feet away until you had finished and then followed you out.

ASFOOR: *(Reading from the book.)* "But also because of those who hid in them."

KHALED: *What?*

ASFOOR: *(Accent, to* KHALED.*)* Excuse me, sir.

KHALED: No.

BARTLETT: Said there may have been an exchange between you.

ASFOOR: *(To* KHALED.*)* I know book you want. I help you find it.

KHALED: That never happened. You don't think I would have remembered that? I'm a terrible liar. It would be obvious if I was lying.

*(*ASFOOR *has put down the book;* BARTLETT *picks it up.)*

BARTLETT: I believe you. But you did find the book.

KHALED: In a book shop, I bought it.

BARTLETT: He never followed you out? Told you where you could find it?

KHALED: *No.*

BARTLETT: Perhaps the librarian did remember it wrong but if we speculated on this encounter that never took place, what might have happened?

KHALED: *What kind of sense is that?*

BARTLETT: He followed you out and:

KHALED: *What am I supposed to speculate on?*

BARTLETT: You're the writer, you tell me.

ASFOOR: Assalam alaykum.

KHALED: *(Disoriented.)* I can't remember what never happened.

ASFOOR: Assalam alaykum.

KHALED: *(Awkwardly.)* Alaykum salaam.

ASFOOR: *(In Arabic.)* I know that book you want.

KHALED: I don't speak Arabic.

ASFOOR: *(In Arabic.)* No?

KHALED: I'm sorry, I'm in a hurry.

ASFOOR: Please. A moment. I would like—my name is Gamal. Gamal Asfoor. Hello.

KHALED: Sorry but I have to go.

ASFOOR: I like to learn English. With you.

KHALED: I—no, I'm sorry.

ASFOOR: You teach me. I pay.

KHALED: I can't. I'm really busy right now.

ASFOOR: *(Hands* KHALED *a piece of paper.)* My number here. I teach you Arabic. You Arab, yes? I watch you. I watch you in the library.

KHALED: No thanks. Thank you, no, good-bye.

ASFOOR: I know book you want. I get it for you.

KHALED: Really, I can't.

(To BARTLETT.*)*

That's ridiculous. There was no encounter. You're making stuff up.

BARTLETT: Well of course I am. You of all people should appreciate the importance of doing that. How that might lead you, stumbling, to a truth or two. Facts aren't the only game in town. Perhaps it never happened, then again, here are the Arabic books. In this story we're making up, maybe he gave them to you.

KHALED: What kind of deductive leap is that? That's worse than guessing.

*(*ASFOOR *goes to sit at the computer.)*

BARTLETT: From his letters we know he shared similar interests with you: writing, poetry, Middle-Eastern stuff, politics, radical books, porn, didn't much like women. Said some nasty things about women in his letters.

ASFOOR: *(At the computer.)* "Unclean."

BARTLETT: God knows what his childhood must have been like.

ASFOOR: "They corrupt. They diminish you. When I die, do not let them touch me."

KHALED: What on earth does that have to do with me?

BARTLETT: Well, Khaled, not knowing you; not really knowing much about you; just from meeting you and casual observance I would have to say your relation to the opposite sex seems to have a kink or two in it.

*(*KHALED *looks at him dumbfounded.)*

Maybe you two commiserated and found solace in the same twisted images and depictions.

KHALED: I don't know who you're talking about anymore; it's not me.

BARTLETT: I'm just saying.

KHALED: *(Overlapping.)* This is beyond making stuff up, this is *Alice in Wonderland.*

BARTLETT: Your girlfriend had a lot to say on the matter.

(A knock on the door.)
KHALED: I knew it. She started this whole ball rolling, didn't she.
BARTLETT: I didn't say that, but she was helpful.
KHALED: She's the one who called you.
BARTLETT: The word *betrayal* came up a lot.
KHALED: *(Continuing.)* Something completely personal gets blown up because an ex holds a grudge. Great.

(There's another knock on the door.)
BETH: *(Off-stage.)* I'm coming.

(BETH enters from the bathroom in a bathrobe. She is drying her hair with a towel. Overlapping with this:)
KHALED: You're going to take the word of someone who's *pissed off with me?*

(BETH has opened the door to CARL.)
CARL: *(Shows BETH his badge.)* Good morning. Ms. Granger?
KHALED: *(Overlapping.)* For something completely unrelated?
CARL: I wonder if we could talk with you a moment.
BETH: What is this about?
KHALED: Jesus, talk about the personal being political; now she gets to drive home that point and nail me with it.
BARTLETT: *(Looking at his notebook.)* She said some interesting things right off the bat.
BETH: So he was involved after all.
CARL: What makes you say that?
BETH: Was he like one of those cells that get activated?
KHALED: *She said that?*
BARTLETT: Why don't you let me finish first.
BETH: That would make sense. His whole life seemed to be one big lie. I don't think he has an honest bone in his body. What did he do exactly?
CARL: We're just trying to get a better idea of who he is at this point.
BETH: When you find out, let me know. Because I sure as hell didn't. You spend two years with someone, thinking you have a pretty good idea of who you're shacking up with, then boom, he pulls some shit that makes you wonder who you're sleeping with.
CARL: Like what exactly?
BETH: And I like to think of myself as an intelligent person.
CARL: What in particular made you—
BETH: *(Interrupting.)* Just everything. He never seemed to come clean about

anything. Always keeping things close to his chest, like he had another life going on. It wouldn't surprise me if he *was* involved. Though I can't imagine he was high up in whatever structure they have. I could admire him if he was. But he's too weak for that. More like a wannabe. Like someone who would be quite willing to take instructions, if you know what I mean.

CARL: I don't; can you explain that?

BETH: Like he knew his life was for shit and something like this would give it meaning. He had that writerly thing of never feeling solid enough about anything. Of being woozy about most things. Of course when you imagine you're in love with someone, all their faults feel like unique traits that give them character. It's disgusting how love can dumb you down. Anyway, what else do you want to know? So like I said, it would just make sense. He never would tell me what he was working on or what he did when he went out. He just shut me out after a while. Could you turn around, please.

(BETH *has finished drying her hair and now selects a dress from the closet. She will proceed to put it on.* CARL *turns around.*)

BETH: And then there was that quarrel we had soon after the attacks.

CARL: What quarrel would that be?

BETH: I almost flipped out because I thought he was actually gloating.

KHALED: That's enough, stop, stop, this is bullshit.

BARTLETT: *(Consulting notebook.)* That's the word she used: "Gloating."

KHALED: I never "*gloated*," that's insane.

BARTLETT: *(Consulting notebook.)* She went on to say that she felt you were almost—

BARTLETT/BETH: Defending them.

BETH: Praising them even.

KHALED: That's a lie.

CARL: Are you sure about that?

BETH: It sure sounded like that to me.

KHALED: She's twisting everything.

BETH: *(To* CARL.) I don't think that would be an exaggeration.

KHALED: *(To* BETH.) That's not what I meant.

BETH: *(To* KHALED.) That's how it sounded.

(*If light changes have been accompanying the transitions of time/new characters, a light change would also signal the shift here.*)

KHALED: I'm just saying we have to look for the "why"? Why did they do this?

BETH: Because they're evil assholes. Are you justifying this?

KHALED: Why are you so frightened of trying to figure this out?

BETH: Because if you go down that road, then you're saying somewhere down the line there's a coherent argument for what they did. A legitimate reason. And there are some things that simply do not deserve the benefit of an explanation, and being "enlightened" on an act like this would just be so fucking offensive. I don't want to know why they did this? *I don't care.*

KHALED: Don't you want to make sure it doesn't happen again?

(At some point, KHALED *moves to help* BETH *zip up her dress, but she refuses his help. The exchange continues over this.)*

BETH: Next you'll tell me this is all *our* fault.

KHALED: Do you or do you not want to make sure this doesn't happen again?

BETH: And your solution is what, we should flagellate ourselves? It's not enough they fucked us over, now you want us to finish the job by beating ourselves up? Paralyze ourselves by examining our *conscience*?

KHALED: Our *policies.*

BETH: That's your idea of defense?

KHALED: We'll finish the job they started if we don't. You've always been able to see the bigger picture, why can't you see it now?

BETH: *(To* CARL.*)* It was more than what he was saying. It was an attitude. The way he looked. And I used to think we shared the same politics.

KHALED: *(To* BARTLETT.*)* That is a complete—I wasn't justifying anything. I was saying let's get at the root causes so we can stop it once and for all. Where do you get "praising them" from that?

BETH: *(To* CARL.*)* There was almost like a gleam in his eye. Like he was saying, "It's just what you people deserve."

KHALED: *(To* BETH.*)* No.

BETH: *(To* KHALED.*)* You all but said it.

KHALED: Why aren't you hearing what I'm saying?

BETH: *It was a rape*, Khaled. It was a rape multiplied by a thousand. You don't go up to the woman who just got raped and say, you know what, I think you probably deserved that because you go around flaunting your ass so what do you expect. And if you want to make sure it doesn't happen again, then maybe you should go around in a fucking burqa.

KHALED: *(Disbelief, then:)* The United States of America is not a woman who just got raped. The United States of America is the biggest, strongest eight-hundred-pound gorilla on the block.

*(*BETH *heads for the door.)*

You can't rape an eight-hundred-pound gorilla, even if you wanted to. Where are you going?

(BETH *doesn't answer.*)
      Beth.

(BETH *starts to open the door, but he shuts it.*)
KHALED: Where are you going?
BETH: You have a nerve. Like you tell me.
KHALED: I just want to know.
BETH: Why? Are you afraid I might say something to someone?
KHALED: What are you talking about?—Beth: speak to me, you're freaking
    me out.
BETH: I followed you, you know.
KHALED: What?
BETH: Those times. When you went out. When you thought I was at work.

(*To* CARL.)
      I should also tell you that I thought he was having an affair. I'm still
not sure he wasn't. I think he was doing personals or a chat room or
something. Or that's what I thought. He certainly was at the computer
a lot. It must have been something steamy because every time I approached him, he would do something to hide the screen.

(BETH *approaches* ASFOOR *at the computer.* ASFOOR *blocks the screen by turning around to face her.* ASFOOR *smiles.*)
      Or he would turn it off. I became convinced he'd hooked up with
someone. Met someone on line. Our sex life . . . well never mind that.
He denied it of course. We had blow-ups about it. So . . . one day, I followed him. I wanted an answer once and for all. So I followed him. To
the park, where he met up with this woman. . . . It was strange. It didn't
last long. He talked. She gave him something, then left. When I asked
later what he'd done, he said he'd been in all day working. The second
time I followed him was the day I was to leave on a business trip. Only
this time the person he met was a guy.

(ASFOOR *stands, goes to the closet, grabs a different hat and jacket, puts them
on, and waits at another point in the room.*)
      Again, it only lasted minutes. And it kind of weirded me out. Later I
thought that was because I was thinking, oh no, Khaled's bi, and we've
been living a bigger lie than I thought. But it didn't have that vibe.
Khaled looked almost—frightened. Once again it was quick. Khaled
left first, then the guy.

(ASFOOR *exits through the front door.*)
     I left for my trip and told myself I'd deal with it later. Then the attacks
     happened, and none of that mattered for a while. But when I confronted
     him, he freaked out.
KHALED: *(To* BETH.*)* You've been what?
BETH: *(To* KHALED.*)* I called. You were never at home when you said you were
     supposed to be.
KHALED: You *followed* me? How dare you?
BETH: Don't turn this around, I'm fucking supporting you while you're sup-
     posed to be writing.
KHALED: That doesn't mean you *own* me.
BETH: Who were they, Khaled?
KHALED: Fuck you, no, it's none of your business.
BETH: I thought you were having an affair; but now I'm not so sure. Now I'm
     actually worried. With the things you've said in the past, and now, and
     these meetings, and your secrecy. Yes, I know you don't like to talk about
     what you're working on, only you've been working on it for as long as
     I've known you, and you have nothing to show for it. Are you having
     an affair? Either you're having an affair or you're up to something you
     shouldn't be. Either one makes you a slimy little shit. So which is it? Tell
     me or I swear to God I will tell someone what I'm thinking.
KHALED: You can't be serious.
BETH: I am, I'm really wondering.
KHALED: Beth. It's me.
BETH: Great, now tell me who that is.
KHALED: We're all freaked out by what's happened. Don't flip out on me.
BETH: Why couldn't you be up to something. Why not? I'm not sure I even
     know you.
KHALED: Okay, stop.
BETH: I'm not sure I've ever known you.
KHALED: You're flipping out, stop it.
BETH: No, tell me. You don't talk about yourself or what you do. Your past
     is a fog. Suddenly you have material on subjects I had no idea you're
     interested in.
KHALED: What are you doing? This is like some fifties' B movie *I Married a
     Communist.*
BETH: Are you fucking around on me?
KHALED: No!
BETH: Then you must be up to something you shouldn't be, and I'm really
     starting to freak out.

KHALED: *(Grabbing her.)* Would you just shut up. You can't talk like that. Not now. Not even for a joke, people take this shit very seriously.

(BETH *just looks at him.*)
>   Beth, Jesus Christ, wake up. I'm not a stranger.
BETH: *(To CARL, looking at KHALED.)* It's funny how people change on you. I mean normally, when you don't think you might be staring at a murderer. How you can be so fascinated and in love with someone and then find all that fall away. And the person stands there naked and butt-ugly, and you get angry at yourself for ever having wanted this man. I really hope these attacks haven't permanently spoiled my views on love.
KHALED: *(To BARTLETT.)* It was a literary group.
BETH: *(To CARL.)* Imagine; that's what he said.
KHALED: For writers; to exchange ideas.
BETH: It was like watching a man hide himself in one box after another; like those Russian dolls.
KHALED: *(Still to BARTLETT.)* I'm not joking, that's what it was.
BETH: I gave up after that. A few days later I asked him to move out.
CARL: Would you still have a picture of him?
BETH: I don't know; I can check.
CARL: I'd appreciate that.

(BETH *exits.* CARL *makes notes.*)
KHALED: Jesus. No wonder you beat a path to my door. For God's sake. She has an ax to grind. It *was* a list-serve for writers. We actually discussed plot lines and books. And yes there was some flirting going on, so what; my moral behavior is not on trial here. And the guy was a jerk because he passed himself off as a woman online, and—he was just an asshole and I left. That's it. The sum total of my secrets. You could frame anything with enough menace and make it seem more than it is.

(Slight beat.)
CARL: Bart.
BARTLETT: Yes, Carl.
CARL: Can I talk to you?

(BARTLETT *and* CARL *move off to talk in private.* CARL *speaks sotto voce throughout this next exchange.*)
BARTLETT: What?
CARL: Look: I'm thinking something.

BARTLETT: Go for it.

CARL: I don't think what we're doing now is getting us anywhere.

BARTLETT: Really? I feel like we're making headway.

CARL: Not—no.

BARTLETT: I think we've loosened his bowels and he's going to shit any second.

CARL: No, he's going to hold off because he's fixated on some idea of procedure. He thinks there's some script we're supposed to follow and that
will protect him. He'll keep us a few facts shy of the truth and piss us
off. The photo *is* too dark. And the clothes are generic. Important, but.

BARTLETT: The receipt is pretty damning.

CARL: We need him to spill his guts.

BARTLETT: What are you suggesting?

CARL: There's an imbalance of authority right now, and we need to correct that.

BARTLETT: I tried that already, and you pulled me off.

CARL: Yes. But with all due respect, I think I know these people a little better.
I've been there. I know how they think. There's some dark shit you have
to know how to access.

BARTLETT: Carl—we're not allowed to do that.

CARL: *(Gets out a small guidebook.)* Actually, if we don't hit any vital organs,
we can.

BARTLETT: No, I don't think so.

CARL: *(Reading.)* "Section 8, paragraph 2. Willful damage is not permitted but
a relaxed, consistent pressure on parts of the body that may be deemed
sensitive is allowed. As long as the suspect remains conscious and doesn't
scream longer than ten seconds at any one time. Some bruising is allowed."

BARTLETT: *(Looks at the guidebook.)* Huh. I need to re-read this. I completely
missed that.

CARL: It has surprisingly useful tips. Especially on how to use simple appliances like microwaves.

BARTLETT: You're suggesting what?

CARL: To bring the full weight of our authority to bear on him. With the aim
of making him adjust his expectations as to what options are available
to him.

(Slight beat.)

BARTLETT: Fine. . . . But gently.

CARL: Thanks.

(CARL and BARTLETT turn to look at KHALED.)

KHALED: What?

170

BARTLETT: *(To* CARL.*)* I'm going to use the john.
CARL: Take your time.
BARTLETT: *(To* KHALED.*)* Can I use your bathroom?—Thanks.

(BARTLETT *exits into the bathroom.* CARL *stares at* KHALED.*)*
KHALED: What's going on?
CARL: Khaled.

(CARL *walks up to* KHALED.*)*
    There's no easy way to segue into this. So I'm not going to try.

(CARL *kicks* KHALED *in the groin.* KHALED *gasps, grabs his testicles, and collapses onto his knees.)*
    First off: that has been coming since we got here because of repeated references to an innocence that is not yours to claim. If you were innocent, why would I have kicked you? Something you've done has given me good cause to assume the worst. The responsibility for that kick lies with your unwillingness to assume responsibility for the part we know you played. We need to know what that was. It might have been a bit part, but never think that makes you a bit player.

(KHALED *doubles over and lets out a strangled cry.)*
    Khaled.—Khaled.

(KHALED *topples over as he lets out a more sustained cry.)*
    Don't overdo it. I didn't hit you that hard.—That's not pain you're feeling, it's shock. You're overwhelmed by the *notion* of pain—that more might follow—not what I actually did.

(KHALED *expresses more of his pain.)*
    Enough with the dramatics or I'll give you something to really scream about.

(BARTLETT *opens the bathroom door. He looks concerned.)*
    It's nothing. We're good.
BARTLETT: What happened?
CARL: He's faking it.
KHALED: *(Strangled.)* No.
CARL: It's shock. I was abrupt.
BARTLETT: Over ten seconds.

CARL: But he's conscious, and it wasn't a sustained cry.
KHALED: What are you doing?
BARTLETT: *(Worried.)* Carl.
CARL: It's under control. Go finish what you were doing.
BARTLETT: Absolutely no bones.
CARL: One more kick and I'm done.
BARTLETT: This has to lead to something.
CARL: The info is in the bag.
KHALED: *(Winded; to neighbors.)* Help.

(BARTLETT gives CARL a worried look before going back into the bathroom. KHALED starts crawling towards the door.)
   Help me.
CARL: If you'd've kept your nose clean, then you wouldn't be here, would you, crawling on the ground, trying to get away from the next hit that's sure to come if you don't tell us what you and Gamal got up to.
KHALED: Please.
CARL: We know you talked with him.
KHALED: No.
CARL: You met up. In the strip joint.
KHALED: I'm not hiding anything. I swear to you.
CARL: We have the receipt. It's as good as a photo.
KHALED: I don't know what you're talking about.
CARL: You really give a bad name to immigrants, you know that. Because of you, we have to pass tougher laws that stop people who might actually be *good for us.*
KHALED: I haven't done anything wrong!

(CARL either kneels on KHALED's chest or else grabs him around the neck.)
CARL: God: I know your type so well. The smiling little Semite who gives you one face while trying to stab you with the other. You're pathetic, you know that. If you hate us, then just hate us. But you don't have the balls to do even that. You bitch and you moan and complain how overrun you are by us, and all the time you can't wait to get here. You'd kill for a visa. That pisses me off. That's hypocrisy. Why not just come clean and own up that you hate everything this country stands for?
KHALED: *(Winded/strangled.)* No.
CARL: No, that's right, because you're too busy *envying us.*
KHALED: *(Winded/strangled.)* Get off me.

CARL: I could snap your neck just for that. What's the expression for "fuck-face" in Arabic? "Hitit khara?" "Sharmoot?"

KHALED: *(Winded/strangled.)* You're crushing me.

CARL: Just how crushed do you feel, Khaled?

(Slight beat, then:)

> Alright, I'm done.

(CARL lets go and stands up. Beat.)

> Now do you want to tell me what you and Asfoor got up to in the strip club? Were you passing a message on to him? Were you the Internet guy? The guy to help him get around? A carrier for something? What? What? Tell me, or I'll—

(CARL pulls his foot back as if to kick KHALED.)

KHALED: *(Flinching at threatened kick.)* No!

CARL: *(Continuing.)* I will. I'll exercise my dropkick on your testicle sack and make you sing an Arabic song in a very unnatural key.

KHALED: I'm going to be sick.

CARL: *You're* going to be sick. I'm the one who's throwing up. Only I have the decency to do it quietly, inside, and not make a public spectacle of myself.

(Perhaps grabbing KHALED by his lapels.)

> What did he want from you? What did he want? What fucked-up part did you play in all of this? What happened with you in there? What happened when you met up with Asfoor? What did he want?

(KHALED opens his mouth as if he's about to vomit. CARL lets go as KHALED dry heaves. Slight beat.)

> You know what I really resent? . . . What you force us to become. To protect ourselves. We are a decent bunch and do not want to be dragged down to your level. But no, you just have to drag us down, don't you. You have to gross us out with your level of crap. I personally hate this, you know that. I hate it when I have to beat the shit out of someone because then by an act of willful horror, whose effect on my soul I can only imagine, I have to shut out everything good about me to do my job to defend and protect. Here I am quickly devolving into a set of clichés I can barely stomach, and you have the nerve to think *you* can vomit. No,

it is I who am throwing up, sir, and if I see one scrap of food leave your mouth, I will shove it back so far down your throat you'll be shitting it before you even know what you've swallowed again.

(BETH *enters dressed in a coat now. She carries a photo.*)
BETH: I found this.

(CARL *steps away from* KHALED.)
    It's pretty crumpled, but. I threw most of them out.
CARL: Thank you. (CARL *looks at photo.*) This will help.
BETH: Look—I . . . I just want to say. . . . I have no idea if he *was* involved in anything. I know I've said things to suggest he might've been. But I'm just telling you what I thought at the time, when we were all upset. Being a major disappointment and a shit doesn't make you a criminal.
CARL: Understood.
BETH: Okay.—Good.—Just so I don't feel I'm—you know.—This isn't about revenge.
CARL: Believe it or not, safeguarding the innocent is as important apprehending the bad guys.
BETH: Good. Okay. Well. . . . Bye.
CARL: Thank you.

(BETH *exits. As soon as the front door closes, the bathroom door opens, and* BARTLETT *enters. He walks over to* KHALED, *who is still prostrate on the ground.*)
BARTLETT: Anything?
CARL: He has a better idea of what's at stake.
BARTLETT: Anything solid?
CARL: Authority has been reestablished. That was important.
BARTLETT: Facts?
CARL: On the verge.
BARTLETT: Verge is where I left him.
CARL: Oh I think he's ready to talk. I think he knows we're not looking for sequential sentences that add up to poop; but details that fit in nicely with what we know happened at the club. (*To* KHALED.) Where you went to get a hard-on while plotting death and destruction.
BARTLETT: Can we get him off the floor? It looks bad.

(BARTLETT *gets the chair as* CARL *moves to pick* KHALED *up.*)
CARL: He's such a drama queen.
BARTLETT: (*Helps* CARL *pick up* KHALED.) The last piece of the puzzle fits, my

friend. You were there. We had surveillance cameras. It wasn't your girlfriend who gave you away. It was your pecker.

(BARTLETT *and* CARL *sit* KHALED *down.*)
You should have followed your religion's advice and avoided all depictions of the human form because that's what did you in.
CARL: Time for exhibit number 4, I think.
BARTLETT: If we absolutely must.
CARL: You completely overlook her patriotism, you really do.
BARTLETT: I must have missed it. (*To* KHALED.) We'll tell you what happened, and you just stop us if we have it wrong, OK?

(*Throughout this next section,* KHALED *remains dazed, in shock.* CARL *will slide open both closet doors.*)
On a Tuesday night, August 21st, at around 10:05, you went to the "EyeFull Tower Club"; where a Ms. Jean Sommers, aka Kelly Cupid, "Dancer Extraordinaire and Stripper Artiste," as she calls herself, was performing.

(*With the doors opened, a dancing pole is revealed. Light change in the closet to simulate club lighting. Perhaps a disco-ball effect and a couple of spot lights.* JEAN SOMMERS *is already at the pole. She is dressed for the act: elements of a cowboy outfit, including two pistols slung on each hip. She might also be wearing a wig.*)
The date on your receipt proves it, and so does Ms. Sommers.
JEAN: I do. Anyway I can help, gentlemen.
CARL: Much appreciated.
JEAN: Will you want to see my act now?
BARTLETT: Is it relevant?
CARL: It might be. Clearly they met here for a reason. Your act may have been a signal of sorts. A series of unintended semaphores that spelt out a message to commence something. Why don't we have a look just to cover our bases.
JEAN: So you do want to see it?
CARL: You bet.
JEAN: You got it. Music.

(*Appropriate music starts, and* JEAN *performs her act. More burlesque and pole dancing than strip tease. After it ends, slight beat.*)
BARTLETT: I don't see how they could have passed messages through that.
CARL: Maybe not but it doesn't hurt to check.

JEAN: That was the shortened version.

BARTLETT: When did you first notice him?

JEAN: The first time he came or the second?

CARL: Are we talking dates, or?

JEAN: *(Smiling.)* Yeah, dates.

BARTLETT: The first.

JEAN: I hardly noticed him at all. Except he was nervous and sweaty. Which isn't unusual when I come on. And he had a couple of books. I thought maybe he was a college grad trying to cram for an exam.

BARTLETT: Hardly a place to study.

JEAN: You'd be surprised. I see more and more people with laptops. We've begun to offer plug outlets in our lap-dance area.

BARTLETT: Anything else, that first time?

JEAN: Not really. I give full attention to my act. I believe in giving your best regardless of what you're doing.

CARL: It shows.

JEAN: Others leave their body when they do this, I don't. To me my body is a celebration of who I am, and I give it to others as a revelation. I try to be your average Joe's desire incarnate. With a little extra thrown in for the more discerning. Nobody leaves my act feeling shortchanged.

CARL: Kudos.

JEAN: Thanks.

BARTLETT: Anything else at first glance?

JEAN: No, he was just a set of eyes. It was later. When he asked for a lap dance that I had more time to observe him.

CARL: *(Showing her* KHALED's *photo.)* And you're sure it was this guy.

JEAN: Yeah, kinda. It was dark, and he was wearing a baseball cap. But I'm pretty sure. And he was wearing this fatigue jacket.

(BARTLETT *picks up the baseball cap and fatigue jacket to show to* KHALED.)

BARTLETT: Any chance you remember the book titles?

JEAN: Yes, as a matter of fact. I'm always curious what other people are reading so I looked. One was on tattoos, and the other had something, something in the title—ending with God, which I thought was an odd combo. I plan on going back to college, you know.

BARTLETT: So what happened next? When you went one-on-one?

JEAN: Well . . .

(JEAN *moves towards* KHALED. *Appropriate music for a lap dance fades in quietly in the background.)*

I began my routine. The usual. I was feeling less than on that day. I had been groped earlier and was not feeling well-disposed to the horny. But I do have a work ethic, like I said, and so I danced. I always give my best.

(JEAN *starts to sketch in some of her moves.*)

Even to people who turn out later to be scum who want to do us harm. Did I tell you my father was a marine?

CARL: No.

JEAN: Highly decorated. My outfit in many ways is a salute to him. That's what he was before he joined up. A cowboy, out west. At night, sometimes, he'd let me wear his medals.

BARTLETT: What can you tell us about Khaled?

JEAN: That's his name, huh?

BARTLETT: Yes.

JEAN: *(While dancing over a seated* KHALED.*)* If I had him again . . . I know what I'd do with him. Coming here to do that to us.

BARTLETT: Well, we don't know for sure if he's—

JEAN: *(Interrupting.)* I'd say touch me, Khaled, so the bouncers can come and smash your stupid face in. Coming here to get off on me while all the time wanting to do shit to us. Wrapping your women in black and then sneaking in here and getting your rocks off. I could pluck your eyes out. I could bend your dick 'round and fuck you up your own ass.

BARTLETT: Your sentiments are understandable. But if you could tell us what happened next.

JEAN: I should have known something was up. I thought he was extra sweaty because he was just too close to something he couldn't have. But it wasn't that. He was always looking around to check for something. It kinda pissed me off he wasn't giving me his full attention. At one time I stuck my boobs in his face, and he actually moved his head, like I was blocking his view. I thought, what the hell are you doing here then? I take pride in what I do and expect some respect. Don't act like you're bored. I decided then and there to make him come. But then this guy shows up. Stands a few feet away and stares. Just stares. Like he'd paid for this show as well. "Do you mind?" I say to him.

BARTLETT: *(Shows her* ASFOOR's *photo.)* This guy?

JEAN: Yeah. It was dark, but yeah. Both of them were Middle Eastern, that I know. So I tell him to piss off, but he just stands there, and this Kaled is looking at him. Suddenly his attention is full on him. And he's changed. Like he's frozen or something. And this guy just stares, and he's looking at Khaled and me. And I say again, "Do you mind?" And he looks at me and his eyes—they're like, I'm-going-to-get-you eyes. Only they're smiling, and it's creepy. And then he leaves to the rest room. And Khaled starts to rise like he wants to follow. Only I push him back down. I'm really pissed off at this point, like I've been insulted. Like my skills have been called into question. So I did something I never usually do. I reached down and squeezed.

(JEAN *does so.*)
 Just one time. And that did the trick. I finished him off. So easy. . . . Then he springs out of that chair and into the rest room.

(*The music stops;* JEAN *moves away from* KHALED.)
 And that would have been it; I would have moved on, onto the next customer, but something about them really annoyed me. So I looked for them to come out; to say something, like have some manners the next time, the both of you, and don't come back. But fifteen minutes later, they're still in there. And I say this to Stewart, one of the bouncers, and he says let me check, and I say, no, let me do it. If I can embarrass these guys I will, so I go in.

(JEAN *opens the bathroom door.*)
 And . . .

(*A laugh.*)
 Damn if I don't see both of their legs under one of the stalls. And—they must have heard me, because Khaled comes shooting out and runs, just runs past me. And out saunters Mr. Creepy after him. Calm as can be, like he'd just been holding a meeting in his office. And I'm think-ing—no, I actually say to him: "Take that shit somewhere else." And he stares at me again, and this time it's scary. Real scary. Like he's telling me he could snuff my life out with his pinkie if he wanted to. So I get out of there and tell Stewart about it, only they're both gone when he goes round to check. . . . And that's my story.

BARTLETT: Did you get a sense of what they might have been doing in the stall?
JEAN: Not a clue. Might have been sucking each other off for all I know. Or shooting up. Who knows. At least one of them's dead. Have you got the other one yet?
CARL: We're working on it.

JEAN: I wouldn't mind getting him in that chair again. Give him a good thwack from me if you find him, care of Kelly Cupid.

CARL: Will do.

JEAN: Anything else I can do for you?

CARL: Not at the moment.

JEAN: Well . . . I'd better get ready for my act then.

CARL: Maybe we'll come back to check out the longer version.

JEAN: I'd like that. I'd hate to think my routine was being used for a nasty purpose.

(JEAN *smiles at* CARL, *then exits.* CARL *closes the closet doors.* BARTLETT *and* CARL *turn to* KHALED. BARTLETT *drags a chair and sits opposite* KHALED. CARL *either sits on the edge of the table, next to* KHALED, *or stands over him.* KHALED *looks at them.*)

(Beat.)

KHALED: She's lying.

BARTLETT: Here's where I have to pry a little more than I like to. Can we—look at your pecker? Please? Very briefly. To clear something up. 'Cause this thing about tattoos keeps coming up.

(KHALED *makes to bolt out of his chair, but* CARL *pins him down, wrapping his arms around* KHALED's *chest, immobilizing his arms.* BARTLETT *puts on a latex glove.*)

BARTLETT: I'm sure it's nothing. I bet it's nothing. But it sure does make me wonder.

(BARTLETT *starts to undo* KHALED's *trousers.* KHALED *writhes in his chair in protest. This can be done with most of* KHALED's *back to the audience. Alternatively, this can take place on the futon, with the agents blocking most of the audience's view of* KHALED.)

KHALED: No.—No.

BARTLETT: *(Overlapping.)* What with that e-mail he sent about tattoos, and the book, and doing it where the skin folds, where you can hide it.

KHALED: *(Half in tears.)* Stop it. No.—No.

BARTLETT: *(Overlapping.)* Was there like some secret mark you each showed yourselves? To ascertain something? Membership? Commitment? What *were* you doing in there for fifteen minutes? Excuse me. This is embarrassing for me, too.

(BARTLETT has yanked KHALED's pants down far enough for him to look.)
What's that? Is that a birthmark? Or?

(CARL also looks.)
What is that?

CARL: Liver spot?

BARTLETT: *(Still looking; slight beat.)* Yeah. . . . Yeah. It's what it looks like. . . . That couldn't be a tattoo, could it?. . . . I wish we'd bought our camera with us. . . . Next time.

(BARTLETT continues to peer, then: a light slap on the thigh to indicate he's finished.)
Alright.

(BARTLETT stands.)
Thank you. Apologies for that. Not a part of the job that I like.

(CARL lets go, KHALED covers himself with his hands and starts to pull up his trousers, but BARTLETT prevents him from doing so by placing his foot on his trousers.)
But it still leaves us wondering what you did all that time in the bathroom with one of the more hideous individuals we've come across? Now would be the time to fess up to any deviant sexual inclinations. It might get you off.

(Slight beat.)

KHALED: *(Quiet.)* I was never there.

BARTLETT: *(Slight beat.)* Alright. . . . We're going to leave you to think about it. Come back later, tomorrow. We'll take a few things with us now.

(BARTLETT nods to CARL to take the laptop.)
Look them over. Assess what we have. What needs filling in.—What might have occurred to you overnight.

(BARTLETT picks up books from the pile.)
And then talk some more. You're not taking any long-distance trips, are you?

(BARTLETT looks at KHALED, then moves to the door.)
Here're your choices, Khaled, that you can think about. Either you're innocent. In which case proving that might be difficult. Or you're guilty, in which case telling us now would score you points because we'll find

out soon enough. Or: you're innocent of being guilty. You didn't know what you were getting into. Stumbled into it. Through deception. Other people's. Your own stupidity. And that would be okay, too. We can work with that. We can work with you to make that seem plausible.

(BARTLETT *is at the door now.* CARL *carries the laptop.*)
    Think about it. And about those evaluation forms: they're no joke. It's your chance to respond. That's what this is all about. At the end of the day, we're fighting to safeguard that right. It sounds counterintuitive. But that's the struggle for freedom for you. It's never as straightforward as you'd like it to be.

(Slight beat.)
CARL: *(To* KHALED.*)* "Ma'salamma."
BARTLETT: *(Turns to* CARL.*)* What does that mean?
CARL: Peace be with you.
BARTLETT: I can go with that.

(To KHALED.*)*
    Peace be with you.

(BARTLETT *and* CARL *take one last look at* KHALED, *who remains slightly bent over, covering his crotch.* BARTLETT *and* CARL *exit and close the door behind them.*)

(Beat.)

(KHALED *pulls up his trousers. Beat.*)

(The closet doors slide open revealing ASFOOR. *He enters the room.*)
ASFOOR: You . . . you help me, yes? You and me, private class. I have . . . I have need to—to learn. Quickly. Yes? . . . When first I come to this country—I not know how to speak. How . . . even to say anything. How one word best is placed with what word next. Yes? But in my head? It is a river of beautiful speech. Like in Arabic. Arabic is. . . . It is the way into my heart. But everywhere, when I open ears, first thing, everywhere now, is English. You not get away from it. Even back home, before I come, I hear it more and more in people who do not speak it. I say, I must learn language that is everywhere. Language that has fallen on our heads and made us like—like children again. What is this power? What if I know it? I say to them, send me there so I learn this. I want to learn. And in

my heart, I say I want to write. I want to write a book. In English. That is goal, yes? And one day, I say . . .

(While accent is maintained, the broken English gradually starts dropping.)
    I might even teach it. . . . I will teach language back. I will make them speak their own language differently. I will have them speak words they never spoke before. I will make them like children, too, speaking words over and over to make sure they understand it. And soon my language will also fall on their heads. Like theirs falls on ours. Exploding in our brains till we can't even dream in peace.

(Slight beat.)
    And so they sent me. . . . They send me.

(ASFOOR draws closer to KHALED. KHALED does not look at him.)
    And now . . . my tongue . . . it wants to rise. Soar. As it used to. It wants to take off in this new language and conjure up brilliant words. It wants to do things in English that seemed so impossible for so long. I can help you find your voice, too. . . . You're stuck. I know you are. You've lost your way. I can feel it. I can help. Most of all . . . above all else, Khaled . . . I know how to inspire. . . . I know how to inspire.

(Beat. Blackout.)

Caution

Inc. and paying the requisite fee. Inquiries concerning all other rights should be addressed to Abrams Artists Agency, 275 Seventh Avenue, Twenty-sixth Floor, New York, New York 10001, Attn: Morgan Jenness.

Special Note

Anyone receiving permission to produce *Back of the Throat* is required to give credit to the author as sole and exclusive author of the play on the title page of all programs distributed in connection with performances of the play and in all instances in which the title of the play appears for purposes of advertising, publicizing, or otherwise exploiting the play and/or a production thereof. The name of the author must appear on a separate line, in which no other name appears, immediately beneath the title and in size of type equal to 50 percent of the size of the largest, most prominent letter used for the title of the play. No person, firm, or entity may receive credit larger or more prominent than that accorded the author. The following acknowledgments must appear on the title page in all programs distributed in connection with performances of the play:

For my mother

Author's Notes

A few suggestions: Try to make sure the actor playing Khaled keeps it light and welcoming for as long as he can. Refrain from playing Khaled too indignant or fearful for at least a quarter of the play up until he first opens the door and asks them to leave. And even then, he's still trying to be civil. As are the agents. The longer we can keep it civil, the better, the more the humor, grounded, will come out, and prepare the audience for when the tension increases. Yes, Khaled is anxious, but I think the character is working to overcome that. I've noticed that if the audience sees Khaled as being under the gun too soon, sees that he's fearful, they will become fearful and anxious on his behalf, and the humor will be squashed.

For the same reason, the agents need to be genuinely civil, and real, and not come off as caricatures. That is, we can't give the audience an out, a way to dismiss the agents as not real. It also helps if the actor playing Carl has a sense of comic timing. (Actually, that applies to all the actors, except perhaps for Asfoor.)

Sound: For the very same reason, keep the preshow music and/or sound effects "light" in the sense of avoiding creating discomfort/tension in the audience as the lights go down. This is by way of suggesting that a play as tone sensitive as this is going to be spun one way or another by something as mundane as preshow music/sounds. The entrance of Asfoor should be accompanied by some sort of sound effect. Past productions have used the sound of an airplane flying by. Also, the tail end of Asfoor's last speech, at the end of the play—or right after he finishes—has often been underscored by music or sounds. This is optional but can be effective. It could also just be an ominous rumbling sound that comes in.

Pacing: Keep the play moving. Especially as we enter the second half of the play, with the entrance of Asfoor and Shelly and the others. Stitch these two halves together by maintaining the energy and drive of the first half when we only have Carl, Bartlett, and Khaled onstage.

Handling the violence: It is a shift in the play, and the more you can smooth that transition, the better. Be careful not to go over the top and badger the audience too much. It's a little bit like shouting onstage. Too much of it can be off-putting. . . . And when Carl does his number on Khaled, it is important that the actor playing Khaled modulate his pained reactions. Yes, be real, but don't go over the top in terms of conveying the physical pain of Khaled; otherwise, again, it will push the audience away.

Finally, in a couple of productions, I found myself acting as Khaled's lawyer, defending his innocence. It's important for the actor playing Khaled to move forward with a sense of his character's innocence. Having said that, the ending is intentionally ambiguous. Perhaps this encounter actually took place (in which case the agents have good cause to feel Khaled is a "person of interest," if not more.) Or, it is a mental/emotional projection of Khaled's. Either way, the idea with the ending is to say that innocent or guilty, Khaled will forever be associated with Asfoor and the attacks and that nothing he can do or say will ever clear him.

For its premier, *Back of the Throat* was coproduced by Thick Description (Tony Kelly, artistic director) and Golden Thread Productions (Torange Yeghiazarian, artistic director) in San Francisco, California, opening on April 18, 2005. It was directed by Kelly; the set design was by James Faerron; the costume design was by Isabella Ortega; and the lighting design was by Rick Martin. The cast was as follows:

KHALED	James Asher
BARTLETT	James Reese
CARL	Paul Santiago
SHELLY/BETH/JEAN	Chloe Bronzan
ASFOOR	Brian Rivera

Back of the Throat was produced at Theater Schmeater (Rob West, artistic director) in Seattle, Oregon, opening on May 19, 2005. It was directed by Mark Jared Zufelt; the set design was by Corey Ericksen; the lighting design was by Lynne Ellis; the costume design was by Colleen Gillon; and the sound design was by Maurice "Mo" Smith. The cast was as follows:

KHALED	Alex Samuels
BARTLETT	Chris Mayse
CARL	Erik Hill
SHELLY/BETH/JEAN	Kate Czajkowski
ASFOOR	Johnny Patchamatla

Back of the Throat was produced at Manbites Dog Theater (Jeffrey Storer, artistic director) in Durham, North Carolina, opening on November 3, 2005. It was directed by Jay O'Berski; the set design was by David Fellerath and John Galt; and the lighting design was by Lionel Mouse. The cast was as follows:

KHALED	Bart Matthews
BARTLETT	David Berberian
CARL	Jeffrey Scott Detwiler
SHELLY/BETH/JEAN	Dana Marks
ASFOOR	Ken Wolpert

Back of the Throat was produced at Cyrano Theater Company (Sandy Harper, artistic director) in Anchorage, Alaska, opening on January 6, 2006. It was directed by Dick

Reichman; the set design was by Doug Frank; the costume design was by Kris Root and Company; the lighting design was by Root; and the sound design was by Erick Hayden. The cast was as follows:

KHALED	Brandon Lawrence
BARTLETT	Dean Williams
CARL	Mark Stoneburner
SHELLY/BETH/JEAN	Veronica Page
ASFOOR	Bowen Gillings

Back of the Throat was produced at The Flea Theater (Jim Simpson, artistic director; Carol Ostrow, producing director) in New York City, opening on February 2, 2006. It was directed by Simpson; the set design was by Michael Goldsheft; the costume design was by Erin Elizabeth Murphy; and the lighting design was by Benjamin C. Tevelow. The cast was as follows:

KHALED	Adeel Akhtar
BARLETT	Jason Guy
CARL	Jamie Effros
SHELLY/BETH/JEAN	Erin Roth
ASFOOR	Bandar Albuliwi

Back of the Throat was produced at Silk Road Theatre Project (Jamil Khoury, artistic director; Malik Gillani, executive director) in Chicago, Illinois, opening on April 4, 2006. It was directed by Stuart Carden; the set design was by Lee Keenan; the costume design was by Janice Pytel; the lighting design was by Kurt Ottinger; and the original music and sound design were by Robert Steele. The cast was as follows:

KHALED	Kareem Bandealy
BARTLETT	Sean Sinitski
CARL	Tom Hickey
SHELLY/BETH/JEAN	Elaine Robinson
ASFOOR	Madrid St. Angelo

Back of the Throat was produced at Furious Theatre Company (Brad Price, Sara Hennessy, Eric Pargac, Vonessa Martin, Shawn Lee, and Damaso Rodriguez, artistic directors) in Pasadena, California, opening on June 24, 2006. It was directed by Rodriguez; the set design was by Lee; the costume design was by Rachel Canning; the lighting design was by Dan Jenkins; and the sound design was by Cricket Strother Myers. The cast was as follows:

KHALED	Ammar Mahmood
BARTLETT	Anthony Di Novi
CARL	Doug Newell
SHELLY/BETH/JEAN	Vonessa Martin
ASFOOR	Aly Mawji

THREE NIGHTS IN PRAGUE

Allan Havis

Production Notes

THREE NIGHTS IN PRAGUE had performance readings in September 2003 at New York's Rattlestick Theatre (Artistic Director David Van Asselt, Director Suzanne Agins; featuring Daoud Heidami); February 2004, Duke University (Director Jody McAuliffe); July 2005, New York's Labyrinth Theatre (Director John Gould Rubin, co–artistic director of Labyrinth); and May 2007, University of California, San Diego's Center for the Humanities (Director Cynthia Stokes; featuring Peter Wylie).

CHARACTERS

ATTA, Egyptian Al Qaeda member, age thirty-seven, ringleader of the 9/11 Trade Towers terrorist flight

PAVEL, Czech citizen, age forty-five to fifty, hired by Al-Ani for odd jobs and favors

AL-ANI, Iraqi consulate official, age fifty-three, under suspicion for spying by the Czech government

DOLNI, Czech youth, age seventeen, who sells drugs, does sexual favors, and steals

(The play takes place within the city of Prague, and the time is April 2001. Scenes are not in proper chronology. The prologue is also optional and can be omitted for production.)

Prologue—Atta's Will

This is what I want to happen after my death.

(Pause.)

> I am Mohamed, the son of Mohamed El Amir Awad El Sayed. I believe that the prophet Mohamed is God's messenger and God will resurrect those in their graves. I want my family and everyone who reads this will to fear Almighty God and don't fall to deception and to follow God and his prophets. I don't want any women to go to my grave at

all during my funeral. In my memory, I want all people to do what the prophet Ibrahim told his son to do, to die as a good Muslim.

Scene 1

(The second night. Atta's hotel room. ATTA, *just out of the shower, is in a bathrobe. There is a knock at his door. He goes over.)*
ATTA: Who is it?
DOLNI: Dolni.

(Pause.)

        A friend of Pavel's. Not really a friend, but I work for him.
ATTA: What do you want?
DOLNI: You asked for a woman.
ATTA: I changed my mind.
DOLNI: That's not right.
ATTA: Go!
DOLNI: Don't be an asshole. Open the door. Fuck! You asked Pavel, and he sent me. The whole night is wasted now.

(Pause.)

        Hey! Come on!
ATTA: *(Opens door slowly.)* Are you alone?
DOLNI: Yes!
ATTA: Keep your voice down.
DOLNI: Okay.
ATTA: I need some cigarettes.
DOLNI: I don't smoke when I work.
ATTA: Go out and buy me a pack.
DOLNI: It's raining out.
ATTA: So?
DOLNI: It's raining out!
ATTA: Rain is a beautiful thing.
DOLNI: I don't want to get wet!
ATTA: Put a bag over your head.
DOLNI: It's going to rain all night.
ATTA: How old are you?
DOLNI: Seventeen.
ATTA: Fourteen?
DOLNI: Does it matter?
ATTA: I don't know. I'm not used to doing this.

(DOLNI *enters.*)

DOLNI: You have money?

ATTA: Of course I have money. Sit down.

DOLNI: (DOLNI *sits on a chair by the bed.*) You look angry.

ATTA: Call me, Mr. Atta.

DOLNI: Mr. Atta.

ATTA: I saw the man who came with you downstairs.

DOLNI: So?

ATTA: You said you were alone.

DOLNI: Now I am.

ATTA: I'll kill your friend if he comes to the door.

DOLNI: Pavel's not my friend. So kill him.

ATTA: Take off your jacket.

DOLNI: Do you have money?

ATTA: Yes.

DOLNI: Show me. And your passport. Put it on the table.

(ATTA *slowly takes out cash.* DOLNI *removes his jacket.*)

ATTA: You don't get to see my passport. I am sorry to be so rude.

DOLNI: No, you're not.

ATTA: I need to frisk you for weapons.

(DOLNI *submits with a degree of flirtation.* ATTA *is quick and thorough.*)

DOLNI: That man won't bother us tonight if I come down in an hour. He's
　　　　my father.

ATTA: What?

DOLNI: Pavel's my stepfather. Same thing. His business failed.

ATTA: You are a liar.

DOLNI: Yes, I am a fucking liar, but this happens to be true. He had a video
　　　　shop. Why would I lie? His customers never returned the inventory.
　　　　Never rewound the tapes. He caught me having sex with a very big boy
　　　　in the back room, too. And I told him, "Papa, stock up on DVDs now."
　　　　Here's a picture of him.

ATTA: That boy is not less than thirty years old.

DOLNI: He dyes his hair blond and works out at the gymnasium. A vain boy
　　　　is a vain boy. Are you vain?

ATTA: No.

DOLNI: I sense that you are. A little, yes? You are a boy as much as you are
　　　　a man.

(Pause.)

Do you want drugs before or after sex? Do you want sex before or after drugs?

ATTA: No drugs.

DOLNI: You seem like a guy who likes hashish.

ATTA: No hashish.

DOLNI: When I can't sleep, I smoke a small pipe. I cough. What strange dreams. Dreams that free me from boredom. I leave my human form and become a wild bird with excellent eyesight. I love having good eyes. I get very hungry when I smoke. Peanut butter is delicious. Chocolate cookies, too. Do you like peanut butter? Do you like poppers? Pavel says you are here on a special mission.

ATTA: I am a merchant, yes.

DOLNI: *(Shaking out a marijuana joint.)* Can I smoke a Mary Jane?

ATTA: What?

DOLNI: Grass. Weed. Marijuana.

ATTA: No.

DOLNI: Please. Just one cig.

(Pause.)

Are you in a hurry? I can cancel the other men tonight.

(Silence.)

Do I talk too much?

ATTA: Yes.

DOLNI: I'll shut up.

(Pause.)

I can spend the entire night. I just have to tell him downstairs.

ATTA: You call this freedom?

DOLNI: I call this business.

ATTA: Where is your sense of pleasure?

DOLNI: I know. Pleasure is more important than business. That's why I need to get high.

(Pause.)

Tell me one secret.

ATTA: I haven't had pleasure in a long time.

DOLNI: We all *crave* a little pleasure. I want to go to Egypt and see *your* pyramids. How *big* they are. And wide-open desert.

ATTA: Like any other desert.
DOLNI: Why don't we sit together on the bed?

(Crosses to the bed.)
>You can take off your bathrobe.
ATTA: Why?
DOLNI: I want to see your chest.
ATTA: *(Reluctant to disrobe.)* I studied to be an architect and an engineer. That means something to me.

(Pause.)
>I'm going to keep my robe on. Maybe you should leave now.
DOLNI: You are hard. I can see that. You are getting very hard under the robe. I can see the jewelry you wear hidden inside. I can see what you had for breakfast today.
ATTA: What did I have for breakfast?
DOLNI: Coffee and dry toast.
ATTA: That's correct.
DOLNI: I can see who you want to fight.
ATTA: And who is that?
DOLNI: Rich Americans.
ATTA: Pavel told you.
DOLNI: He told me the Jews. Isn't it always the Jews?
ATTA: Yes.
DOLNI: Jews don't bother me. And I don't bother them. Why not just fuck the Jews?
ATTA: Let's not talk about Jews tonight.
DOLNI: All right. Who do you want to fuck? *(Silence.)* Are you planning to have children?
ATTA: No. And you?
DOLNI: I don't know.
ATTA: You have thought about it.
DOLNI: All the time.
ATTA: Then it is about finding the right husband.
DOLNI: That's easy for you to say. Men have it easier. I can't have children.
ATTA: Why?
DOLNI: My tubes are scarred.
ATTA: Are you certain?
DOLNI: Two doctors have told me this. There's nothing I can do.
ATTA: I am sorry for you.

DOLNI: Don't be. I would be a monster of a mother. Little brats bring out the worst in me.

ATTA: There are worse things to worry about.

DOLNI: Children make a selfish person evil.

ATTA: It is not in the Koran.

DOLNI: Are you in the Koran?

ATTA: We are all in the Koran.

DOLNI: You should have a son.

ATTA: What?

DOLNI: He would serve you with affection and finish the work you started. It is in your imagination, Mr. Atta. You should have a daughter. She would finish your noble work. Excuse me, please. Was that the wrong word? What is the opposite of noble?

ATTA: Ignoble.

DOLNI: You are gifted in language.

(Pause.)

When I touch you, think of me as your son and as your daughter. If you're mad at one, love the other. I have an addiction, and I am fighting my addiction. You will not catch my addiction. I tell you this because I took a liking to you. Please do me this one favor.

ATTA: What favor?

DOLNI: Think of me as a clean soul.

ATTA: I will do my best to think of you as a clean soul.

DOLNI: *(In innocence.)* Thank you.

Scene 2

(The first night. Evening. April 2001. Airport lounge.)

ATTA: Airports have no sense of architecture. Any idiot knows this. People walk fast and look tortured. People in airports are uncomfortable. All negative public space. The acoustics are miserable. Can you hear the echo? And the lighting can make you blind.

PAVEL: You meet Al-Ani tomorrow.

ATTA: Not today?

PAVEL: The deputy consulate officer. He won't call my cell phone at this hour. He's very strict with his time. You will like him.

ATTA: I know you.

PAVEL: *(Submissive but ironic.)* Do you?

ATTA: I use instinct.

(Grabs PAVEL's *hand and person.)*

    Here. Dirty fingernails. Stains on your collar. Wax in your ear.

PAVEL: Yes, three days a week I am a laborer in the mills. But I had a year of night school.

ATTA: A laborer?

PAVEL: Hard work.

ATTA: The less you tell me, the better.

PAVEL: I'm tired most of the time. A family tradition.

ATTA: Laziness kills the soul.

PAVEL: Does it?

ATTA: Drink. Then we'll talk.

PAVEL: Don't you want to leave the airport now?

ATTA: Not yet.

PAVEL: But I was told to . . .

ATTA: *(His finger to his lips.)* Shhhhhhhhh . . .

PAVEL: The police scare you?

ATTA: Why do you ask that? I respect the police.

PAVEL: Bribes don't work like they used to.

ATTA: A bribe insults Allah.

(Pause.)

    I'll tell you when we must leave the terminal.

PAVEL: My car is in short-term parking. Very expensive.

ATTA: I'll pay for parking.

PAVEL: Actually the car is blocking a service truck. They could tow me.

ATTA: You saved Al-Ani's life?

PAVEL: Who told you?

ATTA: My friend.

PAVEL: It embarrasses me.

(Pause.)

    He was leaving a restaurant late at night, and a thief came up behind him.

ATTA: You chased the attacker away.

PAVEL: I was probably crazy drunk.

ATTA: He trusts you. Al-Ani.

PAVEL: Yes.

ATTA: *(After a silence.)* How is the airport security?

PAVEL: Okay.

ATTA: Do you know what I'm asking?

PAVEL: I do.

ATTA: Talk to me.

PAVEL: My cousins work at this airport. Security is what you see.

(Pause.)

>   For smugglers, the airport has obvious holes. Things can be irregular. But we're not as bad as Athens or Rome. Closed circuit monitors. German shepherds. Plainclothesmen all around. Cargo flights have bigger problems, and many Turks serve as ground crew.

ATTA: And for those travelers who look Middle Eastern?

PAVEL: Iraq enjoys special circumstances in Prague. Oil benefits everyone here. And Prague is Europe's emporium for black-market gun sales.

ATTA: You know a lot of shit.

PAVEL: One day the world will run out of oil. And then what? Who's fucking who?

(Pause.)

>   I wasn't supposed to meet you.

ATTA: Al-Ani didn't dispatch you?

PAVEL: This was a favor for someone else. A dear friend, actually. Dr. Franz Klinger. He has only one eye, and it's color-blind. He lost his medical license. Klinger's a loan shark who gives each client a free pocket calculator. The doctor has a hernia and cannot get out of bed.

ATTA: This is not Turkish coffee.

PAVEL: Armenian coffee. More aromatic on the tongue. You grew up with this coffee.

ATTA: No.

PAVEL: What are you then, Mr. Atta?

ATTA: Egyptian.

PAVEL: Of course. You look like a great pharaoh with short legs. People must tell you that all the time. Now I have offended you. Forgive me.

(Pause.)

>   I can't make coffee like my wife. She brews coffee like she's in the climax of sex. You see, she stirs and stirs the grounds vigorously and
>   . . .

(He sees that ATTA is turned off by this.)

>   What city in Egypt?

ATTA: Cairo.

PAVEL: Cairo, yes. A city of certain forbidden beauty. A fantastic city in celebration of itself. Car headlights never on at night. Streets teeming with disfigured vendors. A city of eternal tragedy. There was a travel video in our public library. *Alive in Cairo!* And I was.

(Pause.)

Here, I buy cigarettes, the package is already open.

ATTA: Always count what's missing. Your friends, your blessings, your money.

PAVEL: My mother said the very same thing. Friends are blessings. She died before Havel won election. In her memory, I quit smoking. Coughed up blood for months. God gives you one warning.

ATTA: *(Distracted.)* One warning is enough.

PAVEL: Blood in the toilet. A clear sign from God. It's late.

ATTA: Nine o'clock.

PAVEL: I quit smoking. My only vice is shoplifting tomatoes at the market.

ATTA: In some countries, you could lose a hand for that.

PAVEL: Iran?

(PAVEL smiles perversely.)

ATTA: Your eyeglasses are broken.

PAVEL: I put a pin to hold the stem. Saved a day's pay.

ATTA: Take off your glasses.

PAVEL: Do you think it has a radio transmitter?

ATTA: No.

PAVEL: My wife is pregnant.

ATTA: Congratulations.

PAVEL: Second time, and I'm scared to death. I have no idea how this happened.

(Pause.)

We have a strange teenage boy who has a cocaine habit.

ATTA: I'm not interested in your family.

PAVEL: It's just small talk.

ATTA: Punish him.

PAVEL: Easy to say, hard to do.

(Pause.)

My wife's a Kurd. From Turkey. Talks too much but a very good cook.

ATTA: Lucky man.

PAVEL: When I get drunk, I feel lucky. My wife does not like when I drink. And that's the only way I can get her to stop talking.

(Pause.)
        You hear the barking dogs?
ATTA: No.
PAVEL: In the distance. The moon's full.
ATTA: And my patience is on the wane.
PAVEL: This city has very intelligent dogs, Mr. Atta.
ATTA: Oh?
PAVEL: Yes, they piss in front of our best stores and shit below the black gargoyles at the police headquarters.
ATTA: All living things shit, my friend.
PAVEL: Dogs don't pay taxes. I envy them. I pay too many taxes, and there's absolutely nothing to eat. I want to bark at the moon. What would you do?
ATTA: I would not bark.
PAVEL: I knew a rich woman who never could shit.

(PAVEL suppresses a laugh.)
        In Prague, rich women fight nature. It is their dream never to shit for the rest of their lives. And there is some rationale for this.

(Pause.)
        Yet I can't visit the toilet enough.

(Pause.)
        You're very serious, sir.
ATTA: I am.
PAVEL: I always make people smile, laugh. But not you.
ATTA: Not me.
PAVEL: Don't you like being here?
ATTA: I don't. Shadows don't grace Prague.
PAVEL: Prague is more a state of mind than a city.
ATTA: Oh?
PAVEL: Intellectuals say that, yes. All the time at the best pubs. "State of mind. It's a state of mind. A great state of mind." And what is your state?
ATTA: I don't like to travel.
PAVEL: Neither did Stendal.
ATTA: Stendal?

PAVEL: The novelist. He pissed in his pants in Italy. I'm well read. Was trained as an architect's draftsman, and I was a good one, too. But I can't compete with the computers they now have.

ATTA: And I was trained as an architectural engineer.

PAVEL: Really?

ATTA: I'm very good.

PAVEL: Do you think there is meaning to coincidences?

ATTA: No.

PAVEL: I do. I write them down. People don't realize the signature of their fate.

ATTA: People are extensions of architecture.

PAVEL: Yes, of course.

ATTA: They have no true fate. They just take up space.

PAVEL: You don't like people.

ATTA: I don't like crowds. I don't like people when they lie. I hate liars.

PAVEL: Of course.

ATTA: When I travel, I can sense the truth, no matter how clever the lie.

PAVEL: A clever lie is the foundation of modern philosophy.

ATTA: Yes.

PAVEL: So I ask myself: Does man shape philosophy? Or does philosophy shape the man?

ATTA: Are you are liar?

PAVEL: No.

ATTA: Are you really married?

PAVEL: My wife says we eloped, but I don't remember.

ATTA: Are you joking?

PAVEL: I'm not joking.

ATTA: Then get rid of her. She's a cunt. This woman lies to you. She is your burden.

PAVEL: I wear an expensive wedding ring.

ATTA: Sell the shitty ring.

PAVEL: But how? I love her still.

ATTA: You put on your shoes and hat, then go through the fucking door.

PAVEL: Obviously, you were never married. Well, you are still a young man. Anything can happen.

ATTA: I want a woman tonight.

PAVEL: A woman? For pleasure or for business?

(ATTA *smiles sweetly.*)

   Money buys pleasure and business, Mr. Atta.

ATTA: I want a young virgin.

THREE NIGHTS IN PRAGUE

PAVEL: A virgin? How beautiful!

ATTA: Smooth and sweet between her legs. I don't care what she shaves.

PAVEL: Smooth and sweet between her legs. I am only the chauffeur.

ATTA: Listen, Pavel.

(Pause.)

Dark eyes. Long legs. Hairless body. No disease. Clean. Very clean. Silent.

PAVEL: You are describing an angel from an old Italian canvas.

ATTA: I shall have a woman tonight. I am allowed to have one.

PAVEL: Okay.

(Pause.)

You want hashish, Mr. Atta?

ATTA: No.

PAVEL: Two little smokes last the whole night. Happy hour.

ATTA: No hashish. No drugs.

(Pause.)

What is your last name?

PAVEL: Frisch.

ATTA: Born in Prague?

PAVEL: I've never moved away. Can't understand why Martina Navratilova left.

ATTA: Frisch? German name. I know many standard German names.

PAVEL: I have Swiss and German blood.

ATTA: *(Pause.)* Will this be a good hotel, Pavel?

PAVEL: I think so.

ATTA: But not a very good one?

PAVEL: We pay twice for what we really need.

ATTA: There's nothing wrong with luxury.

PAVEL: Yes.

ATTA: Don't you like luxury?

PAVEL: If it's affordable.

ATTA: Are there whores in the lobby?

PAVEL: There are many guests who dress like whores.

ATTA: How does your wife dress?

PAVEL: Like a sweet Polish nun.

ATTA: *(Laughs tightly.)* And how am I dressed?

PAVEL: Very well, sir.

197

ATTA: Thank you.

PAVEL: Smart jacket. Good shoulders. V cut.

ATTA: I like the V cut. That's why I exercise each day.

PAVEL: An obese man cannot wear a V cut. Except Pavarotti, and he cheats with a scarf.

ATTA: So you find me someone for tonight.

PAVEL: I'll try.

ATTA: You will try hard.

PAVEL: I will try hard.

ATTA: I'm tired. Long flight.

(Pause.)

What exactly is Al-Ani's rank at the embassy?

PAVEL: Very high. Number two in command.

ATTA: Does Al-Ani pay you enough?

PAVEL: Yes.

ATTA: But you need more . . .

PAVEL: Well, who doesn't? I don't get tips, Mr. Atta, except from the charming rich Jews that own tourist agencies and clothing stores.

ATTA: Fuck the Jews.

PAVEL: Are these games, Mr. Atta?

(Pause.)

You terrorize people, don't you?

ATTA: No.

PAVEL: Do you hurt people?

ATTA: No. Look, Pavel . . . I'm a businessman. Import, export.

(Pause.)

Clean. Beautiful. As pure as snow.

(Pause.)

No more mistruths.

PAVEL: Beautiful and clean, yes. When she comes, you'll pay holiday rates.

ATTA: What is the holiday?

PAVEL: The economy is fucked here.

ATTA: Send the girl to my room. 10 P.M. Alone.

PAVEL: Alone? It's not safe.

ATTA: Why?

PAVEL: Violent crime.

ATTA: In the heart of the city?

PAVEL: Worse than ever.

ATTA: Okay, you escort her to my door, and I'll pay you for your efforts.

PAVEL: Thank you.

(Pause.)

>You will fly back to Germany?

ATTA: Yes.

PAVEL: You like to fly?

ATTA: Not much.

PAVEL: I hate planes. The food is miserable, lice in the seats, and someone always steals your luggage. Do you tip the pilot? Will he get insulted?

(Pause.)

>I tell you, I don't leave Prague.

ATTA: They pay you directly at the embassy?

PAVEL: Most times, yes. Never with checks.

ATTA: In dollars or korunas?

PAVEL: Yes, in korunas and sometimes in British sterling.

ATTA: Where do you exchange money?

PAVEL: Banks, unless . . . well, at your hotel, the concierge's desk. That's why we picked this hotel.

ATTA: Please take off your glasses.

PAVEL: Why?

ATTA: I want to see your face clearly. Maybe you work for the Czech police?

PAVEL: The Czech police? They would never hire me. I married a dark foreigner, and I work for the Iraqis.

(Removes eye glasses.)

>I know I'm a miserable European. Always in debt.

ATTA: Tell me something about the embassy.

PAVEL: It's newly painted. The aged chief cook is going senile. They love hand-dripped candles and velvet ropes. The royal state piano is a recent gift from the Saudis.

ATTA: And Al-Ani?

PAVEL: He replaced Jabir Salim.

ATTA: Why?

PAVEL: Scandal.

(Pause.)

      Al-Ani's more prudent and influential. Aromatic Cuban cigars. Rare caviar. Opera tickets in the best boxes.

ATTA: I hate the opera.

PAVEL: You have to be very cultivated and homosexual to truly enjoy the opera. Jabir Salim could not hide his sexual nature. There are some homosexuals who look into the mirror and see Mother Nature posing as something quite different. *(Pause.)* And that's high culture.

(Pause.)

      Al-Ani doesn't like boys, but he does like mirrors.

ATTA: I see.

PAVEL: Al-Ani won't tell you anything personal. His predecessor was altogether different. Salim lusted after young boys without facial hair. Black and white boys. Good and bad boys. Experienced boys. Boys with cock rings and piercings. I've been told that even Saddam likes boys—to supplement all his beautiful wives and mistresses. I've learned this at the consul. Yes, Iraqis can be decadent, Mr. Atta. Not like dignified Egyptians. Not like you.

(Pause.)

      And Al-Ani isn't religious.

ATTA: Are you?

PAVEL: I know God created me. And He did his work imperfectly.

Scene 3

(Later that evening. Prague café, outdoor seating.)

ATTA: No. I wanted to walk.

AL-ANI: Much too far.

ATTA: The driver . . .

AL-ANI: Pavel.

ATTA: Yes, Pavel. He talks too much. Over the phone you said he was reliable.

AL-ANI: Pavel is, 'though he doesn't always stop at traffic lights.

ATTA: Odd habit.

AL-ANI: Does he annoy you?

ATTA: Yes, but he's amusing.

AL-ANI: And quite bright. For some curious reason, the police tend not to notice him.

ATTA: Perhaps he works for them?

AL-ANI: I doubt it. He has an arrest record.

ATTA: What were the charges?

AL-ANI: Tax evasion. Petty stuff, really.

(Pause.)

> Your overcoat is rumpled.

ATTA: I do not travel well.

AL-ANI: Insomnia?

ATTA: Yes.

AL-ANI: Warm milk at night. Quiet classical music. Flannel pajamas.

(Pause.)

> Without rest you will make mistakes.

ATTA: I don't make mistakes.

AL-ANI: Without sleep you'll become clumsy.

ATTA: What is your rank at the embassy?

AL-ANI: *(Laughing.)* Senior custodian.

ATTA: Are you not a chief officer and second in command?

AL-ANI: At the reception desk, you can see my name on the board. Second consul member.

(Pause.)

> You know, Atta . . . you resemble Kafka. How uncanny. Bullet black eyes, taut skin, tight thin lips, and cold grey complexion. A death mask looking for a proper grave. I don't mean to insult you. Franz Kafka. You know the name?

ATTA: No.

AL-ANI: A psychotic Jew from Prague with great literary pedigree.

ATTA: Don't patronize me. You made some intentions very clear to me in an e-mail. Why this lack of cooperation now?

AL-ANI: You are mistaking my good will.

ATTA: I have printed your letters. Do you think I'm gullible?

AL-ANI: How can I answer that?

ATTA: Things you had said over the phone.

AL-ANI: You and I never spoke over the phone.

ATTA: Who did I speak with? Your tailor?

AL-ANI: I've a staff of five.

ATTA: I did not come for idiotic conversation, Al-Ani.

AL-ANI: Why did you come?

ATTA: To exchange favors.

AL-ANI: Favors?

ATTA: I don't know how else to say it. My colleagues and I need your help.

AL-ANI: You are here to ask for my personal favor?

ATTA: You represent a powerful Arab nation.

AL-ANI: You say that to my face, but what do you say in private?

ATTA: If Saddam can fund $25,000 to each Palestinian family who offers a suicide bomber, then it is equally reasonable for Iraq to bond with us.

AL-ANI: Unfortunately my president does not see it like that.

ATTA: Why?

AL-ANI: When Arafat dies, power will go to a man in a three-piece suit.

ATTA: Maybe. Who cares?

AL-ANI: I do.

ATTA: The Jews will all one day die from the plague.

AL-ANI: Does your Imam teach you that?

ATTA: Yes.

AL-ANI: Even with a more radicalized Palestine, there would be some turmoil for many Arab nations.

ATTA: I understand.

AL-ANI: Bin Laden is a different problem altogether.

ATTA: Not really.

AL-ANI: Bin Laden is stateless and lawless and friendless. Your organization wins little sympathy.

ATTA: That will change after we turn the industrial world upside down. That is our talent.

AL-ANI: Yes, and better to trace dirty work back to an Afghan cave than to our Presidential Palace. Better for Iraq. So what exactly are you thinking?

(Silence.)

World War I began within four hundred miles of where we sit.

ATTA: Then World War III will be conceived in Prague.

AL-ANI: *(Cordially.)* You are either naïve or very insane. We have no uranium in my consulate.

ATTA: You have my references within the House of Saudi.

AL-ANI: Unconfirmed names on a paper.

ATTA: Call them.

AL-ANI: I am not making long-distance calls on your behalf.

ATTA: Use my cell phone.

AL-ANI: You give me orders?

ATTA: No.

AL-ANI: I hear your tone very clearly.

ATTA: You can give the orders. You have a rich country.

AL-ANI: And you have cheap invisibility.

ATTA: We are not afraid to die.

AL-ANI: Everyone should fear death, my son.

(Pause.)

I wish I knew you better.

ATTA: You could know me for twenty years and . . .

AL-ANI: And what?

ATTA: Know me like a stranger. I have no personality, Al-Ani. You can give the orders.

AL-ANI: I only have one imperative, Atta.

ATTA: I realize.

AL-ANI: My government wants to know what your people are planning. Nothing can be traced to Baghdad.

ATTA: Nothing comes from nothing.

AL-ANI: I can only help you if you disclose everything.

ATTA: Tell your government that we plan to kill an entire city of infidels.

AL-ANI: Well, then, I can only grant you a visa and a handshake.

(Pause.)

Why are you frowning?

ATTA: We can win the war. Join us.

AL-ANI: You need a hobby, Atta. Fishing or stamp collecting.

(AL-ANI *offers cigarette and lights his own.)*

Drinking is a wonderful hobby.

ATTA: *(Accepting the cigarette, he lights his own.)* Your chauffeur says the mongrel Jews in Prague are in ascendancy.

AL-ANI: The Jews have successful businesses, yes. I am tolerant of Jews. I have a Jewish doctor, and I must say that he is brilliant.

ATTA: You let him put his filthy Jewish hands on your body?

AL-ANI: I do, and I am in good hands. One day you might demand a Jewish doctor.

(Pause.)

We have to find how to trust each other, Atta.

ATTA: If you trust the Saudi contact, then you can trust me.

AL-ANI: Do you trust yourself, Atta?

ATTA: I trust Allah first.

AL-ANI: Allah appreciates your "modesty."

ATTA: Your man seems to know a lot about my affairs. I think that's dangerous.

AL-ANI: Nonsense. I live in this city. I know what's dangerous.

ATTA: Do you really?

AL-ANI: I told you before, Pavel's harmless. You need money, Atta, and classified intelligence. How long can you rely on Al Qaeda?

ATTA: We're lucky.

AL-ANI: I don't think you are.

ATTA: We've survived the last five years, and we'll survive the next five.

AL-ANI: Most of your men are ignorant Saudis, taking orders from an arrogant Egyptian. I think that is very unsafe.

ATTA: We came together as brothers.

AL-ANI: Let me be candid with you. I laugh at religious zealots.

ATTA: Why?

AL-ANI: They have no sense of irony.

ATTA: My men and I are not simple zealots.

AL-ANI: But have you a concept of irony? *(Pause.)* Atta, do you have a concept of irony? What are you?

ATTA: Devout men of Islam.

AL-ANI: Then I salute you. An enlightened culture needs humor.

(AL-ANI *shows the first sign of fatigue.*)
	You know I'm not well.

ATTA: May Allah watch over you.

AL-ANI: Even if Allah isn't, Czech authorities are.

ATTA: No stain here. I'm clean, legal. No guns, no weapons.

AL-ANI: Why not go back to engineering, Atta?

ATTA: I'm in Prague for one more night.

AL-ANI: You look lonely.

ATTA: I have books with me.

AL-ANI: A hermit occupies a hovel and soon hates the hovel.

ATTA: A hermit is not a martyr.

AL-ANI: A martyr is not a hermit.

(Pause.)
	The Muslim Brotherhood pulled you in.

ATTA: You're barking up the wrong tree.

AL-ANI: My embassy thinks you are not even Mohamed Atta.

ATTA: Who am I then?

AL-ANI: Israeli secret service? An Iranian operative?

ATTA: I am Atta. I am as much me as you are you. You invited me here.

AL-ANI: How was life in America?

ATTA: I had an apartment in Virginia.

AL-ANI: Near the CIA headquarters?

ATTA: No.

AL-ANI: Can you fly a Cessna?

ATTA: I can fly many planes. Allah guides the sincere pilot.

(They sit at the table. ATTA *looks off to the distance.)*
> Is that a man by the door . . .

AL-ANI: Yes. Look at my face. Smile. Everything is wonderful.

ATTA: *(Low voice.)* A Czech agent?

AL-ANI: Kapchek. Bright and intuitive. Deaf in one ear, but he reads lips and speaks seven languages. He masturbates in his Volkswagen and is two years away from his pension. Now smile, and give him only a tight profile.

(Pause.)
> Smile, Atta. Look social. Touch my shoulder gently.

ATTA: I understand you're leaving Prague soon.

AL-ANI: I want to retire, go back to Baghdad.

*(*AL-ANI *eyes the Czech agent leaving.)*
> He's going.

ATTA: *(Normal volume.)* We've been in training for over eighteen months. You will never see anything of this scale.

AL-ANI: I believe you.

ATTA: We will surpass Pearl Harbor. This I do swear.

AL-ANI: And this excites you?

ATTA: Yes.

(Pause.)
> You do not respect Bin Laden.

AL-ANI: No, I don't.

ATTA: He acts with intelligence.

AL-ANI: Does he? (Sardonic:) Bin Laden uses his personal wealth to purchase pawns.

(Pause.)
> You know how Saddam views him.

ATTA: Who is Saddam to judge?

AL-ANI: Saddam is a brilliant tactician. To him, Bin Laden is a hypocrite who speaks to the weak. Actually, he's a hypocrite who likes to fuck sheep.

ATTA: Bin Laden's inspiration keeps thousands of men together on five continents.

AL-ANI: I met him, Atta.

ATTA: *(Skeptical.)* Have you?

AL-ANI: 1994. In Saudi Arabia, at his father's offices.

(Pause.)

His handshake is effeminate, and he has the eyes of a jackal. Have you met him?

ATTA: Yes.

AL-ANI: Did you shake his hands? You have to touch the flesh.

ATTA: How much do British and American intelligence know about us?

AL-ANI: The German authorities know more than you would like, so it is wise to stay outside Hamburg. But no one is about to catch you in Prague. The government is afraid to hit first.

ATTA: Good. We want ten vials this month.

AL-ANI: Ten vials?

ATTA: OK, five vials. And I swear nothing will be traced back to your consulate.

AL-ANI: When you barter, you have to have the goods in hand or have collateral. You have neither.

ATTA: Baghdad knew about the VX project with Bin Laden. The Sudanese method of making VX was always of Iraqi provenance. I know a lot, Al-Ani. Have faith in this exchange.

AL-ANI: There is anxiety in your face.

ATTA: I am your mirror.

(Pause.)

If you cannot give us biological agents, then at least give us the equipment to neutralize transponders for commercial jets. We need to cloak everything in the sky for one hour.

AL-ANI: A month ago I would have been more sympathetic.

ATTA: What could possibly happen to you in one month's time?

AL-ANI: My health is worse. My thinking has changed. I hear God's voice. Iraq was a powerful nation ten years ago. And then the Gulf War changed the equation. Yes, we didn't need Kuwait. I am saddened by the international chorus against Saddam, but the Arab Street looks up to my President. Saddam is not irrational like Kaddafi. You must understand that.

ATTA: I do.

AL-ANI: Saddam has learned from his own errors and the errors of Egypt's Nasser. Saddam has mellowed.

(Pause.)

Transponders are easier to obtain than vials, and still I have strong reservations.

(Pause.)

I have to disappoint you, Atta.

ATTA: I won't allow you to.

AL-ANI: We had an interesting correspondence. But all things do end. Please, I want to be in position to advise you before you leave Prague.

ATTA: Two anthrax vials then and I'll make no trouble for you.

AL-ANI: Don't you understand what I'm saying?

(Pause.)

I'm turning my back on you. I'm going back to Baghdad. I have no choice. The Czech agents will catch me soon. The same Czech agents a dozen years ago who sold Iraq military arms. Take my advice, Atta.

(Pause.)

Al Qaeda hates all Arab governments, except the Taliban. That is why Saddam will never be an ally. You can terrorize America, and Saddam will smile. If you terrorize Saudi Arabia, then things become worrisome for Iraq. You know what I'm saying. Pick your fights carefully.

(Sensing difficulty with ATTA.*)*

I can give you classified intelligence reports. I can give you cash. I can provide you and your group with sensitive maps. But respect our limitations.

(Pause.)

I believe you are Mohamed Atta, and I believe that you have a mission.

ATTA: And I believe you are Al-Ani.

AL-ANI: Then stop talking like a fucking ghost.

ATTA: We want a pathogen. I don't give a damn if you're about to quit your office. I can hurt you with this news.

AL-ANI: And risk exposing yourself?

ATTA: Listen to me. We have four teams in place. They are willing to die. I will lead them. Five months from today. So this is it. A very fine grade of anthrax in aerosol. Iraq has received antiaircraft missiles and guidance systems from the Czechs. All with export licenses for Syria and Yemen. We can expose this and embarrass you.

(AL-ANI *smiles ruefully.*)

You must support Al Qaeda. The West cannot strike back at Al Qaeda. We are Iraq's best sword.

AL-ANI: If I do what you ask, I'll be hunted down.

ATTA: Al-Ani, we want the same thing.

AL-ANI: We define success differently, Atta. You will kill children, and I cannot.

ATTA: I do not kill children.

AL-ANI: You are like the Iranian mother who sends her dear children into minefields in search of bombs and Paradise. Al Qaeda should follow Allah's instructions. Address your faith, and cease the attack.

ATTA: We shall hit America like a glorious bolt from the sky.

AL-ANI: And you will die.

ATTA: Like a thunderbolt.

AL-ANI: Don't talk to me about Saladin and seventy-two exquisite virgins who await you in Heaven.

ATTA: You once hated the Jews, and you ridiculed America.

AL-ANI: I ridiculed the royal Saudi family. Yet, I work with them cordially.

(*Pause.*)

You found Saudi madmen who wait by the phone for your suicide call. Isn't that tragic, Atta? You do have a sense of the tragic?

(*Pause,*)

Such a stone face.

(AL-ANI *rises and crosses the room to* ATTA.)

Let me tell you about my infamous predecessor. Jabir Salim, forty-three years old. Family man and intelligence officer. Very religious. He defected to Britain. Risked his life and his family. In his debriefings by M16, he told the British that Baghdad gave him $150,000 to command a car bombing. . . . Salim told the British that Radio Free Liberty in Prague was the military object. This is the American facility that broadcasts into Iraq.

ATTA: And why did he defect?

AL-ANI: My predecessor compromised himself with a homosexual tryst. Terribly sad. Certainly this behavior is not endorsed in the Koran. And what did Salim learn out of this humiliation?

ATTA: *(Impatient.)* Only love Allah.

AL-ANI: The Czech authorities know I've made large wire transfers. They know when I go to the grocery store, when I go to the bank, and when I have a bowel movement. Salim has made it impossible for me here. I am useless. Prague waits for me to finish Salim's mission. The British leave me friendly notes. Baghdad is still furious with Salim. To all factions, I am no different than Salim except I don't share his rancid sexual vice.

(Pause.)

So I cannot help you, Atta, even if I had the means.

ATTA: I don't believe you.

AL-ANI: Believe what you wish.

(AL-ANI checks his watch.)

ATTA: You're a man who has never seen real combat.

AL-ANI: You are calling me a coward?

ATTA: Yes.

AL-ANI: Atta, I fought in the Iranian war. You know nothing about my life.

ATTA: If I could, I would go over your head, but Aziz won't meet with me.

(Pause.)

I'm staying one more night before I go back to the United States. At the Maximilian Hotel, near Old Town Square and Parizska Street. Call me after you talk things over with your supervisors. I will hurt you in some capacity. That I do promise as Allah is my holy witness. You have less than twenty-four hours. I will not back down, brother.

Scene 4

(The second night. Consulate office.)

AL-ANI: How is your wife?

PAVEL: Fine. She bought a hat that covers her bald spot. You know my cousin's exotic-hat shop downtown.

AL-ANI: Where I bought my hat?

PAVEL: Yes.

AL-ANI: My hat wasn't very exotic. How is your son?

PAVEL: Not bad.

AL-ANI: He still has a medical problem?

PAVEL: Yes.

AL-ANI: For over a year?

PAVEL: Yes. It seems to be getting worse.

AL-ANI: Then I should help you.

PAVEL: Why?

AL-ANI: What is the trouble with the boy?

PAVEL: His heart valve. He needs an operation before the end of the year.

AL-ANI: My god! Is this true?

(Pause.)

    If you love him dearly you should have told me sooner.

PAVEL: Everything about my teenage son is difficult. I have no control over him anymore. But you're right. I should have said something before.

AL-ANI: I'll speak to our consul's medical adviser.

PAVEL: Thank you, sir.

AL-ANI: How much will it cost?

PAVEL: I'm afraid to say.

AL-ANI: Pavel, please know I care. Whatever it is, Iraq will cover half of it.

PAVEL: That's absolutely wonderful, sir. But what of the other half?

AL-ANI: I know you are a good and loving father.

(Silence.)

    I will personally cover the rest.

PAVEL: Dear Jesus . . .

AL-ANI: Your wife tells me all the good things that you do for your family. How soon can your son have this operation?

PAVEL: I'll ask the hospital tomorrow.

AL-ANI: Good. Delays will make everything impossible.

PAVEL: Sir.

AL-ANI: Yes?

PAVEL: I wish I were a good man.

AL-ANI: You are.

PAVEL: I'm selfish, and I have failed as a father.

AL-ANI: You judge yourself too harshly.

PAVEL: If hell exists, I will be sent there with chauffeur's cap one day.

AL-ANI: And so will the best chefs in Prague. When we all get there, at least we'll eat well.

PAVEL: This Atta is a Arab—

AL-ANI: There is no target in Prague.

PAVEL: His visit means more risk for you.

AL-ANI: For me?

PAVEL: A Romanian vampire has softer eyes.

AL-ANI: *(Amused.)* A vampire?

PAVEL: He has fangs.

AL-ANI: The police will be following you.

PAVEL: That will not help much.

AL-ANI: When you're the chauffeur, you should always trust the police.

PAVEL: Perhaps you don't care because you are leaving Prague. London is safer than Prague.

AL-ANI: I do not care for fish and chips.

PAVEL: Someone packed all your bags for England last week.

AL-ANI: How do you know such things?

PAVEL: A cousin of mine works in your apartment building.

AL-ANI: How many cousins do you have?

PAVEL: Forty-three.

AL-ANI: Tell your cousin to shut his damn mouth.

PAVEL: I will. Would you harm him?

AL-ANI: No, it's not in my character, and you know that.

(PAVEL nods his head in agreement.)

Then why do you look so afraid?

PAVEL: Saddam Hussein killed his brother-in-law at a palace banquet.

AL-ANI: It was a *public suicide.*

PAVEL: *(Doubting.)* Sir . . .

AL-ANI: I was present.

PAVEL: How sad.

AL-ANI: Pavel, I stand by you, and you know that. I will give you employment for years to come. I am not moving to London. No more speculation, please. But I ask a special favor. Follow Mohamed Atta until he leaves Prague. He may be on foot, or he may take cabs. He may rent a car or jump a bus. He'll go through stores and buildings just to throw you. I want to know who else he's meeting here. Or if he decides to leave for the airport early.

PAVEL: You have Iraqi professionals to do such things.

AL-ANI: I don't want a professional. I have miserable luck with Iraqi professionals.

PAVEL: And if he catches me?

AL-ANI: Tell him I gave you these idiotic instructions. Tell him this was our way to keep the authorities off his tail. If he's arrested or detained in Prague, it will be a nightmare.

(Sensing PAVEL's reluctance.)

And if any harm comes to you, I guarantee that your widow and family will be provided with a lifetime pension. This I do promise, and I will put in writing.

Scene 5

(Later that evening. Prague lounge near ATTA's hotel.)

AL-ANI: This is a late hour for me.

PAVEL: I know, sir. And you're not well. You didn't have to drive here. I have things under control.

AL-ANI: He's still up in his hotel room? Alone?

PAVEL: No.

AL-ANI: With another Arab?

PAVEL: No.

AL-ANI: With a prostitute?

PAVEL: Yes.

AL-ANI: Is he safe?

PAVEL: He is.

AL-ANI: Is she safe?

PAVEL: The prostitute carries a crucifix and a can of mace.

AL-ANI: *(Dry.)* A crucifix, Pavel?

PAVEL: It can't hurt, God knows.

AL-ANI: What does God know?

PAVEL: God knows that we are accidents.

AL-ANI: Did you arrange the prostitute?

PAVEL: He insisted.

AL-ANI: A pretty one?

PAVEL: Yes,

AL-ANI: Did Atta pay you?

PAVEL: Yes.

AL-ANI: Isn't that beyond your job description?

PAVEL: Well . . .

(Correcting himself.)

Yes, it now seems so.

AL-ANI: You can be arrested for procuring.

PAVEL: I know.

AL-ANI: Is she a member of your family?

PAVEL: Yes. It's safer that way.

AL-ANI: Another cousin?

PAVEL: No.

AL-ANI: Dolni?

PAVEL: If you know, why pretend?

AL-ANI: I am sorry.

PAVEL: This is how I control my child.

AL-ANI: You put your child in danger.

PAVEL: Money is on the table.

AL-ANI: I was genuine about offering to help Dolni's medical needs.

(Pause.)

Does your wife know?

PAVEL: She looks the other way.

AL-ANI: She must know.

PAVEL: My wife is not Dolni's mother.

AL-ANI: I don't care. Talk like a responsible father.

PAVEL: Dolni is my flesh and blood.

AL-ANI: A lost little boy . . . that is your Dolni . . . with strangers for the price of an expensive meal?

PAVEL: Dolni defies my word all the time.

AL-ANI: So?

PAVEL: Perverse as it seems, I'd rather pick his clients and stand by in case he's in trouble. Can you control your own children, I ask you?

AL-ANI: I can and I do. But now your boy will create trouble for you and for me.

PAVEL: Atta is enjoying himself.

AL-ANI: How do you know?

PAVEL: Otherwise, Dolni would be at the window with a signal.

AL-ANI: That proves nothing.

PAVEL: Atta is with a "young woman" who is not "a woman" so he can still feel clean. To his God—Allah—there is no woman in that hotel room. And Allah is happy. Everyone is happy.

AL-ANI: I am not happy.

PAVEL: I'm sorry, Mr. Al-Ani. Atta told me what he wants. For in bed he cannot have sex with a woman. For it is his pure love of Islam. Dolni is smart and has talent about these things.

AL-ANI: Dolni enjoys this work?

PAVEL: I swear he does.

AL-ANI: How can he?

PAVEL: He feels power over other people. He's like a circus lion tamer. To him, sex is power. And he only uses his hands or a riding crop, never his mouth.

AL-ANI: He is attracted to older men?

PAVEL: Yes.

AL-ANI: You know, he'll go through Atta's personal things.

PAVEL: I clearly told him not to.

AL-ANI: Dolni can be a thief.

PAVEL: Only at the vegetable market.

AL-ANI: Your child has a death wish, Pavel.

PAVEL: Yes, and sometimes it simply kills me.

AL-ANI: If I were you, I would take him to a mental-health clinic immediately.

PAVEL: Yes.

AL-ANI: I need to talk to Dolni tonight.

PAVEL: Dolni has a cell phone. Just ring after midnight.

AL-ANI: I need to look at his eyes. I have a few questions for him. All we need is for the police to pick them up.

PAVEL: He won't say a word to the police.

AL-ANI: Can you be so certain?

PAVEL: Dolni won't talk to the police. He has had very bad experiences with them.

(Pause.)

Dolni always wanted to be a girl. He had so many girlfriends, and they loved his sensitivity.

AL-ANI: When did drugs come into the picture?

PAVEL: Age thirteen.

AL-ANI: And when did Dolni lose his virginity?

PAVEL: He hasn't, Mr. Al-Ani. Trust me. That's why no harm will come to him tonight. He is the first of the seventy-two celestial virgins for Atta.

Scene 6

(Later that evening. ATTA's hotel room.)

DOLNI: Euro-trash is crap. I need an island in paradise. Tropical birds along the window of a wooden cottage. Violet flowers open at night. That is where my love finds shelter. Maybe I am alone. Maybe there is someone else in pain . . . like you. A chance to give life to a new birth. Maybe my mother rises from her bed. I am barefoot, and I am blood.

ATTA: You are not an accident.

DOLNI: Exactly what I said. I am a flower. I am a butterfly. I have purpose. Your purpose. I am yours tonight. And you are mine.

ATTA: *(Reaching far below.)* I can't touch you?

DOLNI: Not yet. Let me first touch you. Let me feel the mood. The mood will come. You are handsome, and I know you have sweetness inside.

(Pause.)

I visit the Betlemska kaple—the finest chapel in the city. From the fourteenth century. Of all the buildings, that is my identity. My inner core. Nothing gothic or tacky in Betlemska.

ATTA: I don't know Betlemska.

DOLNI: Tomorrow let's go there. I know you love architecture. It will bring out your sweetness.

ATTA: It's time to go to sleep.

DOLNI: Yes, that would be nice. I like to sleep. My dimples are smiling.

ATTA: Take off your clothes, please.

DOLNI: When you take off yours.

ATTA: All right.

DOLNI: We do this together.

(Pause.)

Go ahead. Shower if you must. You have a little odor.

(Pause.)

Soap and water. Simple.

(Pause.)

Pavel said that you might be an assassin. Is this really true?

ATTA: He's wrong.

DOLNI: I thought assassins only exist in the movies. Who are you after?

ATTA: I am not an assassin.

DOLNI: But if you were, who would you kill?

ATTA: I'm not a killer.

DOLNI: I would leave you if you kill people.

ATTA: Nobody is going to die.

DOLNI: You're lying to me.

ATTA: And so I am. Better to hear my lies.

DOLNI: Pavel said you know how to fly a jet. I love jets. Take me away. In your jet plane.

ATTA: I cannot.

DOLNI: High and fast and far.

ATTA: No.

DOLNI: I will bring you good luck in big jets. I give good luck and good head.
ATTA: I have Allah. I don't need luck.
DOLNI: How do you know?
ATTA: Allah squeezes my hand.
DOLNI: I am squeezing your hand.

(Pause.)

You know I am right.
ATTA: It doesn't matter.
DOLNI: It does matter. You might die.
ATTA: I could say the same about you.
DOLNI: Is Allah the God of pain?
ATTA: Absolutely not.
DOLNI: Listen. You must listen.

(Pause.)

I can please you for years. So take me. I know you like me. You have never met anyone like me before. Children know more than adults. I am a child. We forget. Each day. Your black eyes are signs from God. God makes torment. To see Paradise, but we fail Paradise. Sweet Eternal Paradise. In your jet plane, you take me away. I give happiness, Atta.
ATTA: *(Softly.)* Silence.
DOLNI: I can give you a son. He will fight for your good name. I can also be your son and your lover.
ATTA: I need no son.
DOLNI: You require an heir. He will know your hidden thoughts, and that will please you. And Allah knows your hidden thoughts, and that does not please Allah.

(Pause.)

I am very sorry for I see the pain inside.
ATTA: My father is very educated, and yet he taunted me. To him, I was girlish. More girlish than my two sisters.
DOLNI: Yes.
ATTA: He thought I was another daughter to him, and he didn't want any more daughters. My beard did not come in until I reached eighteen.
DOLNI: I understand.
ATTA: Do you?
DOLNI: We can't live a lie.
ATTA: Yes, yes.

(Pause.)

I have a sick fantasy.

DOLNI: Why is it a sick fantasy?

ATTA: I don't know.

DOLNI: Maybe it is a curse.

*(*ATTA *murmurs.)*

A curse is not a fantasy. A curse can be lifted.

ATTA: There is no curse.

DOLNI: There is no fantasy. Quit your mission. Make me your new mission.

ATTA: Who really is your father?

DOLNI: I already told you. We only get one father in life.

(Pause.)

My mother rises from her bed. The wiser parent. She instructs me on the acts that I am chosen to do. I adore her.

ATTA: All women will go to Hell. That may be the only true thing.

Scene 7

(Later that night. PAVEL *drives* DOLNI *in his car. It is 3 A.M.)*

DOLNI: Why don't you let me drive? Look how exhausted you are.

PAVEL: We'll stop for coffee. I'm very hungry.

DOLNI: You've lost weight.

PAVEL: I know.

DOLNI: You look funny.

PAVEL: Funny good or funny bad?

DOLNI: Just funny.

(Pause.)

I saw a doctor this week. Did you hear what I said?

PAVEL: I heard you.

DOLNI: He was a strange doctor, Pavel.

PAVEL: Why do you wear this expensive make-up?

DOLNI: For security.

PAVEL: I don't understand.

DOLNI: Evil spirits cannot see my true face.

PAVEL: You're crazy.

DOLNI: Maybe a year ago, but I'm sharp as a tack today.

PAVEL: What did the doctor say?

DOLNI: He said my stockings were too tight, and my veins need more living space.
PAVEL: Please don't play with me, Dolni.

(Pause.)

I love you. You are my child no matter what you think.
DOLNI: He said my stockings were cutting off my blood flow. Such a stupid, rude thing to say. A young doctor with a bad leg. He walked like he had polio. I wanted to ask him about his injury. The doctor did some blood work, and he checked my glands. Rough hands for a doctor. He was trained in Hungary. Maybe he was a horse doctor there. Maybe the joke's on me?

(Pause.)

Whooa! Mother of Christ! You almost hit that car. Let me drive, Pavel.
PAVEL: You don't have a license.
DOLNI: It never bothered you before when I drove.
PAVEL: The police are following me.
DOLNI: Shit.
PAVEL: How could he be a horse doctor?
DOLNI: He inserted a big fat sugar cube between my lips and stroked my mane.
PAVEL: I will find the right doctor for you.
DOLNI: It costs money.
PAVEL: I know. We will get enough money from the Iraqi consulate.
DOLNI: Really?
PAVEL: Yes. I trust them.
DOLNI: *(Pause.)* I have money for you.
PAVEL: I don't need your money, Dolni. Save it for the doctors.
DOLNI: You do. You have old debts.
PAVEL: Do you care for me?
DOLNI: I love you. You know that.
PAVEL: But you don't respect me.
DOLNI: I try to respect you.
PAVEL: These drugs are ruining you.
DOLNI: Don't blame the drugs.
PAVEL: What should I blame?
DOLNI: The Gods of our fears.
PAVEL: All right. Let's blame them.
DOLNI: And they will blame us.
PAVEL: Did Atta pay you?

DOLNI: Yes.

PAVEL: Good.

DOLNI: I think he's going to fall apart. He's the most injured person I ever met.

PAVEL: He's angry. He smacked himself on his knuckles and said a million ugly things in Arabic.

DOLNI: He can't make his life better. So he will make strangers feel his pain. Maybe that's the scar inside the Arab mind. I told him that, Pavel. I really did.

Scene 8

(The following morning. PAVEL *sits alone at a café and is started by* ATTA's *greeting.)*

ATTA: Is this your breakfast?

PAVEL: I don't eat in the morning.

ATTA: But you look very hungry.

PAVEL: I can't help it, Mr. Atta.

ATTA: Because you're hungry.

PAVEL: Cigarette?

ATTA: Thank you.

(Accepts.)

PAVEL: You want to know something?

ATTA: Yes.

PAVEL: About my family?

(Pause.)

      Dolni is my child.

ATTA: Very hard to believe.

PAVEL: We don't resemble each other.

ATTA: No, you don't.

PAVEL: We comb our hair differently.

ATTA: You don't worry about someone harming Dolni?

PAVEL: I worry all the time.

ATTA: Your child needs help.

PAVEL: I know.

ATTA: How are you going to help?

PAVEL: I'm saving money for his medical needs.

ATTA: Why bother?

PAVEL: You don't believe me.

ATTA: My father always lied to me.

PAVEL: I'm sorry.

ATTA: Why do you think he lied?

PAVEL: I don't know.

ATTA: He lied because he was ashamed of God. And God was ashamed of him.

PAVEL: I see.

ATTA: My father used to beat me with his shoe.

PAVEL: I have never hit Dolni in all these years.

ATTA: You're not a proper father.

PAVEL: I know.

(Pause.)

I never knew my own father.

ATTA: That is no excuse.

PAVEL: I am not a cruel man, Mr. Atta.

ATTA: I didn't say you were cruel, but I'm going to change the picture.

PAVEL: There's no cruelty inside me. I toss coins at the church beggars. I've spent every Christmas with Dolni, and Dolni has seen me cry all too many times.

ATTA: And if you cry tonight?

PAVEL: What?

ATTA: I like your child, Pavel.

PAVEL: Many people like my child.

ATTA: I am going to take Dolni with me.

PAVEL: Why?

ATTA: Because I want to. I decided an hour ago.

PAVEL: Dolni will only get in your way.

ATTA: That's my problem.

PAVEL: It's my problem, too, Mr. Atta. Believe me.

ATTA: No more strange men for your child. No more cheap hotels. No more rats and no more sin.

PAVEL: That is my daily prayer.

ATTA: Give me cash in korunas.

PAVEL: Why?

ATTA: I will look after your child.

PAVEL: You must be crazy, Mr. Atta. I have enough money to buy stale bread and a newspaper.

ATTA: I said, I will look after your child. Give me dollars.

PAVEL: You cannot steal Dolni from me.

ATTA: I do not steal, Pavel. Don't mistake me. Give me British Sterling.

PAVEL: If you need more, Al-Ani is your source.

ATTA: Al-Ani is a fraud. He gives me shit.

PAVEL: Again, I am sorry.

ATTA: Do you want to die?

PAVEL: No.

ATTA: Then prove yourself.

PAVEL: What, are you going to kill me in front of all these people?

ATTA: I could take you out anyplace. I have no fear.

PAVEL: Then do it here. Do it now.

ATTA: I want you to tell Dolni that he has to go with me.

PAVEL: And if I do?

ATTA: I will let you live.

PAVEL: I don't know what to say to you, Mr. Atta. My tongue is tied, and my hands are very weak.

ATTA: Take out your cell phone, and call your sweet child.

PAVEL: *(Takes out cell phone.)* Am I to believe you?

ATTA: Yes, I would not lie to your face.

PAVEL: But I will never see Dolni again?

ATTA: I don't know. Probably not.

(Pause.)

> Dial the phone.

PAVEL: I can't.

ATTA: I will ask you only once more. Dial the phone, Pavel.

(PAVEL dials.)

> Good man.

PAVEL: *(To phone.)* Dolni, it's me. I'm with the Egyptian. He says good-bye to you.

(PAVEL hangs up.)

> That is the best that I can do, Mr. Atta, because my flesh and blood is everything.

Scene 9

(Third night. Iraq consulate.)

DOLNI: The man downstairs strip-searched me.

AL-ANI: Standard procedure.

DOLNI: I have no weapons.

AL-ANI: Precautions . . . it's the way you dress.

DOLNI: I know you, Mr. Al-Ani.

AL-ANI: And I know you, Dolni.

DOLNI: Always following me day and night.

AL-ANI: That's my job when I'm off duty.

DOLNI: My father doesn't care.

AL-ANI: I care. Your father is so sad.

DOLNI: You have made him even sadder.

AL-ANI: I'm fond of your father.

DOLNI: Should I believe you?

AL-ANI: I line your father's pockets with money. He paid no taxes on this money. Your father loves tax-free money.

DOLNI: Where is he?

AL-ANI: I don't know.

DOLNI: I'm worried.

AL-ANI: No reason to worry. Why not ring his cell?

DOLNI: I tried.

AL-ANI: He'll call you back later today.

DOLNI: You must be feeling what I am feeling.

AL-ANI: No, I don't feel anything, Dolni.

DOLNI: There's a feeling of horror.

(Pause.)

   You won't manipulate me.

AL-ANI: Actually, I'm surprised that you're here.

DOLNI: And I'm surprised that you are willing to see me.

AL-ANI: You know next time you must phone before you come to this building.

DOLNI: Where is my father?

AL-ANI: Is he really your father?

DOLNI: I swear to God, yes.

AL-ANI: He usually acts like your father.

(Pause.)

   Where is he, you ask? Probably at his other job.

DOLNI: He didn't report to work.

AL-ANI: Well, sometimes he does that.

DOLNI: His apartment door is unlocked, and the phone was off the hook.

AL-ANI: Did you ask your mother?

DOLNI: My mother does not live in Prague.

AL-ANI: Maybe he's with another woman?

DOLNI: No. You sent him someplace.

AL-ANI: No.

DOLNI: You were angry at him, and you fired him.

AL-ANI: I don't think so.

DOLNI: His job was finished with Atta's visit.

AL-ANI: That is true.

DOLNI: Atta is sick.

AL-ANI: I know, Dolni. I will try to stop Atta from doing harm. I have phoned the Czech police today. Maybe the Czech authorities will do their responsibilities and spare some innocent lives.

DOLNI: You're lying.

AL-ANI: On my mother's grave.

(Pause.)

The police should be picking him up in Prague. Believe me, they know his whereabouts. I will tell you something in confidence, even at the risk of sounding unprofessional. My superiors have encouraged Atta with money and with fantasy. I cannot support these actions any longer. And it is time to get Pavel out of harm's way.

DOLNI: You're not telling the truth.

AL-ANI: I have no cause to lie to you.

DOLNI: My father is not gullible.

AL-ANI: I know that. He's very loyal to me. He once saved my life. Tell me: Where is Atta?

DOLNI: Gone.

AL-ANI: You were the last one to see him at the hotel.

DOLNI: Atta had other visitors. *(Pause.)* He checked out of his hotel, and your dirty business is done.

AL-ANI: Why did you take up with Atta? Clearly, you knew he was trouble.

DOLNI: I knew he was Egyptian with a fake passport.

AL-ANI: Pavel told you more than that.

DOLNI: I'm going to the police.

AL-ANI: Don't do that, Dolni.

DOLNI: Fuck you.

AL-ANI: Why spend an hour with this man? Did you really need the money?

DOLNI: I did.

AL-ANI: But who made you do something against your will?

DOLNI: You did.

AL-ANI: I did no such thing.

DOLNI: I know heroin once came from your diplomatic pouch.

AL-ANI: No. I never trafficked heroin.

DOLNI: Pavel told me you did.

AL-ANI: Your father lied to you.

DOLNI: I believe him over you. Let's see what the police believe.

AL-ANI: I know what you will tell the police. Word for word. What you will say will ruin your father's good name, and he will be sent to prison. Why do that to your father?

DOLNI: Enough shit! Atta did something to my father.

AL-ANI: Did he say he was going to hurt Pavel?

DOLNI: When I was walking out the door, he made it known to me.

AL-ANI: I am certain that Pavel will turn up and that Atta did nothing to your father.

(Pause.)

Yes, I know what Atta is *capable* of doing. But he is a contradiction. He hates his sexuality.

DOLNI: How do you know?

AL-ANI: My job is to read character. Did you disrobe?

DOLNI: Not completely.

AL-ANI: Then you have a guardian angel. Consider yourself lucky to be alive.

DOLNI: Atta is part of you and your embassy.

AL-ANI: No.

DOLNI: He is part of Iraq.

AL-ANI: He's Al Qaeda.

DOLNI: Then Al Qaeda is part of your gang.

AL-ANI: There is no gang, Dolni. Everyone is a free agent. You have acted like a free agent, too.

DOLNI: You'll give him legal immunity.

AL-ANI: Iraq cannot give him anything useful.

DOLNI: Find my father.

AL-ANI: All right. I will do my best to find him.

DOLNI: You owe my father this favor.

AL-ANI: I do. You're absolutely right. I owe your father safety. And by extension, I must offer you safety. You must stay in this building until we know that Atta has left for Germany. Look, if Atta has harmed your father, he might try harming you.

(Pause.)

Promise me that you will stay here?

DOLNI: You have the means to stop Atta from what he's planning.

AL-ANI: What is he planning?

DOLNI: He's going to kill a million infidels.

AL-ANI: If you know that to be true, why come to me? Why didn't you kill him, Dolni, when you had the chance?

(Silence.)

I just have two arthritic hands. These hands are exceedingly weak. I was once a beautiful young man. As beautiful as you are now. I can understand how Mohamed Atta felt in your arms.

(Pause.)

Will the world really miss a million infidels?

DOLNI: As much as I will miss my father.

Scene 10

(Later that night. Czech police headquarters.)

DOLNI: I am reporting a missing person. My father has been missing for thirty-six hours. I fear that he is no longer alive. My name is Dolni Frisch. I am the son of Pavel Frisch, 28 Valec Street, near the central public school. I dropped out before graduating. I am fifteen years old. I am his only child. I have no job at the moment, but I often paint homes and apartments. I don't pay taxes. I know I should. The Ilka Brothers hire me when they need help. They have a large ad in the telephone book. They have been very good to me. Call them, and they will tell you the same.

(Pause.)

I had a disturbing dream last night. My dreams always come before dawn. A plane hits a building. The great hand of God turns green. I know the pilot.

(Pause.)

My father is not missing. He was killed by a raving foreigner.

(Pause.)

Yes, I am sober. He strangled Pavel Frisch and left him to rot inside his car alongside the cargo road to the airport. I wish for you to save others before he completes his mission.

(Pause.)

Yes, I know who the murderer is. He still is in this city. Maybe for another night. I know his name and what he looks like. He has many names. This is one of his passports. I stole it from his jacket. It says Ahmed Ali

225

Said, but that is not his photograph. Like the photograph, he's a thin, muscular man. But his eyes are reptilian. And that is not his real name. The murderer is from Egypt and has an apartment in Hamburg. He speaks German, yes. An architect by profession. His name is Atta. He is very educated. But he is a killer. You can hear it between each sentence. Yes, I had sex with him. In his fancy hotel. And I was high on drugs.

(Pause.)

At the Iraqi consulate, there is an officer named Al-Ani. My father did small jobs for him. Al-Ani has been good to my father. Al-Ani knows the murderer. I swear to you these two men are working together. Atta is the monster, but Al-Ani is the manipulator.

(Pause.)

My name is Dolni Frisch. Yes. Yes. These are my clothes. I paid for these clothes. I am a boy. No criminal record except for being expelled from school.

(Pause.)

Yes, I will sign a statement.

(Pause.)

Yes, I have a drug addiction. Yes. Yes. At my age. It will end. Someday. God knows. But this man Atta. He is very sick. Dangerous. Maybe he is buying sarin or anthrax to destroy innocents. Maybe a truck. Maybe a helicopter. He has a goal. He will succeed because he is smart and crazy and smart. Very crazy. Very serious. And smart.

(Pause.)

Yes, I will go to jail if need be. I learned how to steal when I was a child. But don't blame my father. I stole from my father, too.

(Pause.)

Show me photos, and I will point him out. Atta can pilot a plane. Atta's anger is real. There is a devil inside his eyes. What will you do to stop him? I know your secret police has been tailing him!

(Pause.)

This awful monster from Cairo—Mohamed Atta—killed my dear father. And you will do nothing about it!

Background Notes on the Incidents in Prague, April 2001

The investigation of the September 11 attack has produced to date only a single instance of an observed liaison between one of the nineteen known hijackers and a hostile, governmental intelligence service. It was the meeting in April 2001 between Mohamed Atta—the alleged ringleader of the hijackers—and Ahmed Khalil Ibrahim Samir Al-Ani, the second secretary of the Iraqi consul in Prague and an officer in the Iraqi foreign intelligence service. This meeting was observed through the surveillance of the Czech counterintelligence service, BIS, and was reported subsequently to major news organizations such as the *Washington Post*, *Wall Street Journal*, *Czech Post*, and the *New York Times*.

The Czech surveillance of Al-Ani grew out of an earlier incident. In December 1998, Jabir Salim, a forty-three-year-old Iraqi intelligence officer, serving as Iraq's consul in Prague, was compromised in a homosexual scandal. He defected to Britain and revealed to British Intelligence that Baghdad had provided him money to organize a car-bomb attack on the Prague headquarters of Radio Free Europe, Radio Free Liberty—the American facility in Prague that broadcasts to Iraq. Al-Ani replaced Salim at the Iraqi consul. The Czech officials believed Al-Ani would continue with the original bombing plot and eventually expelled him from the country.

There are unconfirmed reports that Atta had met or communicated with Al-Ani some time before April 2001. There are other unconfirmed reports that Atta received anthrax spores from Iraqi agents in Prague.

In October 2001, the German magazine *Der Spiegel* published a copy of Mohamed Atta's will, dated April 11, 1996, which, according to the Islamic calendar of zoelqada, is 1416. The PBS program *Frontline* provides the following English translation (available at http://www.pbs.org/wgbh/pages/frontline/shows/network/personal/attawill.html).

Mohamed Atta's Last Will and Testament
In the name of God all mighty
Death Certificate

This is what I want to happen after my death. I am Mohamed the son of Mohamed Elamir awad Elsayed. I believe that prophet Mohamed is God's messenger and time will come, no doubt about that, and God will resurrect people who are in their graves. I wanted my family and everyone who reads this will to fear the Almighty God and don't get deceived by what is in life and to fear God and to follow God and his prophets if they are real believers. In my memory, I want them to do what Ibrahim (a prophet) told his son to do, to die as a good Muslim. When I die, I want the people who will inherit my possessions to do the following:

1. The people who will prepare my body should be good Muslims because this will remind me of God and his forgiveness.

2. The people who are preparing my body should close my eyes and pray that I will go to heaven and to get me new clothes, not the ones I died in.

3. I don't want anyone to weep and cry or to rip their clothes or slap their faces because this is an ignorant thing to do.

4. I don't want anyone to visit me who didn't get along with me while I was alive or to kiss me or say good-bye when I die.

5. I don't want a pregnant woman or a person who is not clean to come and say good-bye to me because I don't approve it.

6. I don't want women to come to my house to apologize for my death. I am not responsible for people who will sacrifice animals in front of my lying body because this is against Islam.

7. Those who will sit beside my body must remember Allah, God, and pray for me to be with the angels.

8. The people who will clean my body should be good Muslims and I do not want a lot of people to wash my body unless it is necessary.

9. The person who will wash my body near my genitals must wear gloves on his hands so he won't touch my genitals.

10. I want the clothes I wear to consist of three white pieces of cloth, not to be made of silk or expensive material.

11. I don't want any women to go to my grave at all during my funeral or on any occasion thereafter.

12. During my funeral I want everyone to be quiet because God mentioned that he likes being quiet on occasions when you recite the Koran, during the funeral, and when you are crawling. You must speed my funeral procession and I would like many people there to pray for me.

13. When you bury me the people with whom I will be buried should be good Muslims. I want to face East toward Mecca.

14. I should be laying on my right side. You should throw the dust on my body three times while saying from the dust, we created you from dust and to dust you will return. From the dust a new person will be created. After that everyone should mention God's name and that I died as a Muslim which is God's religion. Everyone who attends my funeral should ask that I will be forgiven for what I have done in the past (not this action).

15. The people who will attend my funeral should sit at my grave for an hour so that I will enjoy their company and slaughter animals and give the meat to the needy.

16. The custom has been to memorialize the dead every 40 days or once a year but I do not want this because it is not an Islamic custom.

17. I don't want people to take time to write things on paper to be kept in their pockets as superstition. Time should be taken to pray to God instead.

18. All the money I left must be divided according to the Muslim religion as almighty God has asked us to do. A third of my money should be spent on the poor and the needy. I want my books to go to any one of the Muslim mosques. I wanted the people who look at my will to be one of the heads of the Sunna religion. Whoever it is, I want that person to be from where I grew up or any person I used to follow in prayer. People will be held responsible for not following the Muslim religion. I wanted the people who I left behind to hear God and not to be deceived by what life has to offer and to pray more to God and to be good believers. Whoever neglects this will or does not follow the religion, that person will be held responsible in the end.

QUESTION 27, QUESTION 28

Chay Yew

Production Notes

QUESTION 27, QUESTION 28 was commissioned by Asian American Theatre Company in San Francisco and received its first workshop production there in June 2003. The world premiere production was produced by Mark Taper Forum in association with the Japanese American National Museum in Los Angeles in February 2004; the production then transferred to East West Players in Los Angeles. Recent productions include the Smithsonian Institution in Washington, D.C., and Silk Road Theatre in Chicago.

Note

Question 27, Question 28 uses and incorporates interviews, transcripts, and testimonials taken from books, archives, newspapers, and magazine journals, listed in the bibliography, which follows. *Question 27, Question 28* was originally commissioned by Asian American Theatre Company, San Francisco; Executive Director, Pamela Wu.

Characters

Four women. Three Asian women and one Caucasian woman of varying ages.

Set

This play should be staged simply as a play reading with actors sitting on chairs and with scripts with music stands. If slides cannot be employed in the production, an actor can simply announce the slide titles.

Act 1

Prologue

EMILY: Yuri Kochiyama.
DIAN: Haruko Niwa.
SHANNON: Kiyo Sato.
TAMLYN: Monica Sone.
EMILY: Chizu Iiyama.
DIAN: Mine Okubo.
SHANNON: Elaine Black Yoneda.

TAMLYN: Mary Tsukamoto.
EMILY: *(Overlapping.)* Miyo Senzaki—
DIAN: *(Overlapping.)* Emi Somekawa—
SHANNON: *(Overlapping.)* Eleanor Gerard Sekerak—
TAMLYN: *(Overlapping.)* Amy Uno Iishi—
EMILY: *(Overlapping.)* Masako Saito—
DIAN: *(Overlapping.)* Yoshiko Uchida—
SHANNON: *(Overlapping.)* Ada Endo—
TAMLYN: *(Overlapping.)* Haruko Hurt—
EMILY: *(Overlapping.)* Noriko Sawada Bridges—
DIAN: *(Overlapping.)* Helen Murao—
SHANNON: *(Overlapping.)* Mabel Ota—
TAMLYN: *(Overlapping.)* Nobu Miyoshi—

1. Slide: Before Sunday

TAMLYN: Mary Tsukamoto.
EMILY: I was born in San Francisco. My parents came from Okinawa and had the Capitol Laundry on Geary Street, where I lived when I was very little. Then my father moved to Turlock.

　　When I was ten, he moved his family to Florin to raise strawberries, and became one of the biggest strawberry farmers there.
SHANNON: Haruko Niwa.
DIAN: My birthplace is Japan. I was born in 1906 in the city of Ueda. I graduated high school there, and then I went to Tokyo. I came here in 1923.

　　After I graduated from two years in business college in Tokyo, my father, who was in San Francisco with my brother, invite me for just one year, for just visit, but I stayed instead.

　　I like San Francisco and the United States and living in United States very much. It's very attractive.

　　And then, I married Mr. Niwa. I married and had two children.
EMILY: Amy Uno Ishii.
TAMLYN: I was born in Salt Lake City, Utah, on December 11, 1920. I'm the fifth of ten children.

　　My father and mother were both born and raised in Japan. My parents met a lot of hardship and discrimination in Japan because of the fact that they were Christians. Those days—the 1800s—very few Japanese were Christians; there were more Buddhists.

　　My father was chased and beaten by children in the neighborhood. He also told of other specific instances where he was discriminated against because he was Christian. He was encouraged to come to America by the missionaries. They told him—

SHANNON: "America is the land of the free and the home of the brave. Money grows on the orange trees in your backyard. The land is vast, not like Japan."

TAMLYN: They told him—

SHANNON: With your intellect, your knowledge of history, and your ability in handing the English language—"

TAMLYN: (Even to the degree that he did at that time, which, I guess was considered quite a bit)—

SHANNON: "You will go far in America. So go to America. Go to America."

TAMLYN: He arrived here in 1906 and worked on the railroad gang.

EMILY: Mary Gillespie.

SHANNON: I lived in this area most of my life, since 1909. My parents homesteaded here. We came from Ohio. My father's health was bad, and he came here. That's how we happened to come here.

DIAN: Helen Murao.

TAMLYN: I was born in Portland, Oregon, in 1926. My parents died within three years of each other in the mid-thirties, my mother dying first. I was still in grammar school when that happened, and we became wards of the state. I had an older sister, Mary, who died after this. So I was the oldest of three of us, me and my two younger brothers.

The Japanese community was very fearful and very reluctant to take us into their homes because Mary had had tuberculosis. There was nothing more fearful to them than that disease. So they did not offer their homes to us—even our very close family friends. It was with Caucasian people that we made our homes.

During those years it was very hard for me to come to grips with the realization that the Japanese people forsook us. They didn't want to have anything to do with us. Just out of fear for their health.

SHANNON: Mary Tsukamoto.

EMILY: I remember we had an annual oratorical contest sponsored by the Native Sons and Daughters, and I ended up one of the nine qualifying competitors. Then the principal and the teacher called me in and told me that I couldn't be in it because of my ancestry.

I was relieved I didn't have to do another oration, but the teacher didn't let me forget. She was upset and so discouraged that the Native Sons wouldn't change their position. That they would discriminate against me, made her very angry. But she couldn't do anything about it.

She was the one responsible for getting me to college because of that experience—to the College of the Pacific. That teacher was poor herself.

But before my dad knew anything about it, she had arranged to get me a $150 scholarship.

She even had to go and ask Dad if he would let me go and not help at home. You see, every child was needed for the strawberries at that time. Every child and everybody in the family worked together to eke out a living.

My dad was so deeply touched. Of course, he let me go.

TAMLYN: Pauline Miller.

SHANNON: Lone Pine? I thought it was a godforsaken country.

But after we were here for awhile—because I came from Los Angeles and missed all my friends, you know, to come to a little town like this—we weren't here very long before we became acquainted, and we liked it very much. I was thirty-five at the time. My husband bought an automobile dealership and a gasoline station.

DIAN: Amy Uno Ishii.

TAMLYN: I was twelve years old when I left home. But it was a different way of leaving home.

I sat down and talked to my mother and said, "Look, this is 1932, and I'm in junior high school now, the seventh grade. You're having a hard time feeding all these mouths, putting shoes on the feet, and putting patch upon patch on the clothes. So, would it help any if I moved out of the house and worked as a domestic? If I worked in a home and went to school away from here, I would come and see you on my days off."

Tears just rolled down my mother's cheeks and she said—

DIAN: "It would really help. If it's one less mouth to feed, one less person to have to clothe and worry about, it would help so much."

TAMLYN: So I said, "Then I will look for a job."

SHANNON: Masako Saito.

DIAN: We were all told we had to study hard, you have to be good, not do anything to shame the family. It was pounded into us—there was favoritism—my sister above me was very smart—we were always told to be as smart as Kiyo.

My mother wouldn't let Kiyo do a lot of things—

EMILY: "Let her study because she's the smart one!"

DIAN: And I was the dumb one. So I had to do a lot of things—running around, helping them, take the wash up to the roof, four floors, and hang it up.

My parents managed to send us to piano lessons, and we had to go to Japanese school. But we think, in spite of it all, we managed to turn out pretty well adjusted.

SHANNON: Yuri Kochiyama.

233

EMILY: I was red, white, and blue when I was growing up. I taught Sunday school and was very, very American.

I got a job at a department store. But for us back then, it was a big thing, because I don't think they had ever hired an Asian in a department store before.

It was hard for Asians. Even for Japanese, the best jobs they felt they could get were in Chinatown. Most Japanese were either in some aspect of fishing, such as in the canneries, or went right from school to work on the farms.

That was what it was like in the town of San Pedro. I loved working in the department store because it was a small town, and you got to know and see everyone. The town itself was wonderful. People were very friendly. I didn't see my job as work—it was like a community job.

Everything changed for me on the day Pearl Harbor was bombed.

2. Slide: That Sunday

TAMLYN: Haruko Hurt.

DIAN: I didn't even know where Pearl Harbor was. I was that naïve. But I soon found out. It was something that was just foreign to me. Something that country over there, Japan, did. It had nothing to do with me, as far as I'm concerned.

SHANNON: Mary Tsukamoto.

EMILY: I was about twenty-six, and we were in church. It was a December Sunday, so we were getting ready for our Christmas program. We were rehearsing and having Sunday School class, and I always played the piano for the adult Issei service. Of course, because there were so many Japanese, all of it was in Japanese. The minister was Japanese, and he preached in Japanese.

But after the service started, my husband ran in. He had been home that day and heard on the radio—

SHANNON: "The Japanese have bombed Pearl Harbor!"

EMILY: We just couldn't believe it. I remembered how stunned we were. And suddenly the whole world turned dark. We began to speak in whispers.

We immediately knew something terrible was going to happen. We prayed that it wouldn't, but we sense things would be very difficult. The minister and all the leaders discussed matters, and we knew that we needed to be prepared for the worst.

SHANNON: Kay Uno.

DIAN: I was nine at the time of Pearl Harbor, and I was in third grade. That Sunday, we were on our way home from church, and we had the radio on in our car.

Everybody was excited. We said "Oh, those Japs. What are they doing that for?"

When the war happened, my parents were really torn. Japan was their country. They were Japanese, and they couldn't have citizenship here. But, in a lot of ways, my parents were Americans. They flew the flag for every national holiday.

We lived six blocks from where I went to school, and I always walked. All the merchants and everyone knew me—

SHANNON: "Hi, How are you?"

DIAN: Monday, they turned their backs on me.

SHANNON: "There goes that little Jap!"

DIAN: I'm looking around. "Who's a Jap? Who's a Jap?"

Then it dawned on me, I'm the Jap.

After Pearl Harbor, the kids began to shun me. My friends. One person started it, and then pretty soon it went throughout the school. My teacher and music teacher were both very supportive all through the time.

When I had to leave, one of them gave me a gift. A gold leaf pin. It was the first real piece of jewelry I ever had.

I still have it.

EMILY: President Franklin D. Roosevelt.

SHANNON: "Yesterday, December 7, 1941—A date which will live in infamy— the United States of America was suddenly and deliberately attacked by naval and air forces of the Empire of Japan."

TAMLYN: Yuri Kochiyama.

EMILY: On that very day, December 7, the FBI came and took my father.

He had just come home from the hospital the day before. For several days, we didn't know where they had taken him. Then we found out that he was taken to the federal prison at Terminal Island. Overnight, things changed for us.

The FBI took all men who lived near the Pacific waters and who had anything to do with fishing. A month later, they took every fisherman from Terminal Island, sixteen and over, to detention centers in South Dakota, Montana, and New Mexico.

The first group was thirteen hundred Isseis—my parent's generation. They took those who were leaders of the community, or Japanese school teachers, or were teaching martial arts, or who were Buddhist priests. Those categories that would make them very "Japanesey"—were picked up.

SHANNON: Mrs. Hama Yamaki.

DIAN: We had to consult a lawyer to get a permit to return home. Two weeks passed before we were able to return.

After we read newspaper articles about Nihonjin in Idaho being shot, we drove right home. We only stopped once at the restaurant to have coffee. Even though the rooms were dark, we could see the others staring at us. No one said anything to us, but we drank our coffees hurriedly and left.

As we were driving home during a snowstorm, our car stalled in the middle of a mountain road. We were very frightened. But a car drove right up, and a Caucasian man offered to help us. Without a word about Pearl Harbor, he brought out his tools and worked on our motor. The car ignition started smoothly!

I wanted to clasp his hand in appreciation. But all I said was, "Thank you! Thank you!"

EMILY: Yoshiko Uchida.

TAMLYN: One evening, some friends and I were having a late snack in a restaurant in Berkeley. Suddenly, an angry Filipino man accosted us and vividly described what the Japanese soldiers were doing to his homeland. His fists were clenched, and his face was contorted with rage. Fortunately, he had no weapon and left after venting his anger on us, but he had filled us with fear. It was the first time in my life I had been threatened with violence and it was a terrifying moment.

DIAN: President Roosevelt.

SHANNON: "The attack yesterday on the Hawaiian Islands has caused severe damage to American naval and military forces. Very many American lives have been lost."

TAMLYN: Masako Saito.

DIAN: I would be walking down to where I was working until the store closed. And people would come by and say—

SHANNON: "Jap."

DIAN: And then they'd split. I couldn't believe it. I mentioned it to my Chinese friends, and they said—

TAMLYN: "We'll lend you our 'I am Chinese' button."

DIAN: "Oh no," I said, "If they're going to hate me for being a Japanese. Well, there's nothing more I can do—they're the ones who're wrong."

SHANNON: Amy Uno Ishii.

TAMLYN: That Sunday morning I was living as a domestic away from home, out in San Marino, and I had just served breakfast to the family when the news came on the radio that Japan had attacked Pearl Harbor. It's hard to describe the shock.

Even the people I worked for treated me and talked to me as though it was my own father who was piloting those planes out there at Pearl Harbor.

I remember they told me that I could go home and how I had better stay home until the FBI could clear me of any suspicion. I said, "Why should I be suspected of anything? I've lived here in your home for many years now, nursed you when you were sick, and fed you. And I never poisoned you once, and I'm not about to do it now."

But they said—

SHANNON: "You had better stay home until we can get the FBI to clear you."

TAMLYN: I felt like an ant. I wanted to shrivel up into nothing, and my mind was going a mile a minute, thinking, "What am I supposed to do? What am I supposed to say? All I know is I am an American, and yet now, at a time like this, people are going to say, 'You are a Jap,' and that turns the whole picture around."

I had never been called a "Jap" in my life. All these things were going through my mind.

By the time I got home, the FBI was at our house.

EMILY: President Roosevelt.

SHANNON: "I ask that the Congress declare that since the unprovoked attack by Japan on Sunday, December 7, a state of war has existed between the United States and the Japanese Empire."

DIAN: Mary Tsukamoto.

EMILY: Then of course, within a day or two, we heard that the FBI had taken Mr. Tanigawa and Mr. Tsuji. I suppose the FBI had them on their list, and it wasn't long before many of them were taken. We had no idea what they were going through. We should have been more aware.

One Issei, Mr. Iwasa, committed suicide.

DIAN: Amy Uno Iishi.

TAMLYN: The FBI were tearing out floorboards, taking bricks out of fireplace, and looking through our attic. Contraband, I guess. Looking for machine guns, munitions, maps, binoculars, cameras, swords, knives, and what-have-you.

And my family, we just stood there. What could we say with military police standing out in front with guns pointing at the house? Telling us to stay right there in a particular room while they went through the whole house?

They didn't have a search warrant. They didn't have any reason to be coming in like this and tearing up our house.

And when the FBI left, they took my father with them.

DIAN: Mary Tsukamoto.

EMILY: Mrs. Tsuji's husband was also taken away by the FBI. But nobody thought about the family left behind needing food and money.

We finally arranged for the welfare office to provide food, and she cried because Japanese people are proud, and they weren't willing to accept handouts. They had never been on welfare before, and she felt terrible because here she ended up receiving food.

But we told her this was different because her husband was taken and because it's what you have to do. She had three children.

TAMLYN: Haruko Hurt.

DIAN: I did domestic work at the time. The employer, Mrs. Dunlevy, whom I was living with, said to me—

SHANNON: "Haruko—"

DIAN: She said, half-smiling—

SHANNON: "I'm going to look under your bed to see if you have a radio transmitter hidden there."

DIAN: I kinda laughed. I thought she was joking.

I said, "By all means, look under there."

Can you imagine? I know she wasn't joking.

SHANNON: Mary Tsukamoto.

EMILY: We were supposed to turn in our cameras and our guns, and they were called in. Every day there was something else about other people being taken by the FBI.

Then gradually we just couldn't believe what people were saying. There was talk about *sending* us away, and we just couldn't believe that they would do such a thing.

DIAN: Amy Uno Ishii.

TAMLYN: There was also a very strict curfew law. We had to be in by five o'clock in the evening. We could not go out before a certain time in the morning.

We could travel only so many miles from our homes. If you worked a little further than that from your home, you had to give up your job.

SHANNON: Emi Somekawa.

DIAN: I think the thing that we felt the most was that the people who stopped in at our store thought maybe we should close it up. For our safety. But my husband said—

EMILY: "No, there's no need to do that. We're American citizens."

DIAN: When April came along, we knew that we had to go. So my husband started selling things in the store.

SHANNON: "San Francisco Examiner! 6 A.M. Extra! Ouster of All Japs in California Near!"

TAMLYN: Mary Tsukamoto.

EMILY: It would be a situation where the whole community would be uprooted. But soon enough we were reading reports of other communities being evacuated from San Pedro and from Puget Sound.

After a while, we became aware that maybe things weren't going to just stop but would continue to get worse and worse.

SHANNON: Amy Uno Ishii.

TAMLYN: It was the most difficult thing, adjusting to having Dad away from home.

My mother and father had just celebrated their twenty-fifth anniversary. It was the first time they had ever been separated.

My mother was home with the children—but to have my father forcibly taken away from her, she was in a state of shock. Her blood pressure was really high, and it was a matter of trying to keep her composure.

She realized that she now had to be the head of the household, the backbone of the family.

It was very difficult when the young ones would say to my mother—

EMILY: "When is Daddy coming home? Where is he?"

TAMLYN: What kind of answers could she give? Could she tell the children truthfully that Daddy will be gone only a couple of weeks or a couple of months or a couple of years? She didn't even know.

The mere mention of my father would just break my mother up. It was just eating away at her.

Then the evacuation order came.

3. Slide: Exodus

DIAN: President Roosevelt.

TAMLYN: Executive Order 9066. SHANNON: "Now, therefore, by virtue of authority vested in me President of the United States, and Commander in Chief of the Army and Navy, I hereby authorize and direct the secretary of war . . . or any designated commanders . . . to prescribe military areas . . . [and to] determine the right of any person to enter, remain in, to leave."

DIAN: Amy Uno Iishi.

TAMLYN: That was really the biggest surprise of all. No one had an inkling as to where we were going to be sent and for how long.

239

DIAN: Mary Tsukamoto.

EMILY: I remember Mrs. Kuima, whose son was thirty-two years old and retarded. She took care of him. They had five other boys, but she took care of this boy at home. The welfare office said—

SHANNON: "No, you can't take him. All families have to institutionalize a child like that."

EMILY: It was a very tragic thing for me to tell her, and I remember going out to the field—where she was hoeing strawberries—and I told her what they told us, that you can't take your son with you. And so she cried, and I cried with her. A few days before they evacuated, they came to take him away to an institution. It was very hard for me to face that family. I felt as though I was the messenger that carried such tragic news for them. It was only about a month after we got to Fresno Assembly Center that they sent us a wire saying—

SHANNON: "He died."

EMILY: All these years she loved him and took care of him. He only knew Japanese and ate Japanese food. I was thinking about the family. They got over it quietly. They endured it. I just felt guilty, you know, just having been involved.

TAMLYN: Emi Somekawa.

DIAN: When we first realized that an evacuation would take place, it was a depressing feeling that's hard to explain.

I didn't know whether we'd come back to our home again, but it was a feeling that all these years we'd worked for nothing. That kind of a feeling, you know, that you're just losing everything.

EMILY: Yoshiko Uchida.

TAMLYN: As our packing progressed, our house grew increasingly barren, and our garden took on a shabby look. My mother couldn't bear to leave her favorite plants to strangers and dug up her special roses, London Smoke carnations, and yellow calla lilies to take to a friend for safekeeping.

One day, a neighbor rang our doorbell and asked for one of Papa's prized gladiolas that she fancied as she passed by.

It seemed like a heartless gesture, and I was indignant, just as I was when the people told me the evacuation was for our own protection.

But Mother simply handed the woman a shovel and told her to help herself.

She said—

EMILY: "Let her have it if it will make her happy."

DIAN: Eleanor Roosevelt.

SHANNON: "Approximately three months after Pearl Harbor, the Western

Defense Command ordered all persons of Japanese ancestry excluded from the coastal area, including approximately half of Washington, Oregon, and California, and the southern portion of Arizona. Later, the entire state of California was added to the zone from which Japanese were barred.

"This separation is taking place now."

TAMLYN: Emi Somekawa.

DIAN: One thing that upset me, that was hard to take, was that we had this German family right next door, and they were as German as German could be, and they were free. They could do anything they wanted, and nobody was bothering them. Why us? I felt like we were just being punished for nothing.

The day we left the house, this German lady came with a cake, and she said—

SHANNON: "If there was anything else we could do for you, call."

DIAN: So twice they came out to the assembly center. I think they were a bit displaced, too. I don't think they could help but feel that way.

TAMLYN: Mary Tsukamoto

EMILY: I worried about trying to buy the right kind of things to get ready for a place I knew nothing about.

They said "camp." I thought "summer camp."

I thought we were going up into the mountains somewhere. I even bought boots thinking there might be snakes!

SHANNON: Amy Uno Ishii.

TAMLYN: We had to dispose of all our belongings. We stood by so helplessly when people whom we thought were our friends and neighbors, came by and said to my mother—

SHANNON: "I'll give you two dollars for your stove—"

EMILY: "A dollar and a half for your refrigerator—"

DIAN: "A dollar for your washing machine—"

SHANNON: "Fifty cents for each bed in the house, including the mattress and all linens."

TAMLYN: That really hurt because we knew—I was old enough to realize—it took my mother and father twenty-five years of hard work to put together a few things. And then to have this kind of thing happen.

We finally got rid of everything except—we had an old-fashioned upright piano that we were very fond of, and there was no way that my mother was going to let that piano go for two dollars. She just refused. She said she would take that piano out in the backyard and take an axe to it before she'd let anyone take it away for two dollars.

DIAN: Miyo Senzaki.

EMILY: I got married in March 1942. My husband used to come after me, and he found out that they were going to be evacuated. They already got their notice. That's when my husband said—

DIAN: "You either marry me or we just won't see each other."

EMILY: So I looked at him and said, "Marry you? You haven't even got a job."

    We got married the day before the old Union Church was going to close. We got married so we could go to camp together.

TAMLYN: Monica Sone.

DIAN: On the day we evacuated, Dunks Oshima had offered to take us down to Eighth and Lane in a borrowed pickup truck. The menfolk loaded the truck with the last few boxes of household goods that Dunks was going to take down to the hotel for storage.

    Puzzled, he held up a gallon of soy sauce—

TAMLYN: "Where does this go, to the hotel, too?"

DIAN: No one seemed to know where it had come from or where it was going, until Mother finally spoke up—

EMILY: "Er—it's going with me. I don't think we'd have shoyu where we're going—"

DIAN: My brother looked as if he were going to explode—

TAMLYN: "Mama, people will laugh at us. We're not going on a picnic—"

EMILY: "Nonsense. No one will ever notice this little thing. It isn't as if I were bringing liquor—"

DIAN: "Well, if Mama's going to take her shoyu, I'm taking my radio along. At least it'll keep me from talking to myself out there—"

TAMLYN: "That's enough! Two suitcases and a seabag a person, that's final! Now let's get going before we decide to take the house along with us."

DIAN: My mother personally saw to it that the can of shoyu remained in her baggage.

EMILY: Eleanor Gerard Sekerak.

SHANNON: I was teaching a criminology class at San Francisco City College when a field trip took us to observe a camp set up at Tanforan by the Immigration and Naturalization Service after Pearl Harbor. This was my first contact with internment.

    Later, in a graduate class on the Berkeley campus, the professor unexpectedly informed us that one of our colleagues would be giving his final oral presentation early. Hiro Katayama bade us—

DIAN: "Goodbye."

SHANNON: And left the classroom—his destination . . . Tanforan.

    During hall duty, I had the occasion to admonish, almost daily, a youngster who always dashed by as though on roller skates. Once while reminding him not to run in the halls, I asked for his name—

TAMLYN: "Bill Oshima!"

SHANNON: After evacuation, the halls seemed very quiet.

EMILY: Nobu Miyoshi.

DIAN: We had chosen "voluntary evacuation."

One Sunday morning in February 1942, my sister Anne received a call from the War Relocation Authority office giving permission for us to leave Sacramento, California. The deadline for leaving was eight o'clock that evening!

The office had kept assuring us that we would have ample time for preparation, so we were shocked by this call.

We had not even collected boxes for packing our household goods. We and about twenty-five friends and neighbors went into high gear to dismantle our home. There were no consultations. Everyone did what they thought was necessary. And there was very little conversation or questions in the constant activity.

Suddenly, Esther Tani said—

TAMLYN: "This is against the Constitution. This is wrong."

DIAN: I was amazed to hear such a purely American expression. I heard no other Nisei openly call our government into question. I think most of us felt that we had no rights.

EMILY: Elaine Black Yoneda.

SHANNON: On the evening of Sunday, March 29th, the radio suddenly blurted out:

TAMLYN: "Attention, attention, all those of Japanese ancestry whose breadwinners are in the Manzanar Reception Center: You are hereby ordered to report to the Civil Control Station at 707 South Spring Street tomorrow from 8 A.M. on for processing to leave for Manzanar by noon, April 2nd."

SHANNON: Had I heard correctly? What of the promise of "last ones out," and here it was only six days since my husband's departure? But soon the announcement was repeated.

I immediately called Army Headquarters but was told to call back after 7 P.M. for an answer to my question: "Does General DeWitt's Manzanar order include a three-year-old Eurasian child living with his Caucasian mother and grandparents?"

EMILY: "You do not have to go, Mrs. Yoneda, nor will you be allowed to go. But your son must go on the basis of the Geneva Accords. That is, the father's ancestry counts, and one-sixteenth or more Japanese blood is the criteria set."

SHANNON: After relating the conversation to my parents, I told them if my son had to go, I would go, too, come hell or high water!

They agreed my decision was correct.

DIAN: Mary Tsukamoto.

EMILY: We never dreamed we would be separated—relatives and close friends, a community. We were just like brothers and sisters. These were our people. And we loved them. We wept with them at their funerals and laughed with them and rejoiced with them at their weddings.

And suddenly we found out that the community was going to split up.

We were just tied up in knots, trying to cope with all of this happening at once and so fast. I can't understand why they had to do this.

TAMLYN: Elaine Black Yoneda.

SHANNON: On Monday morning, my son Tommy and I took our places in the long line already formed outside the station. Suddenly an Army officer and a priest came running to where we stood, telling us to—

DIAN: "Go right in. Don't wait in line."

SHANNON: I protested. But I was ushered in, anyway.

There the captain refused to give me two application forms and the Maryknoll father kept saying—

EMILY: "We will have a Children's Village where our well-trained sisters will take care of your son. You needn't, nor will you be allowed to go. It will be *too hard* for you."

SHANNON: I turned to the officer said, "As sure as we are standing here, my husband will be in a khaki uniform like yours before the year is out! And I'll be there with our son to see him off!"

Then I turned to the priest, "Father, for all you know I may be an atheist, but I took an oath to love, honor, and cherish, NOT OBEY, for better or worse, and that means something to me! I'll be with my child and my husband and never mind the 'too hard' bit!"

I demanded two forms, and they were handed to me. I completed the applications and was given a typhus shot. I also informed them we would take the first train on April Fool's Day.

When we finally pulled into Manzanar, my husband, Karl, and I had a good, silent cry in each other's arms.

DIAN: Mary Tsukamoto.

EMILY: We had been a very happy family. When we left, we swept our house and left it clean because that's the way Japanese feel like leaving a place.

I can just imagine everyone's emotions of grief and anger when they had to leave, when the military police came to tell them—

SHANNON: "Get ready right now. You've got two hours to get ready to catch this train."

DIAN: Aiko Horikoshi.

TAMLYN: I wouldn't describe myself as a resister, but I kept defending my rights. I resisted the evacuation order during a long night prior to leaving for Pomona Assembly Center.

The night before evacuation, I climbed out of my bedroom window to meet my boyfriend, Tom, who was Caucasian. We drove around town for three hours.

I didn't want to be evacuated. I didn't want to leave, and I was rebelling with every fiber in my being.

But we were too young to elope. We talked about how we could get away from all this.

Finally at five o'clock in the morning, I crawled back into my bedroom window and . . .

There was my father.

Waiting for me with open arms.

And he just held me real tight and said—

DIAN: "Thank you for coming home."

SHANNON: Mary Tsukamoto.

EMILY: There were tears everywhere. Nobody could take pets, and this was a sad thing for my daughter. Grandma couldn't leave her flowers. Grandpa looked at his grape vineyard. We urged him to get into the car and leave.

I remember that sad morning when we realized suddenly that we wouldn't be free. It was such a clear, beautiful day, and I remember as we were driving, our tears.

We saw the snow-clad Sierra Nevada mountains that we had loved to see so often, and I thought about God and about the prayer we always prayed.

DIAN: Florence Nakamura.

TAMLYN: Our family number was 19153.

In April 1942, on the day of departure, each member of my family had a cardboard tag with this number attached to his or her coat.

This tag was our identification.

SHANNON: Mary Tsukamoto.

EMILY: On the train, we were told not to look out the window. But people were peeking out. After a long time on the train, somebody said—

DIAN: "Oh there's some Japanese standing over there!"

EMILY: So we all took a peek, and we saw this dust, and rows and rows of barracks, and all these tan, brown Japanese people with their hair all—bleached. Dust had covered their hair. They were all standing in a huddle looking at us, looking at this train going by.

Then somebody on the train said—

TAMLYN: "Gee, that must be Japanese people in camp."

EMILY: We didn't realize who they were before. But I saw how terrible it looked: The dust, no trees—just barracks and a bunch of people standing against the fence, looking out. Some children were hanging onto the fence like animals, and that was my first sight of the assembly center.

I was so sad and discouraged looking at that. I knew, before long, we would be inside, too.

SHANNON: Masako Saito.

DIAN: We did assemble, somewhere on Van Ness Avenue—my brother-in-law Frank came to pick us up. We then went on to the railroad station. We had to stay overnight in the old boxcar train we were on until they decided where to place us.

Finally, they took us to Santa Anita.

We lived in a horse stall.

4. Slide: Somewhere in Between

TAMLYN: Mary Tsukamoto.

EMILY: When we arrived, we saw all these people, peeking out from behind the fence, wondering what group would be coming next, and, of course, looking for their friends, too. Suddenly you realized that human beings were being put behind fences just like on the farm where we had horses and pigs in corrals.

It was hot, and everybody was perspiring. We were tired from the train trip, and here they were staring at us. It was humiliating to be stared at like that. And these were Nihonjin people staring us, Nihonjin people, our people.

We came dragging suitcases and luggage and all our clothing. We felt so self-conscious to be stared at, but of course I looked right back to see if I recognized anybody.

My father and mother and my cousins had gone a day or two ahead of us. I was looking for them, and they came looking for us.

Then we saw each other.

TAMLYN: Emi Somekawa.

DIAN: The Portland Assembly Center was terrible. It's just amazing how people can think of putting another group of human beings into a place like that. There was so much horse and cow manure around.

We were put into a cubicle that just had plywood walls, and it was a horse stall with planks on the floor with about an inch of space between them.

In the corner, we saw this folding bed, an army camp cot, with mattress ticking, and we were supposed to go out there to fill it with straw so that we would have a mattress.

It's depressing we had to go into a place like that.

SHANNON: Mine Okubo.

TAMLYN: The room showed hurried whitewashing. Spider webs, horse hair, and hay had been whitewashed with the walls. Huge spikes and nails stuck out all over the wall. A two-inch layer of dust covered the floor. We opened the folded spring cots and sat on them in the semidarkness.

In the next stall, we heard someone crying.

EMILY: Eleanor Roosevelt.

SHANNON: "To many young people, this must have seemed strange treatment of American citizens.

"One cannot be surprised at the reaction in young Japanese Americans but also in others who had known them well and had been educated with them and who asked bitterly, 'What price American citizenship?' Nevertheless, most of them realize that this was a safety measure.

"The Army carried out its evacuation with remarkable skill and kindness.

"The early situation in the centers was difficult. Many of them were not ready for occupation. The setting up of large communities meant an amount of organization that took time.

"But the Japanese proved to be patient, adaptable, and courageous."

TAMLYN: Haruko Niwa.

DIAN: I was kind of bitter at first. I trust the United States so deeply, its freedom, and this Constitution. We are very proud about the United States, and I trusted this country so much.

But it all owes to wartime. I thought that no matter what, we have to obey military and government's order.

SHANNON: Mary Tsukamoto.

EMILY: We began to realize what it meant to stand in line—long hours standing to eat in the mess hall, standing in line for our bath, standing in line in front of the latrine. That was a shock, but I guess the Army's latrine is the same everywhere.

247

For us women and children, this was something which we couldn't
. . . it was just a shock. I remember we got sick . . . we couldn't go . . . we
didn't want to go. It was smelly, and it was dirty.

In the shower, the water was poured over you, and there were no
partitions, and it was so cramped that we almost touched each other.

It was very humiliating.

TAMLYN: Chizu Iiyama.

DIAN: There was no privacy. And it was like that in camp—and we got over
the feeling of embarrassment.

They had this huge shower room, half for the men, and the other
for women.

Then they said some of the young men had made peep holes. I heard
a lot of giggling that went on.

SHANNON: Monica Sone.

DIAN: The partition wall separating the rooms was only seven feet high with
an opening of four feet to the top.

At night, Mrs. Funai next door could tell when my sister Sumi was
still sitting up in bed in the dark, putting her hair up. Through the plank
wall, Mrs. Funai would say—

EMILY: "Mah, Sumi-chan, are you curling your hair tonight again? Do you
put it up every night?"

DIAN: And Sumi would glare at the wall.

SHANNON: Helen Murao.

TAMLYN: In the late thirties and forties in my neighborhood where I grew
up with Caucasian kids, we were all just one big family. But as we approached our teen years, you know, sex started to become important,
and boys and girls started to pair off. While I was just great as a neighbor
and a friend, all of a sudden, I wasn't right to be dated. So I had very
strange feelings.

In camp, I discovered that among Japanese people I was really kind
of an oddity, because I had lived among Caucasians. When the guys
started coming around, I was thinking, "Boy, this is terrific I was getting offers for dates and stuff like that. This was just going to be great!"

It was this racial thing that I was just beginning to become aware
of. I discovered that among the Nisei people, I was an equal. I could
compete with the other girls for the boys' attention.

That summer I had this sorting out and coming to terms with my
own self and my own life.

It was not an easy time.

DIAN: Yakuri.

EMILY: Plate in hand,
      I stand in line,
      Losing my resolve
      To hide my tears.

      I see my mother
      In the aged woman who comes,
      And I yield to her
      My place in line.

      Four months have passed,
      And at least I learn
      To call this horse stall
      My family's home.

SHANNON: Kiyo Sato.

DIAN: The assembly center was quickly built, temporary. Not a blade of grass, not one tree for the five thousand people living there behind barbed-wire fences. And I wanted to see something growing—I would go around and see trees in the distance—oh—to be able to go out.

One day, I saw a whole bunch of people gathered around. I thought someone got sick or died—what do you do in a place like this if anyone got sick? So I went over to see what happened. You know what it was? A seed had sprouted. A seed had sprouted, and everyone was there to look at it.

Everyday, no matter what time of the day I went, there was somebody there. And they built a little fence around it, so that it would be safe. I think it was morning glory.

It was amazing to me that all the Issei had packed seeds. My mother packed seeds, and they planted everywhere—between the barracks, et cetera. It was green everywhere—sometimes you couldn't see the barracks because the vines were growing. We were there for two and a half months.

SHANNON: Mary Tsukamoto.

EMILY: We had our July Fourth program. Because we couldn't think of anything to do, we decided to recite the Gettysburg Address as a verse choir. We had an artist draw a big picture of Abraham Lincoln with an American flag behind him.

Some people had tears in their eyes. Some people shook their heads and said it was so ridiculous to have that kind of thing recited in a camp.

I know it didn't make any sense, but we wanted so much to believe that this was a government by the people and for the people and that there was freedom and justice.

SHANNON: Yoshiko Uchida.

TAMLYN: One of the elementary school teachers was the first to be married at Tanforan. She wanted to have the kind of wedding she would have had on the outside. She wore a beautiful white marquisette gown with a fingertip veil. We crowded into the church barrack that day, and the wedding was a moment of extraordinary joy and brightness. We showered the couple with rice as they left, and they climbed into a borrowed car decorated with "just married" signs and a string of tin cans. They took several noisy turns around the racetrack in the car. After a reception in one of the recreational centers, they began their married life in one of the horse stalls.

SHANNON: Haruko Niwa.

DIAN: I told Nobu and Aki, "From now on you kids have to be really strong and pray every minute, because whatever happens, you have to decide yourself.

"I cannot watch you constantly, and we don't know from now on what kind of living we going to have. We don't know we can continue as a family unit.

"We cannot protect you, so you have to stand up and protect yourself and decide what is wrong and what is right, because Mommy and Daddy can't follow all over, because we don't know what's going to be. We have to be closer than before."

That's what I told the two boys, you know.

SHANNON: Noriko Sawada Bridges.

EMILY: I recall one girlfriend who decided she was 100 percent American. So when I would speak to her in Japanese, she wouldn't answer because she claimed she couldn't understand. She refused to eat rice because that was Japanese. She refused to use chopsticks because that was Japanese. She was viciously the other way. It's hard to survive in a camp like that, hanging on to those notions.

DIAN: Helen Murao.

TAMLYN: By Labor Day 1942, when we were to be moved inland to Idaho, I guess I was beginning to feel that I had no choice.

I had to quit being so angry and quit being so hateful. I had a job to do with my brothers, so I ran them like a drill sergeant.

People who met me in those years smile and laugh and talk about it now.

They say—

EMILY: "That Helen ran those boys like she was a drill sergeant."

TAMLYN: I wouldn't let them out after nine o'clock. I made them go to school.

I made them study. I made them . . . you know. I had them help me scrub their clothes so that they would be clean.

Then somewhere during that time I came to feel, well, we're going to show these people. We're going to show the world. They are not going to do this to me. Nobody is going to make me feel this miserable. The United States government may have made me leave my home, but they're going to be sorry. You know what I mean.

I'm going to prevail. My will is going to prevail. My own life is going to prevail. I'm not going to kill myself.

I am going to prevail.

SHANNON: Yuri Kochiyama.

EMILY: I couldn't believe this was happening to us. America would never do a thing like this to us. This is the greatest country in the world.

So I thought this is only going to be for a short while. Maybe a few weeks or something, and they will let us go back.

At the beginning no one realized how long this would go on. I didn't feel the anger that much because I thought maybe this was the way we could show our love for our country.

SHANNON: Chizu Iiyama.

DIAN: When we were in a temporary detention center in Santa Anita, my mother cried and cried and said we were all going to get killed. But when she realized in a week or so that they weren't going to kill us—she perked up.

In fact, she took English in camp. She even took a class in American Constitution. And when the time came for her to become a citizen, she was one of the first people to.

TAMLYN: Mrs. Hatsumi Nishimoto.

EMILY: I do not recall any pleasant camp experiences—not even one.

What bothered me most was there was virtually no family dining. Young people ate with their friends. Men dined together. And women ate in their own groups.

Perhaps one positive thing about camp was that life was scheduled— without question. Everything occurred on time.

Life in camp could be described as happy, because we had time on our hands and could attend classes for free.

SHANNON: Yoshiko Uchida.

TAMLYN: I was an assistant at one of the three nursery schools at Tanforan.

Whenever the children played house, they always stood in line to eat at make-believe mess halls rather than cooking and setting tables as they would have done at home.

It was sad to see how the concept of home had changed for them.

SHANNON: Mary Tsukamoto.

EMILY: Soon we learned to cope, and we managed to enjoy whatever we could and got busy. I taught English to Isseis, which was a delightful experience. I also taught public speaking.

This was thrilling to me, because I found out that the Isseis really wanted to learn something that they did not have the opportunity to learn before.

One mother said—

DIAN: "I want to be able to write my son a letter. I'm always asking other people to write for me. When he's in the service and worried, I want him to know I'm all right. I want him to understand from my own letters that I care for him and that I'm okay."

EMILY: We used unfinished buildings for temporary classrooms, and we hastily tried to keep everybody busy. Soon, surprising things began to happen.

The Issei ladies were making crepe-paper flowers. They were taking classes from old Mrs. Nagao, who was a farmer's wife, brown and tanned and wrinkled. All I knew was that she was strawberry grower's wife, and I knew she could pick strawberries. Here she was—a teacher of the crepe-paper flower-making class.

Soon the whole camp was transformed.

Who but Nihonjins would leave a place like that in beauty? It was an inspiring sight. I felt proud that the Nihonjins, who had coped through the heat of the summer, had faith enough to plant a garden.

Of course, it was probably torn down quickly because it was the Fresno Fairground.

DIAN: Eleanor Roosevelt.

SHANNON: "At first, the evacuation was placed on a voluntary basis. The people were free to go wherever they liked in the interior of the country.

"But the evacuation moved very slowly, and those who did leave encountered a great deal of difficulty in finding new places to settle.

"In order to avoid serious incidents, on March 29, 1942, the evacuation was placed on an orderly basis and was carried out by the Army.

"It was an entirely new undertaking for us.

"And it had to be done."

EMILY: Wasco Fujiwara.

TAMLYN: Fresno Assembly Center was just a temporary camp. We stayed there for three months.

We were then sent to a more permanent home in the interior, Tule Lake, because they had just finished that camp.

SHANNON: Monica Sone.

DIAN: When I got to the camp, I noticed a powerful beam of light sweeping across my window every few seconds. The light came from high towers placed around the camp where the guards with tommy guns kept a twenty-four-hour vigil. I remembered the wire fence encircling us.

What was I doing behind a fence like a criminal? If there were accusations made, why hadn't I been given a fair trial? Maybe I wasn't considered American anymore.   Maybe my citizenship wasn't real. Then what was I?

Of one thing I was sure. The wire fence was real.

I no longer had the right to walk out of it.

Act 2

5. Slide: Behind the Fence

TAMLYN: Katarine Krater.

SHANNON: After the bombing of Pearl Harbor, my husband had a grocery store down the main street, and all of a sudden these strange people began to come into the store—we thought we knew everybody in Owens Valley in those days—and these people were very uncouth, very unappealing.

We eventually found out that they were the people who had been brought in to build the barracks for Manzanar for the Japanese who were going to be interned there.

Well, I was very upset, and in those days I expressed myself, and I told these people that I thought this was unforgivable, and I didn't get a very good response. In fact, they were very unfriendly.

My husband told me I had better be quiet and not say anything about it. So, I didn't say very much about it.

EMILY: Haruko Niwa.

DIAN: My first morning in Manzanar, when I woke up and saw what Manzanar looked like, I just cried.

And then I saw the mountain, the high Sierra Mountain, just like my native country's mountain, I cried.

That's all. I couldn't think about anything.

TAMLYN: Katarine Krater.

SHANNON: The camp was enclosed in barbed wire, and there was a tower at each of the four corners. It wasn't a relocation camp. It was a concentration camp, that's what it was. They were prisoners there. They couldn't leave, and they couldn't move around at all. There were ten thousand at the time—it varied—but at one time they had a population of ten thousand, which was more than the entire population of Inyo County.

There were people in Independence who were just frightened out of their wits. They thought the Japanese were going to break out of Manzanar, and we'd all be slaughtered in our beds.

We know of at least two men who slept with guns under their beds all the time the Japanese were at Manzanar.

DIAN: Helen Murao.

TAMLYN: At Idaho's Minidoka, we were assigned our barracks.

At the same time, the camp was giving out bedding. The old and the infirm got beds with mattresses. The younger people got uncomfortable cots and pillow ticking that you had to fill with straw.

The guys in camps were teenagers. They were running down the block saying—

EMILY: "There's one over there!"

DIAN: "There's a good one over here!"

TAMLYN: They were pegging the families that were coming in that had—you know—good-looking girls. Finally, they came running up to me and asked where my parents were.

Since they did not know my parents were dead, I lied and said . . . "They weren't around."

They asked—

DIAN: "How many beds?"

TAMLYN: "Just one."

I managed to finagle a real bed with a real mattress from these guys using feminine wiles.

EMILY: Haruko Niwa.

DIAN: Aki was sitting on the front entrance step, he was crying with a drop of the tear like a marble. I know he missed the school in Westwood. He enjoyed so much, the school activities that I know he missed that—all his friends in school and all that—and thinking about what is going to be his education and his future. Oh, he had the marble-size tear rolling down from his eyes, you know.

My other son Nobu was quiet sitting in the corner of the barracks. He was just sitting, just staring from the corner at nothing.

SHANNON: Noriko Sawada Bridges.

EMILY: When my mother was asleep, I would go to the library that was a block away and bring back books. She would accuse of me meeting boys at the library. She hated the library because I was being encouraged to be delinquent. She wouldn't let me go on dates. She just wouldn't allow anything.

It got to the point where I decided this wasn't worth living for. This was no life. Once I made that decision, I felt powerful and liberated. So then I took all my photographs and cut them up and burned them so she wouldn't have any evidence that I had ever existed.

Then I took a handful of her sleeping pills. But you know, they don't work all that fast. I was lying on the cot, and it was lunchtime, and my father asked me if I wanted some lunch, and I said sure. So he went to the mess hall and brought back my lunch and my mother's lunch, and I ate it. That diluted the effects of the pills a lot.

Then my girlfriend came by and was being very chatty, and I said that I didn't feel much like chatting because I'm really committing suicide and I'm supposed to die any minute now. She ran for the doctor.

The doctor came, and my mother told him that I was pregnant, which I wasn't. He was asking me the name of the boy, and I was saying that I was not pregnant, and my mother was saying I was pregnant. Otherwise, no woman my age would be committing suicide. It was the *haji*, the shame of it all.

All of a sudden, it struck me as being really funny. I mean, here's this big moment in my life, and I'm being accused of being pregnant, and it's all like low comedy. So I began to laugh, and I laughed and I laughed. Of course, they're looking at me like I'm nuts and gone off my rocker totally.

The doctor made me drink some spirits of ammonia and then made my father sit at the foot of my bed. And every time I fell asleep, he poked me in the foot with a needle, and that would wake me up. I was annoyed as all hell about the whole thing and swore I would never do it again.

Oh, my mother was also annoyed because the doctor was paying more attention to me than he was to her.

It was funny.

DIAN: Pauline Miller.

SHANNON: My daughter was just a little girl. I guess she was about four or five years old.

One time, we went for a dinner out at Manzanar, and they served all this beautiful food that they had raised. They raised their own vegetables and everything, and that's what they were showing.

And I couldn't get my daughter to take a bite because she figured they were enemies, you know. She just had that in her mind. They were our enemies, and you just didn't eat their food.

She just sat there.

TAMLYN: Toyo Suyemoto.

DIAN: Mother did not approve of her children "staying out" in the latrine building without parental supervision. Like other mothers in camp, she felt that discipline and respect for parental control were being ignored by the children.

One night, my two youngest brothers were not back from their showers though it was almost midnight.

Then Mother began putting on her cardigan sweater. I realized what she was about to do, and I told her she was not allowed to enter the men's shower area.

All she said was—

EMILY: "I will bring them back."

DIAN: And very quickly, she returned to our barracks with the two boys.

They pleaded—

TAMLYN: "Please don't ever do that again!"

DIAN: After that, she never had to remind them to be home on time.

EMILY: Helen Murao.

TAMLYN: I insisted that my two brothers and I eat together in the mess hall as a family unit. I insisted that we have grace before meals. And I insisted that they be in our room at eight o'clock at night. Not because I wanted to see them but because I thought that's we should do as a family unit— we should be together, spend our time together, and live as a family group—and I tried all the really childish ways to maintain us that way.

SHANNON: Anonymous.

EMILY: In our block, there was a woman whose husband began to beat her. Of course, everyone knew about it. How could you hide such a thing in those barracks? She was so ashamed that she wouldn't come out of her unit for days, even to eat.

Then one day—and I still don't know how she did it—she left camp, left her husband, and her two small children.

She must have suffered a lot to leave her children.

TAMLYN: Masako Saito.

DIAN: My mother was, well, it was hard on her, I guess—she's such an excitable woman—we tried to tell her how to do things, but she refused. When we were in camp, her main goal was to have her floor nice and clean.

But whatever it is—it was fate—as my mother would say. I know it was a feeling of sadness, being confined.

We felt it most when we used to go on Sundays to the grandstand for our church services. And we would be singing our church hymns, and in the background we would see the train wending its way, going around, and we thought, "Wouldn't it be nice to get out?" And that's how all of us felt.

I felt sad especially on a Sunday morning—in Sunday school.

SHANNON: Ada Endo.

TAMLYN: My sister and her husband and family are devoted Christians. I would never think of her doing anything out of line.

One night she came over and said—

EMILY: "You know, there is a lot of lumber down there, and there is only one guard. Let's go down—and get some lumber."

TAMLYN: I looked at her, and I was sure surprised. I said, "Sure, why not?"

So we went down when the guard was not making his rounds or when he was on the other side.

We would go in and grab a piece of lumber, and we would wait awhile. And when the coast was clear, we would run back to the barracks. She held one end, and I held the other end.

I don't know how many pieces of lumber we brought back, but we divided it, and she took it to her barrack. I kept my half, and that is what we made shelves with.

We probably wouldn't ever do it again. We probably wouldn't even steal a penny, but we stole lumber that night.

DIAN: Anonymous.

EMILY: I remember one of my friends got engaged and married in camp. We gave her a shower.

What we gave her were carpenter nails because they were so precious. We went to the dump site and around the construction of new barracks and sifted through the sand for them. I think I stole some from my dad's toolbox. I wrapped them up in crepe paper so they resembled flowers and gave them to her.

She was very touched by it because she had to build furniture from scrap lumber for her new place.

SHANNON: Aiko Yoshinaga-Herzig.

TAMLYN: I never had any sexual experience before going to camp. And so, making love on a straw mattress was noisy for me. Every time you moved a toe . . . you know.

SHANNON: Anonymous.

DIAN: We put up sheets to partition off our bed from the boys' beds. But we were always aware that they could hear everything, even a whisper. So my husband and I had no choice but to take "long" walks in the middle of the night . . .

TAMLYN: Noriko Sawada Bridges.

EMILY: I was trying to let my mother know what a crumb she was, and it wasn't working, and it would never work. When I realized that, I thought that I was sacrificing my life for nothing.

Things eased up a bit because when the doctor came back I told him why I made this suicide attempt, and so he told my mother that she should allow me to go to the library. And she should allow me to have dates.

So when a young man would ask me to go to a dance and I would say yes, and he would show up and he would say—

DIAN: "Hello, Mrs. Sawada."

EMILY: She wouldn't answer.

When we started walking off toward the mess hall where the dance was being held, not necessarily on our block, so maybe we would walk half a mile, my mother would follow us.

You know, walk a few paces behind, and she would wait at the mess hall until the dance was over, and then she would follow us home.

And that cured most guys of asking me the second time.

I was not the belle of the ball.

DIAN: Yoshiko Uchida.

TAMLYN: Sometimes as we walked, we could hear the MPs singing in their quarters, and then they seemed something more than sentries who patrolled the barbed-wire perimeters of our camp. We realized they were lonely boys far from home, too.

Still, they were on the other side of the fence. Although at times they tried to talk to us, we never offered them our friendship.

EMILY: Mary Gillespie.

SHANNON: They built the camp, and these men used to get very much provoked because we had to ration things—we were given just so much coffee, so much sugar—and they got everything, they were treated very good . . . they had all kinds of food, and, you know, the Japs don't really live like that, they're used to fish and rice and their food.

The Japs had ham and bacon and all this stuff, and it was said by some people who worked out at the camp that the garbage cans were just full because they weren't used to that kind of food.

They got the best of everything. They were treated very, very good. I'll say that for them.

EMILY: Teruyo Tamura Mitsuyoshi.

DIAN: The food in the mess hall was terrible. They served a lot of stewed stuff—unidentified meat with rice—and Jell-o.

So whenever the food was unappetizing, we would return to the barracks for cocoa and Spam.

To this day, I hate Spam.

SHANNON: Aiko Horikoshi.

TAMLYN: I remember, in a department store in Powell, there were three Issei women who were looking at the material, and there were two local Caucasian ladies there and me. We were the only ones in the store.

Those two ladies were talking about the three Japanese ladies, and they were calling them—

SHANNON: "Hicks."

TAMLYN: And I got all uptight about that. They didn't know what I was (I was half Japanese, half Caucasian).

I went over and said, "Don't you call us hicks. We are from Hollywood, California. You are such hicks you don't even have an escalator in the whole state of Wyoming."

I huffed and went away. They just stood there with their mouths open. They didn't even answer me.

EMILY: Mary Gillespie.

SHANNON: There were some real rough times at Manzanar because some of the internees tore down the American flag, and they jumped all over civilian cars, but they moved them out to Tule Lake afterwards.

Well, all I can say is that when they were put into camp, they were royally treated—they fished and hunted. They were confined there but . . .

No, I never went to the camp. I had no desire to.

DIAN: Hisaye Yamamoto.

EMILY: Sears and Roebuck and Montgomery Ward catalogues would come in by the truckloads. And I'm sure they did millions of dollars worth of business.

SHANNON: Aiko Yoshinaga-Herzig

TAMLYN: We read those two catalogues from the two companies like bibles. I remember memorizing what page the chocolate candies were on in the Sears and Roebuck catalogue.

EMILY: Mine Okubo.

DIAN: When the cold days came in Tanforan, the War Relocation Authority distributed GI clothes to all those employed, both women and men. It was welcome if peculiar apparel—warm pea jackets and army uniforms. In sizes 38 and 44! They were apparently left over from the First World War!

We also ordered our clothing allotment from the Sears Roebuck summer catalogue. These clothes, with many substitutions, began to arrive.

Because of the catalog orders and the GI clothes, everyone in camp was dressed alike.

EMILY: Eleanor Gerard Sekerak.

SHANNON: When my teaching contract did not arrive, I was informed by the dean that the district had decided to hire a man. This was long before the days one could rush into court claiming discrimination!

Then a telegram arrived, and the wire read—

DIAN: "If you have not yet signed a contract, will you consider a position at Topaz, Utah? We are in desperate need of teachers."

SHANNON: I packed and caught a train for Utah, arriving there October 1st.

When I arrived at the staff women's dorm, a crew of young men delivered my trunk. One of the men shrieked upon seeing me and dropped the trunk on his toes. It was my hall runner from Technical High—

TAMLYN: "Bill Oshima!"

SHANNON: He dashed away shouting—

TAMLYN: "Guess who's here? That strict teacher from Tech!"

SHANNON: By noon, the whole of Topaz knew that a Californian teacher had arrived.

Never was an ordinary teacher made to feel more welcome. People crowded around to ask questions, shake hands, bow, and thank me for being there.

When questioners learned that I was from Oakland and from UC, out the crowd emerged classmates from University High—and Hiro Katayama, who had told us good-bye only six months before.

EMILY: Helen Murao.

TAMLYN: I was still in high school, so I had to go to class.

My two brothers had to go, too, and I lied a lot because I didn't want to go. I would stay at home, because the hot water in the mess mall and in the laundry rooms was available. I would scrub my brother's blue jeans and their clothes on a washboard and try to wring them out and also launder our sheets in the morning.

Then I would write a note saying, "Please excuse Helen for being absent, she was busy." And then I'd sign it, and the teacher would accept it.

I still managed to get good grades.

DIAN: Eleanor Gerard Sekerak.

SHANNON: I wondered how I could teach American government and democratic principles while we sat in classrooms behind barbed wire.

I never ceased to have a lump in my throat when the classes recited the Pledge of Allegiance, especially the phrase "Liberty and justice for all."

On my first day, in our opening discussion, the students and I agreed that the whole evacuation process had been traumatic and could not last forever. And we could not permit academic achievement to be interrupted.

So they arrived for classes on time, with their homework completed. They worked diligently, took their exams, and observed normal classroom standards.

We had one exception.

The day the first snow fell.

All the Californian Bay Area students and I rushed to the window to watch.

EMILY: Anna T. Kelley.

SHANNON: There were also teachers employed out there. Caucasians. They would come into Independence into Lone Pine. They met with a lot of hostility and were called "Jap lovers." Some restaurants refused to serve them.

DIAN: Mary Tsukamoto.

EMILY: During the Christmas season, I renewed my letter writing with vigor and enthusiasm. I even wrote letters to President Franklin Roosevelt and his wife, Eleanor.

One day, the mailman delivered a letter to my barrack at 9-8-E. I wondered why a little parade of curious people accompanied him right up to my door. He handed me a letter, and his eyes were excited.

On the envelope were the gold letters that said, "The White House." Who could possibly be sending a letter to 9-8-E in Jerome, Arkansas, internment camp from the White House?

I carefully opened the envelope—

SHANNON: "Dear Mrs. Tsukamoto,

"Thank you so much for your letter. It was good of you to write to the President and me and your thoughtfulness is deeply appreciated. I am glad for you and wonder what your plans are for the future.

"Very sincerely yours,

"Eleanor Roosevelt."

EMILY: Eleanor Roosevelt wrote a letter to me!

TAMLYN: Mrs. Hama Yamaki.

DIAN: My son Bill was stationed in Minneapolis and could not secure a permit from the army to enter Tule Lake. This was most distressing to me, because I had to wonder when we would meet again.

Shikata-ganai. It was the draft, he was a man, and he had to go.

In a letter, he expressed the thought—

TAMLYN: "It might be a long time before we see each other again."

DIAN: So I replied, "Do your best while on duty."

EMILY: Katarine Krater.

SHANNON: You know, of course, a good many of the Japanese girls are very beautiful, and this one girl was engaged to one of the boys who had enlisted from Manzanar. The girl was in camp, and he was out. The girl was standing by the -wire fence saying good-bye to him, composed and undemonstrative, holding the barbed wire, and she didn't even realize that those barbs were cutting into her hands.

DIAN: Mrs. Tei Endow.

EMILY: My son Sho had originally served in Alaska. And then he was wounded while serving in the 442nd in Italy. Shrapnel missed his spinal column by a fraction of an inch.

When we first heard Sho had been injured, I received a very nice letter from the War Department that we were welcome to visit him.

I cannot help but think that perhaps we were treated more fairly during the war because we had a son serving in the army.

Sho received the Purple Heart.

SHANNON: Mrs. Itsu Akiyama.

TAMLYN: My son, George, was on leave before going overseas. Later, when I saw him off at the camp gate, I broke down crying. I did not know whether I would see him again. Even after I came home, all I could do was cry.

What troubled me most was that I did not really know how to pray for George's safety. In Japan, my parents had been Buddhist and prayed to a local shrine.

Here in America, I had no one to pray to. And I felt a desperate desire to pray.

DIAN: Eleanor Gerard Sekerak.

SHANNON: Just as we were settling down to a stable community, there was an uproar in the media outside the camps over Nisei registration for the draft.

As a consequence, "applications for leave clearance" were combined with registration of every man of military age into a single questionnaire.

The questions were worded for simple "yes" and "no" answers.

Question 27 concerned a person's willingness to serve in the armed forces. Question 28 asked for unqualified allegiance to the U.S. and the foreswearing of allegiance to Japan.

EMILY: Amy Uno Ishii.

TAMLYN: There were bad feelings among the Japanese people in the camps because all the Nisei, the American citizens that were eighteen years and over, were made to sign a questionnaire, to state whether they would be faithful to this country or not. It was a loyalty questionnaire. Everyone called it "Question 27, Question 28."

It was worded something to the effect—

DIAN: "Will you be loyal to this country?"

TAMLYN: What is the justification of the government bringing questionnaires such as that into these barbed-wire encampments where we were being "protected" when we didn't ask to be protected? When we didn't feel we needed to be protected?

They looked upon us as enemies of this country, and yet they dared to bring in this type of questionnaire asking us all to sign those questions saying—

DIAN: "Will you be faithful and loyal to this country?"

TAMLYN: How could we be anything but? They had us where they wanted us, under barbed wire, guard towers, searchlights, and armed guards. So this was really a ridiculous thing!

It was really an insult to the integrity of the American people, to put forth these types of questions to the Japanese internees, and we *were* considered internees. And yet the boys still were forced to sign these questionnaires!

Many, many Japanese people said—

EMILY: "Don't sign it. By golly, they've got us here. If they want us to be loyal Americans, turn us loose, put us back where we were, send us home, and then draft our boys into the service. Then our boys would be justified to go and fight for this country and prove their loyalty to this country."

DIAN: Eleanor Gerard Sekerak.

SHANNON: All activities were suspended for a week while we interviewed the adult residents to complete the questionnaires

There were many meetings, many committees, and much speech-making.

EMILY: Amy Uno Ishii.

TAMLYN: My mother, brothers, and sisters all agreed that the boys volunteer to go into service in spite of the fact that their father was interned in a so-called "hard-core enemy-alien camp."

My mother—who had done nothing against this country except to raise ten children—was behind barbed wire. In spite of all of that, my mother felt—

DIAN: "If you boys go and serve this country and prove your loyalty, maybe they will turn Daddy loose and at least give a chance for Dad to join Mother and the children and bring back the family unit."

TAMLYN: So the boys went to Camp Savage in Minnesota. They entered what you call military intelligence. They went as interpreters.

SHANNON: Florence Ohmura Dobashi.

EMILY: Had I not wanted to leave camp, I might have answered "no" to both 27 and 28. But I chose to be practical and said, "Yes."

It seemed foolhardy to make those sacrifices and feel like a lonely martyr, yet I was bothered by not answering honestly.

It was the only way out.

SHANNON: Chizuko Omori.

DIAN: When the questionnaires came out, my father rejected them and asked for repatriation to Japan. Now that was very devastating for me personally.

I was like, thirteen years old. I think I protested very loudly, and when I would say, "I'm not Japanese! I'm American!" my mother would say to me—

TAMLYN: "Well if you are an American, what are you doing here in this camp?"

DIAN: Well, I couldn't answer that, of course.

SHANNON: Miyo Senzaki.

EMILY: You learn from the time you're a child in school, from the first grade, to salute the flag. You believe in all the words that are said, you know.

And all of a sudden, you're in camp and you see the flag at half-mast, and you see the name of someone who volunteered for the army.

He's dead.

You think, can you salute that flag? Does it really stand for what it means? That was the time in my life when I didn't feel it stood for what it says.

I remember running over every day and see whose name would appear. We would see names of the kids we went to school with who died in the 442nd.

TAMLYN: Sato Hashizume.

DIAN: One family, the Nambas, created a shrine with a photograph of their uniformed son, his medals, and a carefully folded American flag.

At lunch I stood by Mrs. Otaki. Her cheeks were tear-stained, and her shoulders stooped with sorrow. I tried to speak but could only muster up a nod.

SHANNON: Yoshiko Uchida.

TAMLYN: In Tanforan, my sister grew ill and spent many long days in bed, prompting a well-meaning Issei friend to bring her a small container of clear broth. She urged my sister—

EMILY: "Just take this, Keiko San, and you'll be strong and healthy in no time at all. I guarantee it will work."

TAMLYN: It wasn't until after Kay was up and around that the friend came again to see her.

EMILY: "It worked, didn't it? My broth?"

DIAN: "I guess it did—"

TAMLYN: My sister said.

Only then did the woman reveal she had made the brew with earthworms.

EMILY: "It's guaranteed to restore good health."

SHANNON: Emi Somekawa.

DIAN: There was a case at Tule Lake of a lady who was pregnant, and she had a very serious cardiac condition. All through her pregnancy she spent most of her time in bed, under medication. She didn't quite reach full term, but she went into labor.

The baby was in the neighborhood of about five and a half pounds when it was born, and the mother fell into a coma at the time she delivered.

I was there at the time of her delivery. The doctor who was attending her said they didn't think that she would ever come out of it.

The mother wasn't able to nurse the baby or do anything for the baby because she was constantly under an oxygen tent. This went on for about ten days, and she never improved.

One day, her husband came and said—

EMILY: "I just can't stand watching her breathe. That very labored type of breathing, day after day. Will you please take her out of her misery?"

DIAN: I said, "Well, I will talk to the doctor and see what he says."

The doctor said—

TAMLYN: "We have nothing here to offer her, and if that's the wishes of the family, then I'll go along with it."

DIAN: The next day the husband came back again with his family. He had four children, and they were all still little. The first one might have been in grammar school but not much older. They all came.

And the doctor told me—

TAMLYN: "Fix up a fourth of morphine."

DIAN: So I was there. There was a teaspoon with some water in it, and the father told each child—

EMILY: "Give your mother a sip of water."

DIAN: After the last child gave the sip of water, the father did the same thing, and then he was ready for the morphine.

Right away, the oxygen tent was removed, and she just went to sleep. That was it.

SHANNON: Aiko Horikoshi.

TAMLYN: I was a nurse aide at the hospital when I lived at Heart Mountain. We had a Caucasian chief nurse, Anna Van Dirk, who put a proclamation or a bulletin up ordering us to bow to her.

There was a lot of rumble especially among the doctors that they were ordered to bow to her. I was real irritated, and there was a lot of uneasiness in camp. The hospital staff decided to go on strike, and so I went on strike.

We used to call her Anna Van Jerk.

SHANNON: June Tsutsui.

DIAN: I still have the photograph of my first-born son's grave. It always brings back painful memories.

I carried my baby full term. The delivery was intensified by the camp's inadequate medical care and by the doctor's late arrival.

I started hemorrhaging.

I believe that was aggravated by the hasty delivery on a hard flat table. I still think that a better-staffed hospital might have prevented it.

I endured such pain.

EMILY: Mabel Ota.

TAMLYN: I was in labor for twenty-eight hours, during which time no doctor came to check on me. When he finally came and examined me, he said they could not perform the operation because there was no anesthesiologist in camp.

They took me to the delivery room and gave me a local, and I could see the knife he used to cut into me. Then he used those huge forceps, and I kept watching that clock. He really had a hard time yanking her out, and I was conscious all the time. It was a horrible experience.

Then I remember looking at my baby and saying, "Gee, I thought babies were bright red when they were born." And this one was very pale, and they rushed her over to the incubator.

I didn't get to see my baby for three days. They said she was too weak to be moved. When I finally saw her, I noticed she had scabs on her head where the forceps had been used. There's one spot where hair has never grown.

I'm convinced my baby suffered permanent brain damage due to that procedure.

SHANNON: Miyo Senzaki.

EMILY: When I was pregnant with my second, that's when I flipped. I thought to myself, "Gosh what am I doing getting pregnant?"

I told my husband, "This is crazy. You realize there's no future for us, and what are we having kids for? We're behind barbed-wire fence, the war could go on, what are we going to do? It's a crime to have children. We're not doing them any favors. I'm not going to have this child in camp."

Then, that night it bothered me so much, I wanted to get an abortion. I knew where a doctor lived, so I walked by his place.

I just couldn't go in. I thought, "Oh my god, I can't kill this child." But then I said, "If I have it, it's not fair. What am I doing?"

So I walked back. I figured the doctor is going to say "no" anyway. Then I cried, and I told my husband, "I'm having this one in camp, but no more kids, unless you get me out of here."

DIAN: Yoshiko Uchida.

TAMLYN: One of the funerals I attended in camp was for the father of a friend of mine. She had returned from school in Colorado for the occasion, and it must have been devastating for her to see the bleakness of Topaz for the first time, knowing her father had spent his last days in such a place.

The funeral service was brief, and his coffin was decorated with cascades of crepe-paper flowers painstakingly made by some Issei women.

Many of those who died in Topaz were buried in the desert.

And it seemed ironic that—only then, they were *outside* the barbed-wire fence.

6. Slide: Outside the Fence

TAMLYN: Mine Okubo.

DIAN: Relocation programs were finally set up in the center to return residents to normal life. Students left camps to continue their education in colleges and universities willing to accept them. Seasonal workers flowed, to relieve the farm labor shortage.

Much red tape was involved, and "relocatees" were checked and double-checked. Jobs were checked by the War Relocation offices, and even the place of destination was investigated before an evacuee left.

In January of 1944, I finally decided to leave. I plowed through the red tape and through the madness of packing again.

I also had to attend forums on "How to Make Friends" and "How to Behave in the Outside World."

EMILY: Amy Uno Ishii.

TAMLYN: Before we left Heart Mountain permanently, my husband and I left to go to the small town out of Billings, Montana, to top sugar beets. This was when the government and the people on the outside realized that all the young people had fled the country and gone to the big cities to work in defense plants or had gone into the service. Who was there to harvest the crops?

They then realized they had a ready source in the camps. So they recruited us to go these various farms.

The government made a big mistake in rounding us all up. It was costing them a lot more than they could afford to keep us behind barbed wire, so they were encouraging us to leave the camps.

So we asked permission from the WRA for a release, and they said—

SHANNON: "Yes."

TAMLYN: They gave us a one-way ticket to Chicago and twenty-five dollars.

DIAN: Mitsuye Endo, a twenty-two-year-old American citizen, once worked for the Sacramento Department of Motor Vehicles. In 1942, she was first sent to Tule Lake Center and later to Topaz.

In July, she challenged the Constitution by filing a petition for a writ of habeas corpus asking the courts to rule on whether she could be held indefinitely as a prisoner without being accused, tried, or convicted of a crime.

EMILY: Mitsuye Endo.

TAMLYN: I never imagined it would go to the Supreme Court. In fact, I thought it might be thrown out of court because of all that bad sentiment toward us.

While all this was going on, it seemed like a dream. It just didn't seem it was happening to me.

DIAN: December 18th, 1944.

EMILY: United States Supreme Court Justice William O. Douglas.

SHANNON: "It is conceded by the Department of Justice and by the War Relocation Authority that Mitsuye Endo is a loyal and law-abiding citizen. They make no claim that she is detained on any charge or that she is even suspected of disloyalty.

"Moreover, they do not contend that she may be held any longer in the Relocation Center.

"Mitsuye Endo is entitled to an unconditional release."

EMILY: Justice Frank Murphy.

SHANNON: "I am of the view that detention in Relocation Centers of persons of Japanese ancestry regardless of loyalty is not only unauthorized but is another example of the unconstitutional resort to racism inherent in the entire evacuation program.'"

TAMLYN: And that was our good-bye to the camp.

7. Slide: A New Spring

DIAN: Mary Tsukamoto.

EMILY: I knew I would never live here again. The endless nightmare was behind me, and there was only hope for our future.

My last look at the barrack city brought me anguish mixed with exultation. I stood there for a moment taking one last look. Here I was—a tired twenty-eight-year-old Nisei mother with her child, taking this big step onto the train and the gate.

Dad and my cousin were there to greet us at the station. Auntie, Uncle, Mother—they were all there, and it was wonderfully good to see them and hug them, and suddenly I realized I was free.

I was in the real world, and I was free at last!

SHANNON: Helen Murao.

TAMLYN: I felt wonderful the day I left camp.

We took a bus to the railroad siding and then stopped some place to transfer. And I went in and bought a Coke. A nickel Coke.

It wasn't the Coke but what it represented—that I was free to buy it, that feeling was so intense.

You get maudlin, sentimental about freedom. But if you've been deprived of it, it's very significant.

EMILY: Mrs. Hatsumi Nishimoto.

DIAN: When we returned—in February or March 1945—we were distressed to see that our orchard had been neglected, and our dwelling was filthy.

Our caretaker had been promised that our house would remain vacant, but another neighbor told us in confidence that the orchard foreman had lived in our home.

When I saw the condition of our orchards, I was quite downhearted. What was most cumbersome was the two of us had to do all the work. There were plenty of workers around, but we were unable to hire anyone. Our work was so exhausting that I lost six pounds in the first week!

It took us about three years to return our orchard to its normal condition.

EMILY: Amy Uno Ishii.

TAMLYN: Our only problem was we could not go back to our own house.

The house that we had lived in on Thirty-eighth Street was not available to us when we came back. But we talked to the landlady, the Mexican family that owned the property. They wanted us to come back so badly. They were so happy to see us. They came and embraced my mother. Mrs. de la Puente never spoke any English.

When we were forced to leave our home there, the de la Puentes were very, very nice. They helped us. They asked if they could store some of our things for us. They promised us that if we ever came back, the house was always ours to rent again. We lived in that house for eighteen years.

But at the time we came back, the government had frozen the business of housing and things. The people in the house had a lease on the house because they worked for the government, and the government would not allow the de la Puentes to throw them out. So until their lease had expired, they could not be made to move.

In the meantime, we lived out somewhere else. While there, my mother had a heart attack and died. The de la Puentes felt so badly because my mother never got a chance to come back and live in their house.

DIAN: Noriko Sawada Bridges.

EMILY: The Supreme Court decision was in 1944, and so the West Coast was opened, and I came out to San Francisco.

As we were being oriented to the world outside, the relocation office would take groups of us who were going out and give us little lectures on how it was out there.

He would say—

SHANNON: "Don't congregate in groups of more than five.

"Don't speak Japanese.

"Don't be loud."

DIAN: Anonymous.

TAMLYN: We weren't to congregate among our kind. We shouldn't speak Japanese nor be conspicuous. We were not to talk about camp. In other words, we were not to be Japanese in any way.

But to the dominant society we were not only Japanese, we were "Japs." Certainly, not American. So where the hell did that leave us?

DIAN: Noriko Sawada Bridges.

EMILY: When I got on this train the following year to Chicago, I went into the club car to get a drink. I was sitting there, and some soldiers came in, and they spoke to me in Japanese.

You know, all the signals went up, and I was ready to fight or flee, but I looked through beyond them, and they said—

SHANNON: "Oh, aren't you Japanese?"

EMILY: "No."

SHANNON: "Korean?"

EMILY: "No."

SHANNON: "What are you?"

EMILY: "I don't know. My mother was a lesbian."

I apologized to my mother at this point.

I felt like it was the only way I could get out of saying. "I am a Japanese American, I'm proud of it, and fuck you."

But I just couldn't do that.

DIAN: Fumi Kamada.

TAMLYN: Salt Lake City was nice—quiet—clean town. But—I remember one instance when my husband and I—Sunday—walking downtown and this young man in uniform approached us and asked for matches. He want to light the cigarette. So my husband reach in to give it to him.

Instead of taking the matches, he give my husband—you know—slapped him.

And then my husband tried to go back to him, and I pulled him away because I don't want to get mauled, you know—get involved in a fight or anything. And he's wearing a uniform, and you're not supposed to hit a man in the uniform. Although my husband told him, "You know I was in the army, TOO."

But he didn't care because us, you know, Japanese walking downtown, I guess he didn't like it.

He called him—

SHANNON: "You dirty . . . "

TAMLYN: Three word, you know.

EMILY: Emiko Omori.

DIAN: Immediately after leaving camp, I was so busy trying to make ends meet that I had no time to think about what we'd been through.

I do remember being asked about the camps when I went to NYU in 1947 but always in the context of the Holocaust. All my friends were Jewish. You were made to feel apologetic, almost, about complaining of our "treatment."

But I do remember being annoyed during one of these discussions by a remark—

SHANNON: "Well, at least YOU weren't gassed or anything."

TAMLYN: Noriko Sawada Bridges.

EMILY: When the restrictive covenant was being taken off the deeds that ran with the land, I was getting signatures for a petition. I ran into this woman who said—

SHANNON: "Well, this measure, if it passes, means that if you want to live in the house next to mine, and you have the money to buy it, you could move in?"

EMILY: "Yes."

SHANNON: "Weren't you in one of those camps?"

EMILY: "Yes."

SHANNON: "I don't want an ex-con living next to me."

TAMLYN: Haruko Niwa.

DIAN: It was August 15th, 1945.

I was riding a bus downtown coming home, and then all the church bells rang, and whistles and firecrackers and all that, and all the ladies in the seats in the bus kiss me and hug me. We just kept crying.

The war was over!

It was so happy for all of us, and my husband hustle and bustle for going back to West Los Angeles. Day and night he was making a box and putting everything in.

We knew we were coming home.

8. Slide: The Near Distance

DIAN: Helen Murao.

TAMLYN: Camp wasn't a dreadful place. It wasn't a wretched place. I did have some good times at camp. As I said, I met a lot of kids and learned how to interact with my peer group, the Japanese.

But the overriding feeling that I had, without even being conscious of it at the time, was the deprivation of freedom, and that was a very traumatic thing.

You don't appreciate it until you don't have it. As I said, you can flag-wave, and you hear all these people who make it seem so trite, but it isn't.

SHANNON: Chizuko Omori

DIAN: Well, you know what happened in our family. I mean, the fact that our mother died at the age of thirty-four, a year out of the camps, very suddenly of bleeding ulcers, the door on the whole camp chapter of our lives was closed. And we didn't open it again for years. It was like she was somehow connected with that whole sorry incident, and we were not gonna talk about it anymore.

And we never did.

TAMLYN: Cara Lemon.

SHANNON: One of the reasons the internment is able to maintain its obscurity is the absence of education and general knowledge about it. The fact that I had absolutely no idea of the internment when I went to college is a testament to how little attention the subject has received.

Depictions of the Second World War in American public schools still often present United States' efforts in the war as sacrificial and heroic. The American role in the war is often portrayed as representative of democratic reason battling totalitarian regimes and ensuring justice for the future. Because of the United States' victory in the war, it is easier to remember it in that role. As a consequence, education about the Japanese American internment has received little attention.

The Japanese American internment is a reminder that we are not as far removed from racially motivated policy as we might pretend. Unfortunately, this important reminder has not reached many American citizens, especially younger generations.

The danger of not knowing about the Japanese American internment and its consequences is the inability to prevent the occurrence of a similar event.

TAMLYN: Yuri Kochiyama.

EMILY: I was one of these real American patriots then. Back then, I was all American. Growing up, my mother would say we're Japanese. But I'd say "No, I'm American."

At the time, I was ashamed of being Japanese. I think many Japanese Americans felt the same way. Pearl Harbor was a shameful act, and being Japanese Americans, even though we had nothing to do with it, we still somehow felt we were blamed for it. I hated Japan at that point.

So I saw myself at that part of my history as an "American" and not as "Japanese" or "Japanese American." That sort of changed while I was in the camp.

I hated the war because it wasn't just between the governments. It went down to the people, and it nurtured hate.

The evacuation showed us that even though there is a Constitution, constitutional rights could be taken away very easily.

TAMLYN: Mrs. Ethelyne Joseph.

SHANNON: Yes, at the time, I did, because of the war. I thought the Americans were doing a correct thing in incarcerating these people.

The camps were a necessity because when you think of Pearl Harbor, naturally, if they would have made a return on Pearl Harbor, well, we would have been *done*. I think above everything else that it was a necessity. I'm sure we all felt the same way because we were at war. Naturally, we had a feeling of hatred toward them.

Since then, they have proven themselves, after having lost the war, and they're making their place in society, so I figure they're now equals.

But they had a lot of freedom in their little realm in Manzanar. They had their basketball courts and their tennis courts and their swimming pools. So they really didn't live as though they were in an internment camp. Other than the fact they were deprived of their autos and a few personal things. They didn't have it so bad.

And as far as their behavior and the conduct of the camp and as far as Manzanar is concerned, there were beautiful relations.

In fact, internees still come back every year.

TAMLYN: Haruko Niwa.

DIAN: At first, when we have to evacuate, I was kind of hurt, you know. I was hurt, but I thought about it: It's wartime, so I thought, do the best we can whatever situations arise. We thought we do the best for the children.

I decided to stay here. I turned down my father's request to return to Japan, so I chose United States. I will obey the law of United States and everything. This is my country.

TAMLYN: Katarine Krater.

SHANNON: I think that the hysteria ran so high at the time, it went from President Roosevelt down. He was the one who signed the Executive Order, so the fault lies right on his doorstep and right down the line.

I just can't believe this could ever happen again.

Are you familiar with General DeWitt, and his role in the affair? He heavily influenced the decision, and, as a matter of fact, it was his plan, so to speak. It was his recommendation to the President.

And, of course, you read the telegram they sent to the President?

The Japanese American Citizens League sent this.

TAMLYN: "In this solemn hour we pledge our fullest cooperation to you, Mr. President, and to our country. There can not be any question, there must be no doubt, we, in our hearts know we are Americans, loyal to America, we must prove this to all of you."

SHANNON: The telegram was sent on December 7, 1941.

Just *after* Pearl Harbor.

He ignored it.

DIAN: 1976.

TAMLYN: President Gerald Ford.

SHANNON: "February 19th is the anniversary of a sad day in American history.

"It was on that date in 1942, in the midst of the response to hostilities that began on December 7, 1941, that Executive Order No. 9066 was issued—resulting in the uprooting of loyal Americans. Over 100,000 persons of Japanese ancestry were removed from their homes, detained in special camps, and eventually relocated.

"We now know what we should have known then—that evacuation was wrong."

EMILY: Helen Murao.

TAMLYN: My overriding feeling, and I've told my children, is don't let anybody else do something to you that you don't want to have happen to you. Don't let anybody control you. I have not wanted anybody to control me. My first reaction was, "I'll show you."   Well, I did show them.

So I guess I proved something, but I don't want anything to control my life. Hatred and bitterness can control you too, right? I think I resolved it.

But so, you know, we never forget.

DIAN: Mary Tsukamoto.

EMILY: I realized I needed to be angry not just for myself personally but for what happened to our people. And also for our country because I really believe it wasn't just Japanese Americans that were betrayed but America itself.

I'm saying this for the kids—the kids and their children and their friends and all the generations that are coming. For their sakes, we need to be angry enough to do something about it so that it will never happen again. I'm disappointed for America that it had to happen, and I want the record to be straight.

I know many Niseis who say, "That was all so long ago. Let's forget it and leave well enough alone." But I say, "We were the ones that went through it—the tears and the shame and the shock."

We need to leave our legacy to our children. And also our legacy to America, from our tears, what we learned.

TAMLYN: 1990.

EMILY: President George H. W. Bush.

SHANNON: "A monetary sum and words alone cannot restore lost years or erase painful memories. We can never fully right the wrongs of the past.

"But we can take a clear stand for justice and recognize that serious injustices were done to Japanese Americans during World War II."

TAMLYN: Emi Somekawa.

DIAN: I hope that something like this will never happen to another group of people or to us ever again.

But sometimes I wonder.

(Pause.)

(Lights slowly fade to black.)
TAMLYN: Mary Tsukamoto.
EMILY: Yuri Kochiyama.
DIAN: Haruko Niwa.
SHANNON: Kiyo Sato.
TAMLYN: Monica Sone.
EMILY: Chizu Iiyama.
DIAN: Mine Okubo.
SHANNON: Elaine Black Yoneda.
TAMLYN: *(Overlapping.)* Nobu Miyoshi—
EMILY: *(Overlapping.)* Miyo Senzaki—
DIAN: *(Overlapping.)* Emi Somekawa—
SHANNON: *(Overlapping.)* Eleanor Gerard Sekerak—
TAMLYN: *(Overlapping, softer.)* Amy Uno Iishi—
EMILY: *(Overlapping, softer.)* Masako Saito—
DIAN: *(Overlapping, softer.)* Yoshiko Uchida—
SHANNON: *(Overlapping, softer.)* Ada Endo—
TAMLYN: *(Overlapping, softer.)* Haruko Hurt—
EMILY: *(Overlapping, softer.)* Noriko Sawada Bridges—
DIAN: *(Overlapping, softer.)* Helen Murao—
SHANNON: *(Overlapping, softer.)* Mabel Ota . . .

(Slow fade to black.)

Bibliography

Daniels, Roger. *Prisoners without Trial: Japanese Americans in World War II*. New York: Hill and Wang, 2004.

Egami, Hatsuye. *The Evacuation Diary of Hatsuye Egami*. Edited and with an introduction by Claire E. Gorfinkel. Pasadena, CA: Intentional, 1995.

Grapes, Bryan J., ed. *Japanese American Internment Camps*. San Diego, CA: Greenhaven, 2000.

Harth, Erica, ed. *Last Witnesses: Reflections on the Wartime Internment of Japanese Americans*. Hampshire, England: Palgrave, 2001.

Inada, Lawson Fusao, ed. *Only What We Could Carry: The Japanese American Internment Experience*. Berkeley, CA: Heyday, 2000.

Japanese American Project. Oral History Program. California State University, Fullerton.

McKay, Susan. "Young Women's Everyday: Heart Mountain, Wyoming." In Mike Mackey, ed., *Guilt by Association: Essays on Japanese Settlement, Internment, and Relocation in the Rocky Mountain West*. Powell, WY: Western History, 2001. 3–7.

Nakano, Mei T. *Japanese American Women: Three Generations, 1890–1990.* Berkeley, Ca: Mina, 1990.

National Japanese American Historical Society. Seattle, WA.

Ng, Wendy. *Japanese American Internment during World War II: A History and Reference Guide.* Westport, CT: Greenwood, 2001.

Okubo, Mine. *Citizen 13660.* New York, Columbia University Press,

Oral History Project of Japanese American Women's Exhibit. National Japanese American Historical Society. Seattle, WA. June 1989.

Oral History Project. Regenerations. Japanese American Museum of San Jose, CA.

Sekerak, Eleanor Gerard. "A Teacher in Topaz." In Inada, *Only What We Could Carry,* 126–37.

Sone, Monica. *Nisei Daughter.* Boston: Little, Brown, 1953. Rept., Seattle: University of Washington Press, 1979.

"Starting Over: Japanese Americans after the War." Dianne Fukami, producer/reporter. KCSM-TV. 1996. Available at http://distribution.asianamericanmedia.org/browse/film/?i=199.

Takaki, Ronald. *Strangers from a Different Shore: A History of Asian Americans.* Boston: Little, Brown, 1989.

Tamura, Linda. *The Hood River Issei: An Oral History of Japanese Settlers in Oregon's Hood River Valley.* Urbana: University of Illinois Press, 1993.

Tateishi, John. *And Justice for All: An Oral History of the Japanese American Detention Camps.* New York: Random, 1984.

Tsukamoto, Mary, and Elizabeth Pinkerton. *We the People: A Story of Internment in America.* Laguna, CA: Laguna, 1988.

Uchida, Yoshiko. *Desert Exile: The Uprooting of a Japanese-American Family.* Seattle: University of Washington Press, 1982.

CONTRIBUTORS

Kia Corthron's plays include *Moot the Messenger* (Actors Theatre of Louis-ville's Humana Festival), *Light Raise the Roof* (New York Theatre Work-shop), *Snapshot Silhouette* (Minneapolis's Children's Theatre), *Slide Glide the Slippery Slope* (Actors Theatre of Louisville, Humana, Mark Taper Forum), *The Venus de Milo Is Armed* (Alabama Shakespeare Festival), *Breath, Boom* (London's Royal Court Theatre, Playwrights Horizons, Yale Repertory Theatre, Huntington Theatre, and elsewhere), *Force Continuum* (Atlantic Theater Company), *Splash Hatch on the E Going Down* (New York Stage and Film, Baltimore's Center Stage, Yale Rep, London's Donmar Warehouse), *Seeking the Genesis* (Goodman Theatre, Manhattan Theatre Club), *Digging Eleven* (Hartford Stage Company), *Life by Asphyxiation* (Playwrights Horizons), *Wake Up Lou Riser* (Delaware Theatre Compa-ny), *Come Down Burning* (American Place Theatre, Long Wharf Theatre), and *Cage Rhythm* (Sightlines/The Point in the Bronx). Awards include the Rockefeller Foundation's Bellagio Creative Arts Residency (Italy), Play-wrights Center's McKnight National Residency, Virginia Center for the Creative Arts Award for Excellence in the Arts, Barbara Barondess Mac-Lean Foundation Award, AT&T On Stage Award, Daryl Roth Creative Spirit Award, Mark Taper Forum's Fadiman Award, National Endowment for the Arts/TCG, Kennedy Center Fund for New American Plays, New Professional Theatre Playwriting Award, Callaway Award, Connections Contest winner, and in television a Writers Guild Outstanding Drama Series Award and Edgar Allan Poe Award for *The Wire*. She has devel-oped work through the Hermitage Artists Retreat, Norton Island retreat, Sundance retreat at Ucross, O'Neill National Playwrights Conference, Women's Playwrights Festival in Seattle, Hedgebrook retreat, Shenandoah International Playwrights Retreat, and elsewhere. She traveled to Liberia in 2004 under the auspices of the Guthrie Theater's Bush Foundation grant, inspiring her to write *Tap the Leopard*. Corthron is an elected member of the Dramatists Guild Council, a member of the Writers Guild of America, and an alumna of New Dramatists.

Yussef El Guindi won the 2009 M. Elizabeth Osborn New Play Award for an emerging playwright. His most recent productions include *Jihad Jones and the Kalashnikov Babes*, produced by Golden Thread Productions in San Francisco, and *Our Enemies: Lively Scenes of Love and Combat*, produced by Silk Road Theatre Project in Chicago, where it was Jeff-nominated. The play that is part of the current volume is *Back of the Throat*, winner of the 2004 Northwest Playwrights' Competition held by Theater Schmeater. It won *L.A. Weekly*'s Excellence in Playwriting Award for 2006, was nominated for the 2006 American Theater Critics Association's Harold and Mimi Steinberg / ACTA New Play Award, and was voted Best New Play of 2005 by the *Seattle Times*. It was first staged by San Francisco's Thick Description and Golden Thread Productions; and later presented in various theaters around the country, including The Flea Theater in New York. Another play of his, *Ten Acrobats in an Amazing Leap of Faith,* staged by Silk Road Theatre Project, won the After Dark Award for Best New Play in Chicago in 2006. His two-related one-acts, *Acts of Desire*, were staged by the Fountain Theatre in Los Angeles. *Back of the Throat* and the two-related one-acts, now titled *Such a Beautiful Voice Is Sayeda's* and *Karima's City*, were published by Dramatists Play Service. The latter one-acts are also included in *The Best American Short Plays: 2004–2005*. His play *Ten Acrobats in an Amazing Leap of Faith* is to be included in *Salaam/Peace: An Anthology of Middle-Eastern-American Playwrights*, was published in 2009. Yussef holds an MFA from Carnegie-Mellon University and was playwright-in-residence at Duke University.

Allan Havis has had his plays produced at theaters across the country and in Europe, including San Diego Repertory, Old Globe, Vox Nova, Seattle's ACT, Odyssey, Long Wharf, South Coast Rep, American Repertory Theatre, Hartford Stage, Virginia Stage, WPA, Berkshire Theatre Festival, Trapdoor Theatre, Coral Gable's New Theatre, Interact Theatre, Philadelphia Theatre Company, and Rowholt Theater-Verlag (National German Radio). Works have been commissioned by England's Chichester Festival, Sundance, San Diego Rep, Ted Danson's Anasazi Productions, South Coast Rep, Mixed Blood, CSC Rep, Malashock Dance, Carolina Chamber Chorale, National Foundation for Jewish Culture, University of California, San Diego, and San Diego State University. Fifteen full-length published plays include *Morocco, Hospitality,* and *The Haunting of Jim Crow*. His published books include the edited volume *American Political Plays*, the children's novel *Albert the Astronomer*, and a book on ninety years of eccentric cinema, *Cult Films: Taboo & Transgression* (2008). Havis is the recipient of awards from the Guggenheim Foundation, Rockefeller Foundation, Kennedy Center for the Performing Arts / American Express Fund, Foundation for the Dramatist Guild / CBS, HBO / Playwrights USA, and National Endowment for the Arts Foundation; San Diego Theatre Critics Circle 2003 Outstanding New Play for Nuevo California (cowritten with Bernardo Solano); and San Diego's 2008 Patté Best Play award for *The Tutor*. For many years, he has headed the MFA playwriting program at UC San Diego and now serves as provost of Thurgood Marshall College at UC San Diego. He is a graduate of Yale School of Drama.

Naomi Iizuka's plays include *36 Views, Anon(ymous), At the Vanishing Point* (in the current volume), *Polaroid Stories, Language of Angels, Tattoo Girl*, and *Skin*. Her plays have been produced by the Guthrie Theatre, Actors Theatre of Louisville, the Children's Theater Company, the Kennedy Center for Performing Arts, the Huntington Theater, Berkeley Repertory, GeVa, Portland Center Stage, the Public Theatre, Campo Santo + Intersection for the Arts, the Dallas Theatre Center, the Brooklyn Academy of Music's Next Wave Festival, Soho Repertory, and the Edinburgh Festival and have been workshopped at Sundance Theatre Lab, Midwest PlayLabs, the Public Theater's New Works Now, PS 122, Manhattan Theatre Club, and Seattle Rep. Her plays have been published by TCG, Smith and Kraus, Heineman, Playscripts, Theatre Forum, and American Theater. Naomi's play *Ghostwritten* premiered at the Goodman Theatre in Chicago in spring 2009. Her play *Concerning Strange Devices from the Distant West* is scheduled to premiere at Berkeley Repertory in spring 2010. She is currently working on commissions from Cornerstone Theatre, the Huntington Theater, Yale Repertory, and the La Jolla Playhouse. Naomi is a member of New Dramatists and the recipient of a PEN/Laura Pels Award, an Alpert Award, a Joyce Foundation Award, a Whiting Writers' Award, a Stavis Award from the National Theatre Conference, a Rockefeller Foundation MAP grant, an NEA/TCG Artist-in-Residence grant, a McKnight Fellowship, a PEN Center USA West Award for Drama, Princeton University's Hodder Fellowship, and a Jerome Fellowship. She teaches at the graduate MFA Playwriting program at the University of California, San Diego.

Anne Nelson is an author and playwright who specializes in international affairs. Nelson, a native of Stillwater, Oklahoma, graduated from Yale University. Her work spans many genres. She was a prize-winning reporter covering the wars in Central America and served as the director of the Committee to Protect Journalists and the director of the International

Program at the Columbia Graduate School of Journalism. Her 1986 book on politics and human rights in Puerto Rico, *Murder under Two Flags*, provided the basis for the 1990 feature film A *Show of Force*. Her plays include *The Guys* (2001), *Savages* (2006), and the short play *Petra* (2006). Nelson's most recent work is the nonfiction book *Red Orchestra: The Story of the Berlin Underground and the Circle of Friends Who Resisted Hitler* (2009). The book describes a circle of playwrights, academics, and other intellectuals who formed a resistance movement in Nazi Germany. Nelson has been the recipient of numerous honors, including the Livingston Award for journalism and a Guggenheim Fellowship.

Chay Yew's work includes *Porcelain, A Language of Their Own, Red, A Beautiful Country, Wonderland, A Distant Shore, 17,* and *Visible Cities*. His other work includes adaptations *A Winter People* (based on Anton Chekhov's *Cherry Orchard*) and Federico Garcia Lorca's *House of Bernarda Alba*; performance work *Vivien and the Shadows*; and a musical, *Long Season*. His plays have been produced at the Joseph Papp Public Theatre, Royal Court Theatre (London), Mark Taper Forum, Manhattan Theatre Club, Long Wharf Theatre, La Jolla Playhouse, Intiman Theatre, Wilma Theatre, Portland Center Stage, East West Players, Cornerstone Theatre Company, Perseverance Theatre, Dad's Garage, La Mama (Melbourne, Australia), Fattore K (Rome, Italy), Singapore Repertory Theatre, and TheatreWorks (Singapore), among others. He is also the recipient of the London Fringe Award for Best Playwright and Best Play, George and Elisabeth Marton Playwriting Award, GLAAD Media Award, Asian Pacific Gays and Friends' Community Visibility Award, Made in America Award, AEA/SAG/AFTRA 2004 Diversity Honor, and Robert Chesley Award. Yew has also received grants from the McKnight Foundation, Rockefeller MAP Fund, and the TCG/Pew National Residency Program.

THEATER IN THE AMERICAS

The goal of the series is to publish a wide range of scholarship on theater and performance, defining theater in its broadest terms and including subjects that encompass all of the Americas.

The series focuses on the performance and production of theater and theater artists and practitioners but welcomes studies of dramatic literature as well. Meant to be inclusive, the series invites studies of traditional, experiimental, and ethnic forms of theater; celebrations, festivals, and rituals that perform culture; and acts of civil disobedience that are performative in nature. We publish studies of theater and performance activities of all cultural groups within the Americas, including biographies of individuals, histories of theater companies, studies of cultural traditions, and collections of plays.

Other Books in the Theater in the Americas Series

A Gambler's Instinct: The Story of Broadway Producer Cheryl Crawford
Milly S. Barranger

Unfriendly Witnesses: Gender, Theater, and Film in the McCarthy Era
Milly S. Barranger

The Theatre of Sabina Berman: The Agony of Ecstasy and Other Plays
Translated by Adam Versényi
With an Essay by Jacqueline E. Bixler

Messiah of the New Technique: John Howard Lawson, Communism, and American Theatre, 1923–1937
Jonathan L. Chambers

Composing Ourselves: The Little Theatre Movement and the American Audience
Dorothy Chansky

Ghost Light: An Introductory Handbook for Dramaturgy
Michael Mark Chemers

The Hanlon Brothers: From Daredevil Acrobatics to Spectacle Pantomime, 1833–1931
Mark Cosdon

Women in Turmoil: Six Plays by Mercedes de Acosta
Edited and with an Introduction by Robert A. Schanke

Rediscovering Mordecai Gorelik: Scene Design and the American Theatre
Anne Fletcher

A Spectacle of Suffering: Clara Morris on the American Stage
Barbara Wallace Grossman

Performing Loss: Rebuilding Community through Theater and Writing
Jodi Kanter

Unfinished Show Business: Broadway Musicals as Works-in-Process
Bruce Kirle

Staging America: Cornerstone and Community-Based Theater
Sonja Kuftinec

Words at Play: Creative Writing and Dramaturgy
Felicia Hardison Londré

Entertaining the Nation: American Drama in the Eighteenth and Nineteenth Centuries
Tice L. Miller

Stage, Page, Scandals, and Vandals: William E. Burton and Nineteenth-Century American Theatre
David L. Rinear

Contemporary Latina/o Theater: Wrighting Ethnicity
Jon D. Rossini

Angels in the American Theater: Patrons, Patronage, and Philanthropy
Edited and with an Introduction by Robert A. Schanke

"That Furious Lesbian": The Story of Mercedes de Acosta
Robert A. Schanke

Caffe Cino: The Birthplace of Off-Off-Broadway
Wendell C. Stone

Teaching Performance Studies
Edited by Nathan Stucky and Cynthia Wimmer
With a Foreword by Richard Schechner

Broadway's Bravest Woman: Selected Writings of Sophie Treadwell
Edited and with Introductions by Jerry Dickey and Miriam López-Rodríguez

The Humana Festival: The History of New Plays at Actors Theatre of Louisville
Jeffrey Ullom

Our Land Is Made of Courage and Glory: Nationalist Performance of Nicaragua and Guatemala
E. J. Westlake